The Althouse Press
Faculty of Education, The University of Western Ontario
Galway and Dibbon, EDUCATION REFORM:
From Rhetoric to Reality

EDUCATION REFORM
From Rhetoric to Reality

Edited by Gerald Galway and David Dibbon

with a foreword by Benjamin Levin

The Althouse Press

First published in Canada in 2012 by
THE ALTHOUSE PRESS
Dean: *Vicki Schwean*
Director of Publications: *Greg Dickinson*
Faculty of Education, The University of Western Ontario
1137 Western Road, London, Ontario, Canada N6G 1G7

Editor: *Geoffrey Milburn*
Editorial Assistants: *Sarah Burm, Katherine Butson*
Indexer: *Gail Edmunds*
Cover Designer: *Louise Gadbois*

Library and Archives Canada Cataloguing in Publication

Galway, Gerald James, 1957-
    Education reform : from rhetoric to reality / Gerald Galway and David Dibbon.

Includes bibliographical references and index.
ISBN 978-0-920354-74-2

    1. Educational change—Newfoundland and Labrador. 2. Educational law and legislation—Newfoundland and Labrador. 3. Church and education—Newfoundland and Labrador. I. Dibbon, David C., 1958- II. Title.

LA418.N4G36 2012   370.9718   C2011-908074-5

Printed and bound in Canada by Aylmer Express Limited, 390 Talbot Street East, Aylmer, Ontario.

This book is dedicated to the memory of my good friend and colleague, David Dibbon.

G.G.

Contents

Reflections and Conclusions

Contributors

Gerald Galway
Gerald Galway is an educator and researcher at Memorial University's Faculty of Education and a former senior executive with the Newfoundland and Labrador Department of Education. Over a sixteen-year career in government, Dr. Galway led a series of provincial research and policy initiatives and is the recipient of several education and research awards. His research interests include educational policy and governance, educational change, public sector accountability, and educational reform.

David Dibbon
David Dibbon was dean of education at Memorial University until his untimely death in 2010. Prior to joining the Faculty of Education in 2000, Dr. Dibbon had a productive twenty-year career in the public school system as classroom teacher, assistant principal, and principal. As a school principal, he was recognized, both locally and nationally, for his innovative leadership. He was also a successful researcher who published in the areas of teacher supply and demand, education reform, teacher working conditions, educational technology, and classroom innovation and change.

Roger Austin
Dr. Roger Austin has held leadership roles in the School of Education at the University of Ulster, Northern Ireland and is currently the co-director of the Dissolving Boundaries program which uses Information and Communications Technologies (ICT) to link schools in Northern Ireland and the Republic of Ireland. He has published extensively on modern French history, the teaching of history, and the role of ICT in teaching, learning, and policy implementation. His most recent co-authored book was *E-schooling: Global Messages from a Small Island* (2008).

Jean Brown
Jean Brown is a professor of education at Memorial University where she teaches graduate and undergraduate courses in educational leadership. Dr. Brown's research interests are focused in the areas of e-learning and community partnerships. She is author of numerous papers and reports and most recently has been leading a project to build a research alliance between the university and the community.

Bonaventure Fagan
Bonaventure Fagan is a former educator and educational administrator in the Newfoundland and Labrador education system. He received M.A. and M.Ed. degrees from Memorial University and a Doctor of Arts degree from Idaho State University. Dr. Fagan has authored several articles in the fields of curriculum and educational reform. Best known as a strong advocate for Catholic education, Dr. Fagan's publications include *Trial: The Loss of Constitutional Rights in Education in Newfoundland and Labrador—The Roman Catholic Story*, an account of the erosion of Catholic minority rights in education.

Mary G. Green
Mary Green is an adjunct professor in the School of Education, Acadia University. Dr. Green has served in a number of leadership roles including teacher, curriculum specialist, assistant superintendent, and visiting professor. She earned B.A., B.Ed., and M.Ed. degrees from Memorial University and received her Ed.D. degree from the University of South Australia. She is currently working on a new book examining the turbulence associated with educational reform.

Edward Hancock
Edward Hancock is executive director of the Newfoundland and Labrador Teachers' Association (NLTA), a position he has held since 2001. He is a former staff officer with NLTA, high school teacher, and administrator. Mr. Hancock holds bachelor's degrees in science and education as well as a master's degree in education from Memorial University. He also holds a Certificate in Industrial Relations from Queen's University. Mr. Hancock is the author of several articles and commentaries relating to teachers and the law and has written numerous articles for *The Bulletin*, the NLTA's membership publication.

Bryce Hodder
Bryce Hodder is a former teacher and consultant for the Newfoundland Department of Education. Over his career he has worked on numerous curriculum projects developing programs and resources for religious education. After the reform of the denominational education system in Newfoundland and Labrador, Mr. Hodder was charged with overseeing the development of a new religious education program. He now teaches religious studies methods at Memorial University's Faculty of Education.

William J. Hunter
William Hunter is a professor and former dean of education at University of Ontario Institute of Technology. Previously, he held academic posts in Ohio, Rhode Island, Alberta, and Nova Scotia. His current research interest is in the field of educational technology and policy. He has served as reviewer, board member, and editor for academic journals—most notably as editor of the *Canadian Journal of Education*. Dr. Hunter received a Ph.D. in educational psychology from Kent State University in 1974.

Benjamin Levin
Benjamin Levin is a professor and Canada Research Chair in Education Leadership and Policy at the Ontario Institute for Studies in Education (University of Toronto). He is a former senior public servant and held the post of deputy minister of education in the province of Manitoba and later in the province of Ontario. Dr. Levin is an internationally recognized scholar, having published an extensive body of work in educational reform, educational change, educational policy and politics.

Glenn Loveless
Glenn Loveless has had a broad-ranging professional career as teacher, principal, school district administrator, senior public servant college dean, and university professor. Much of his work has been focused in the areas of language education and governance. Dr. Loveless holds undergraduate and graduate degrees in arts and in education from Memorial University and a Ph.D. in linguistics from Université Laval.

Phillip McCann
Dr. Phillip McCann is professor emeritus in the Faculty of Education at Memorial University where he began his career in 1967. He has published several books and articles on the history of education in Britain and Newfoundland. His *Schooling in a Fishing Society: Education and Economic Conditions in Newfoundland and Labrador, 1836–1986* (1994) is well recognized as a seminal work on education in Newfoundland and Labrador.

Bruce Sheppard
Bruce Sheppard is a professor in the Faculty of Education at Memorial University. He has served as CEO/director of education in two school boards and has been associate dean of graduate programs and research in education at Memorial University. His research interests include educational

leadership, educational change, and e-learning. He has been a recipient of a number of awards throughout his career including the CEA-Whitworth Award for contribution to research and scholarship in Canada.

John J. Stapleton
John Stapleton is Principal of St. Mark's College and President of Corpus Christi College (University of British Columbia) in Vancouver, British Columbia. Prior to his Vancouver appointment, Dr. Stapleton was a professor in the Faculty of Education at the University of Manitoba and has served as Dean of the Faculty of Education at both Lakehead University and the University of Manitoba. Dr. Stapleton has written extensively on educational leadership and Catholic education and has been recognized with numerous awards and distinctions for his contributions.

Philip Warren
Dr. Philip Warren has had a rich career in education both provincially and nationally. Educated at Memorial University and the University of Alberta, Dr. Warren began his career in the 1950s and served as a school principal, university professor, university administrator, and policy researcher. From 1964–1969 he chaired the Royal Commission on Education and Youth and, in the Wells government, served as Minister of Education from 1989–1993 . Dr. Warren retired from political life in 1993. He was named an Officer of the Order of Canada in 2002.

Acknowledgments

There are many individuals and organizations, without whose support and encouragement, this book could not have been completed. We sincerely appreciate their time, support, and encouragement. First and foremost, we thank the contributing authors for their thoughtful contributions. We especially thank Dr. Benjamin Levin for taking time to read the manuscript and for writing the Foreword to the book.

We also thank our colleagues at Memorial University. We appreciate the financial and moral support of the Faculty of Education, Memorial University, and, in particular, former Dean, Dr. Alice Collins, for her personal support of the project. We also gratefully acknowledge the Leslie Harris Centre of Regional Policy and Development, Memorial University, for the provision of a research grant, and especially Dr. Robert Greenwood and Mr. Michael Clair for partnering with us on the project. Finally, we are grateful to Ms. Katherine Butson and Mr. Will Oxford for reading many of the chapters and for providing helpful comments.

You are never dedicated to something you have complete confidence in. No one is fanatically shouting "The sun is going to rise tomorrow". They know it's going to rise tomorrow. When people are fanatically dedicated to political or religious beliefs or other kinds of dogmas or goals it's because these are threatened.

Robert Persig

Foreword

Benjamin Levin

Newfoundland holds a unique place in Canada. Although the first Europeans arrived on the island more than 500 years ago, Newfoundland has been a part of Canada for only sixty years—a status change still regretted by some! In most of Canada the history of the last 200 years is largely the expansion of European settlement primarily for agriculture, but the pattern in Newfoundland was quite different. Its people, like the Québécois, think of themselves as a "distinct society" in a way that most other Canadians do not.

Yet in some other ways, Newfoundland reflects many of the quintessential themes of Canadian history—the colonization of remote and often inhospitable places, the displacement of the Aboriginal inhabitants, and the mixing of different religions, ethnicities, and cultures to form something new and different—and not without plenty of tensions! The salient issues in Canadian education history are mirrored by those in Newfoundland's education history, in particular the extent to which the school system would recognize or reflect differences in ethnicity and religion.

Canada's efforts to understand and accommodate diversity in its schools are a key part of our history. The biggest debates and conflicts in Canadian education have been about the ways in which differences in culture, language, and religion would be reflected in our school systems. The fact that the country's original terms of confederation paid explicit attention to minority rights in education is a prime indicator of the importance of this topic. A couple of decades later, the Manitoba Schools Question threatened to destabilize the entire country in a heated debate over education, language, and religion.

Nor have these issues gone away since that time. In the early part of the twentieth century, the role of schooling in assimilating huge numbers of immigrants was a focus of much discussion. Despite the constitutional guarantees, the education of the francophone minority created much political conflict in many parts of the country. As Canadian society became more secular, language came to play an increasing part in the debate, although religion in education has always been, and remains, controversial.

Virtually every province has struggled with questions of diversity in education. Quebec had twenty years of debates, laws, and court cases to redefine the place of language and religion in the organization of its school districts, involving several Supreme Court cases. Ontario has faced continuing legal challenges to its practice of funding of "public" and Catholic schools. The extension of full funding to Catholic schools in the 1980s was highly controversial, as was the short-lived tax credit for private schools a few years ago, and the issue of funding for private and religious schools also dominated the 2007 provincial election. Other provinces have also had changing arrangements to recognize and fund various kinds of private and religious schools. In Alberta, changes in local funding in the 1990s triggered court cases regarding the rights of Catholic school boards. In Manitoba, the creation of two Aboriginal-focus schools early in the 1990s was a huge public issue, as was a Black-focused school in Toronto more recently. These varying efforts and policies across the country show how contentious the issues are.

Another important element of Canadian education has been the arrangements for the education of Aboriginal people. Residential schooling is now widely recognized as a disastrous policy, but there is still much debate about how best to organize and support effective education for our indigenous people. Issues of jurisdiction are just as difficult here as they are and have been in regard to religion and language. Aboriginal people are by no means a homogeneous community with a single point of view, and the increasing urbanization of Aboriginal people has made the political challenges more difficult. One thing that is clear is that we have not yet created the appropriate policies or arrangements for education of Aboriginal people, because there are still large gaps in outcomes between Aboriginal children and other Canadian children.

These issues of the accommodation are now increasingly evident in the rest of the world. Across Europe, countries are worried about how to

organize schooling in the face of much more diverse populations. On a recent trip to Europe, I was told that the student population in Madrid and
Oslo were both more than twenty-five per cent foreign-born—an unprecedented situation in both countries. Ireland, which for centuries exported
people, had a large influx of Poles and Africans and little idea of what this
might mean for their schools. Switzerland is now more than twenty-five per
cent foreign-born, including many visible minorities. Malaysia and Singa-
pore are trying to figure out the role of their main languages in their school
systems. The list goes on and on.

In most of the world, Canada is seen as a beacon for the peaceful and
effective accommodation of diversity in education and social relations.
Our results on international tests such as PISA (the OECD's Programme
for International Student Assessment) show high levels of achievement
and smaller (although still substantial) degrees of inequity than virtually all
other countries. In PISA, Canada and Australia are the only countries in
which foreign-born do as well as native-born students. Because virtually all
countries are now facing growing levels of population diversity, many look
to Canada to see how to manage these challenges successfully, even though
Canadians know that we have made many mistakes and have much that
still needs improvement.

All of this is to indicate the importance of this book. It is easy to talk
about "Canadian" policy or approaches to diversity, but all Canadians
know that our country is highly decentralized in this regard, and provinces
have found quite different pathways. Although there is a substantial Canadian scholarship on diversity in education, there is not nearly enough re-
counting and analysis of the details of how our current arrangements have
been shaped. Canada's scholarly community is small, especially given the
diversity of our education systems and experiences. It is therefore a plea-
sure to see a collection of thoughtful and interesting chapters that focus on
recent education policy in Newfoundland and Labrador. As someone
whose first degree was in history, and who sees how powerfully history
shapes the present, I welcome the rich and varied discussions of important
issues that these chapters represent.

One suspects that most Canadian educators would know relatively
little about the education system of Newfoundland and Labrador; at best,
people might know that the province had quite a few separate education
systems based on religion that were recently, with difficulty, merged into a
single public system. This book will provide interested readers, not just in
Canada but internationally, with insight into the complexities of education

change even in a relatively small jurisdiction. The various chapters examine the political, administrative, legal and other elements that were part of this change, and place them in their larger historical context. Some of the authors seem to think that this change was positive and needed. A few clearly have the opposite view. Others are neutral in expressing their own stance, but nonetheless provide illuminating comments on how it all happened. The events in question are mostly recent enough that people remember them quite well, yet also now far enough away that there is a certain degree of objectivity and distance.

This book, I am sure, will be a standard source for many years to come on the development of education in Newfoundland and Labrador. It should, however, be more than that. As I have tried to show, the themes and issues in this book are of national and international significance, and the province's struggles and challenges, while in many respects particular to that unique (and wonderful) place, also have much to say to all of us about how we can and should undertake the appropriate organization of our schools.

Introduction

Gerald Galway and David Dibbon

Education systems have always been in the vanguard of those organizations impacted by social change. Shifts in demography, family structures, and economic conditions are first felt in schools. Economic uncertainty, new technologies, new forms of competitiveness, and changing public expectations all translate into policy issues for school systems. To help navigate the changing educational landscape, governments have turned to various forms of expert advice and enacted a range of political-democratic processes. In Canada, like other Western countries, some of the most tangible and public demonstrations of government legitimation in the past quarter-century have been reflected in the widespread reform of education systems. Over the past 25 years, most Canadian provinces introduced a broad array of education reform initiatives aimed at meeting the demands of higher public expectations and broadening definitions of the purpose of education. Many provinces undertook a series of commissioned studies, large-scale program reviews, new accountability frameworks, performance indicator systems, internal and external scans, and strategic plans, all of which fed significant restructuring and reorganization. Many of these adjustments and reinventions—packaged under the broad banner of "restructuring"—were heralded as a means of keeping education current, relevant, and responsive as policy-makers tried to negotiate new expectations for schools. One of the most fundamental reorganizations took place in Newfoundland and Labrador, where, by constitutional amendment, the 150-year-old denominationally-based system of education was replaced by a public system.

In 2009, the province of Newfoundland and Labrador turned 60 years old. Since 1949, when Newfoundland became Canada's tenth province, its education system has undergone profound changes, including several major amalgamations leading up to the 1997 reforms. In early 2007, while discussing resources for a course on the history of education, we realized that there had been no recent scholarly work that broadly examined the reform of the denominational education system from a critical and historical perspective. Although we found some excellent historical accounts of general educational development, we could find no independent appraisal of government's reform agenda of the last 20 years. Within Newfoundland and Labrador, the historical accounts of educational development generated by such authors as Rowe (1964), Warren (1973a), Andrews (1985a), McKim (1988), and McCann (1994) were prepared before the structural reforms of the last two decades. Other than those discourses produced by governmental authorities, we could find no recent independent scholarly account of the transition to educational secularism, either in the province of Newfoundland and Labrador, specifically, or in Canada, generally. The time seemed appropriate to revisit and critically examine these events.

Using the reorganization of education in Newfoundland and Labrador as a point of departure, *Educational Reform: From Rhetoric to Reality* examines religious, social, economic, humanistic, and political dimensions of educational reform that are relevant to educational contexts across Canada and abroad. The recent socio-economic and demographic experience of this isolated province makes it an ideal archetype for the study of many of the organizational, governance, and delivery issues now facing other jurisdictions. Against a backdrop of unprecedented enrolment change, economic rationalism, and a new secularism, this book contextualizes the antecedents to educational reform, its processes, and its consequences. The book places emphasis on the transition to secularism and explores questions relating to religious minority rights, legal and constitutional aspects of reform, economics, student learning, school board autonomy, centralization, and the often overlooked humanistic side of educational change.

The idea for this book coincided with our interest in hosting a symposium to revisit the reform events culminating in 1997—10 years after the constitutional amendment of Term 17 of the Newfoundland Terms of Union with Canada. The symposium was held at Memorial University in May, 2008, and represented an extraordinary opportunity for educators, researchers, and policy makers to consolidate their knowledge of educational reform over the last several decades, and to engage in constructive discourse to chart the future. Our goal was to bridge the *rhetoric* of educational reform and to examine the *reality* of how reform is operationalized in school and school board contexts.

As it turned out, not everyone shared our enthusiasm for this kind of forensic audit. Although the symposium did draw a strong contingent of academics, NGOs, and graduate students, most of the education officials and policy advisers from the provincial government whom we had expected to attend, were noticeably absent. We relate this occurrence not to express disapproval or to raise questions about the priorities of the government; indeed, one of us served as a senior education ministry official for half of his career. But, it bears pointing out here that from the perspective of governmental authorities, educational reform is risky business—even restructuring that may have been implemented more than a decade earlier, by a different government.

As Ozga (2000) observes in *Policy Research in Educational Settings: Contested Terrain*, "policy...is struggled over, not delivered, in tablets of stone, to a grateful or quiescent population" (p. 1). Educational reform policy is complex and almost always contested; it involves multiple actors across time and space. It is argued, debated, and disputed by almost everyone from teachers and academics to politicians, industry leaders, advocacy groups, and parents. Many issues in Canadian society are cast as educational problems, requiring immediate intervention by policy makers. Public expectations for education have never been higher, and there are many competing claims about what social and economic outcomes the education system should deliver. In short, the education agenda is constantly being constructed and reconstructed by special-interest groups, the mass media, industry, and the general public. No wonder forays into public policy areas that have, more or less, reached some form of settlement tend to be avoided by policy makers. As will become evident throughout the book, denominational reform is one of those "sleeping dogs" that few political advisers would want to see awakened.

Nevertheless, documenting the evolution of education systems is important scholarly work. We are, therefore, pleased to have compiled this comprehensive and diverse set of perspectives on the reform of education in Newfoundland and Labrador. Our hope is that this work can be of value to educational leaders and policy makers in other jurisdictions, both within Canada and further afield.

The book is organized in three sections. Part One includes presents a set of five chapters that provide an analysis of the precursors to the reform events of the 1990s in Newfoundland and Labrador. In Chapter One, we (Galway and Dibbon) present an argument that relies on a political-social-historical review of antecedent policy influences. Using the metaphor of a "perfect storm" of policy drivers, we suggest that the secularization of education and the reform of the denominational system were inevitable. Our conceptualization of educational reform draws on the work of Kingdon (1995) who explains significant policy change in terms of agenda setting and decision making under conditions of ambiguity where there are multiple discourses at play. We suggest that education is an example of a policy arena that is continually evolving without necessarily settling into stasis and where there are multiple—macro and micro—policy streams. Multiple streams theory can be applied here as a way of understanding how major policy shifts, such as educational governance change, come about.

In Chapter Two, Philip Warren, noted professor of education, author of the *Royal Commission on Education and Youth* (Government of Newfoundland and Labrador, 1967, 1968) and former education minister (1989–1992) in the Clyde Wells government, analyzes the politics of reforming Newfoundland's denominational education system in the 1990s. Beginning with a brief history of the system, he identifies five forces that influenced the reforms: the work of the Williams Royal Commission, the changing demography and economy of the province, the growth of secularization and the declining influence of the churches, the influence of various special-interest groups and the media, and sustained leadership by several political leaders. These are some of the same influences we discuss in Chapter One, but Warren provides us with a unique insider perspective. Throughout a 40-plus year career he gave advice on educational reform to several governments, and later, as education minister, sat at the policy tables where significant reform decisions were taken and implementation strategies devised. We are fortunate to be able to include his thoughts and reflections on some of the challenges, opportunities, and outcomes of the transformation from religious to public schooling.

The next chapter describes the involvement of teachers in the reform process. Starting with its brief to government, entitled *Exploring New Pathways* (1986a, 1986b), the Newfoundland and Labrador Teachers' Association (NLTA) was a prominent voice in public debate about changing the province's denominational education system. Through its activities during this time, the NLTA played a pivotal role in drawing attention to the difficulties associated with denominationally-based school governance. Edward Hancock, a long-time teacher advocate and current executive director of the NLTA, revisits the organization's involvement in the call for an end to church-run schools.

Chapter Four examines the changes in the world economy that took place during the later 1980s and early 1990s, in particular, the rise of globalization and its ideology—neoliberalism—and their impact on Canadian and Newfoundland society. Phillip McCann, professor emeritus of Memorial University, is a prolific author who has written extensively on the history of education. He contends that during the latter part of the last century the neoliberal dispositions of governments, bolstered by strong representation from the business sector, created pressure on schools to become less concerned with Christian humanism and more oriented towards competitiveness and entrepreneurialism. His review of government and industry publications—most calling for a new educational focus on scientific and technological competence and a "competitive edge"—suggests that these new policy directions radically affected the educational landscape in Newfoundland and Labrador and led to changes in the aims of education, the organization of schooling, and the focus of the school curriculum.

We conclude this section by taking a closer look at the economics of school board consolidation. In Chapter Five, Gerald Galway reviews the economic arguments that tend to be brought forward by governments and their agents whenever there is an impending restructuring of schools or school districts. He examines how, in the post-war period, governments managed their economies using Keynesian economic policies which are widely believed to have led to excessive public debt. Subsequently, in the 1980s, market principles were adopted by many governments throughout the world as an alternative to regulation and a means to debt reduction. As new sets of governance arrangements matured, there emerged a press for smaller, more effective, and efficient public service delivery mechanisms—a new, "corporate" approach to public management. Within this global-competitive discourse, Galway argues that education systems were targeted as one social sector where efficiencies could be gained. The chapter explores how the language of competitiveness, effectiveness, and accountability dominated the public domain, as one of the principal drivers of the 1990s reform movement, and how such ideas have permeated education systems across Canada, leading to a widespread reconstruction of the way education was conceptualized. He raises a number of key questions about how a corporate managerialist approach to education came about, and why economic considerations seem to have trumped the social costs of educational restructuring.

In Part Two, we explore the contested nature of educational change. We begin with a counter-argument to the claim that the reform of the denominational education system in Newfoundland and Labrador was necessary and warranted. Bonaventure Fagan (Chapter Six) has written extensively about the period leading up to and immediately following the two referenda that led to the dismantling of the Church-governed school system. Taking the perspective of the Catholic denominational authority as it existed in the mid-1990s—the Catholic Education Council—Fagan contends that the structural changes required to achieve economic efficiencies could have been made with the cooperation of the denominational authorities. If the government had been more willing to work within the existing structure, or a variation of the existing structure, he suggests, wholesale restructuring could have been avoided and the religious character of at least some schools could have been preserved. His careful chronicling of the events surrounding the amendment of Term 17 provides an important alternative perspective on educational reform and raises moral questions such as: what rights are important?; under what circumstances should the will of the majority supplant the rights of minorities?; and, should economics or political expediency supersede constitutionally-entrenched rights?

John Stapleton's examination of religion and schooling in Canada (Chapter Seven) reminds educators of the fact that in many jurisdictions in Canada, publicly-funded denominational education still enjoys constitutional protection. He outlines the arguments for and against continuing with the present publicly-funded denominational systems in Ontario, Saskatchewan, and Alberta, and offers his insights on the future of denominational education.

In Chapter Eight, Glenn Loveless explores legal and constitutional factors related to educational reform in Canada with particular reference to the governance rights of Christian churches. He reviews the processes required to enact constitutional change, with specific reference to education in Newfoundland and Labrador and Quebec. He then discusses how the constitutional provision for separate (Catholic) schools in Ontario particularly, has become a political issue, given the emerging cultural-religious mosaic of Canada.

In the absence of denominationally-based religious education, the Newfoundland and Labrador government of then Premier Brian Tobin (1996–2000) was faced with the daunting task of developing a single religious education program to be offered at all grade levels to children from all Christian denominations. Bryce Hodder was the education consultant at the ministry of education charged with overseeing the development and implementation of much of the new program. Contrary to the prevailing view, in Chapter Nine Hodder argues that religious education became more—not less—accessible to students. Although religious instruction in the post-reform system was not denominational in character, religious education, in fact, became mandatory, thereby advancing the educational objective of better preparing students to live in a multicultural and multi-faith world. That is not to suggest that this was a seamless process; nor without opposition. There are still several foundational questions that remain unanswered and these questions are posed in Hodder's conclusions.

In Part Three of the book, authors offer their insights on educational governance in post-reform Newfoundland and Labrador. These are accounts of the experiences of those affected by educational restructuring and lessons learned from the process. They provide a unique set of perspectives that will be instructive to any jurisdiction contemplating structural and/or governance reform. In Chapter Ten, Bruce Sheppard examines the district-level fallout from large-scale structural change. Although such changes may improve efficiency and fiscal accountability, Sheppard argues that these initiatives have frequently been found to negatively impact authentic student learning. He explores a growing body of empirical evidence supporting the idea that school districts, and not governmental authorities, are best positioned to facilitate meaningful, learner-focused educational reform. When school districts function as complex, adaptive professional learning communities, the educational goals of reform—enhanced student learning—can best be met. Unfortunately, he suggests, regressive government policies, regulations, and aggressive reform agendas have inhibited school districts from functioning in this manner. Even though school districts are able to overcome the more typical challenges associated with their accountability arrangements with government, Sheppard believes it is not possible for them to sustain a meaningful educational agenda without longer term stability.

Following on Sheppard's arguments, David Dibbon, Bruce Sheppard, and Jean Brown, in Chapter Eleven, examine the changing relationship between school boards and government and the impact of educational reform in Newfoundland and Labrador on school board autonomy. Their data suggest that the restructuring that took place in 1997 and again in 2004 resulted in a fundamental shift in the power relationships among the ministry, schools boards, and directors of education. Although this shift may be evident to those closely connected to the governance and administration of education, they assert that the gradual and subtle centralization of school governance has not been as clear to parents and members of the general public. They contend that placing school boards and their directors of education in a position of subservience to governmental authorities does nothing to advance the technical core of schooling—teaching and learning.

Mary Green, in Chapter Twelve, maintains that one of the greatest governance tasks for education organizations is caring for its people—energizing, motivating, and encouraging them so that they feel valued, continue to learn, and contribute to the achievement of organizational goals. Drawing on research conducted in one school district, she explores how individuals are positioned in contradictory ways, and how they manage multiple and competing agendas while implementing mandated educational restructuring. The chapter examines the difficulties of practising caring relationships and offers possibilities for improving the quality of employees' lives while also contributing to reform and improvement within educational organizations.

Chapter Thirteen presents an outsider perspective on educational reform. Roger Austin and William Hunter are two colleagues working in very different educational contexts from each other and from the education system in Newfoundland and Labrador. Newfoundland and Ireland share a unique religious, ethnic, and cultural heritage as two "states" with remarkably parallel denominational and economic histories under British rule. One reflection of this shared background is the similarity in the role of religious denominations in school management. This chapter examines elements of these common backgrounds and describes initiatives currently under way in Ireland and Northern Ireland to bring children from different religious traditions together through curricular projects using new technologies. Austin and Hunter rely on the notion of the "second record"—that is, the physical evidence that exists in document form—to complete their analysis and to tease out any lessons from the Newfoundland and Labrador experience that may be brought to bear on the policy choices available to other jurisdictions. Their stance, as detached observers, provides a rich external perspective on denominational reform, and shows how lessons learned in both Newfoundland and Ireland may serve to inform practice in other jurisdictions.

In Chapter Fourteen, we offer some final thoughts on how the reform of education systems, which is normally a divisive and contested process, could be different. We suggest that meaningful and beneficial change must include humanistic considerations, and that centrally-mandated large-scale reform, even in the face of continued enrolment decline, is a blunt instrument and leaves scars that are difficult to heal. Our final analysis, based on our own work and the work of our colleagues, calls for different approach to educational reform—one that respects the need to be efficient and accountable, but also accounts for the social, cultural, and humanistic costs of re-engineering education systems.

This book represents new scholarly work that closely examines a Canadian case study in large-scale structural educational reform. We are fortunate to have such a strong assemblage of contributing authors for this volume. Our colleagues have made this work unique in that it is a systematic attempt to consolidate research and discourse on the impacts of educational reform with its basis on the "lived experience" of a Canadian school system. The book offers ideas about how schools and school districts can navigate these new arrangements. This is, in many ways, a collective reflection on the outcomes of reform—intended and unintended—and a point of departure for further research on large-scale reform.

Part One

Secularizing Educational Governance—
Demographic, Political, Ideological
and Economic-Competitive Influences

Chapter One

A Perfect Storm: Conceptualizing Educational (Denominational) Reform in Newfoundland and Labrador

Gerald Galway and David Dibbon

Sixty years ago the people of Newfoundland made a decision which set into motion a series of events that would change the very fabric of their history and culture as a fishing community dominated by European economic interests. The decision to become the tenth province of Canada had an immediate and profound impact on the state of education in Newfoundland and Labrador. By most accounts, in 1949, relative to most of its sister provinces, the education system in Newfoundland was poorly developed and inaccessible to many of its citizens (Rowe, 1964). Inhibited by early foreign-imposed restrictions, government instability, economic uncertainty, and religious segregation, its system of schooling was slow to emerge. At the time of Confederation with Canada in 1949, only about three-quarters of school-aged children were enrolled in elementary-secondary school, while university (college) enrolment, in a province with a population of approximately 350,000, was fewer than 400 (Statistics Canada, 1999). Rowe (1964) articulated the problem as being rooted in colonialism, economic exploitation, and religious intolerance. The British west-country merchants exerted their considerable political influence to resist the establishment of Newfoundland as a permanent settlement; it was not granted colonial status until 1825 and did not introduce a functional Schools Act until 1843. These factors, combined with early-twentieth-century economic turbulence—brought on by a crushing war debt, overspending on the railway system, the failure of world export markets for fish—geographic isolation, and poverty created almost insurmountable obstacles for the development of a modern education system.

Since those early days, when Newfoundland first became part of the Canadian confederation, the social and educational landscape has changed dramatically. The province has made exceptional gains on measures of general educational attainment (literacy, post-secondary participation, and graduation), and on most national and international measures of achievement it ranks at or near the national average (Statistics Canada, 2004, 2007a). Today in Newfoundland and Labrador, schools are staffed with a well-educated teaching force. Virtually all teachers hold university degrees while two-thirds of teachers have earned two or more degrees and about one-third hold master's level degrees or higher (Government of Newfoundland and Labrador, 2009). The standard of schools and educational infrastructure has also improved. Particularly since the late 1990s, when responsibility for infrastructure was no longer under the control of the denominational authorities, successive governments have poured hundreds of millions of dollars into construction, maintenance, and consolidation and renovation of buildings.

But the past 60-year period in the province's history has also been punctuated by a number of turbulent events. Changing birth patterns, out-migration, and urbanization have generated one of the most significant demographic shifts in the Western world. The dramatic downturn and diversification of the fishery in 1992 and the rise of energy as a significant economic driver have contributed to significant social upheaval. Once a fishing society with a way of life described by McCann (2002) as "localised, god-fearing, [and] socially conservative" (p. 2), Newfoundland and Labrador is emerging as a global presence in the energy sector with annual oil production valued at more than $10 billion (Government of Newfoundland and Labrador, 2008a). The changing labour market has resulted in widespread migration to larger centres, while recent trends towards participation in high-paying itinerant work arrangements means that for some families, one or both parents may be separated from their children and communities for long periods—months at a time. Continued economic uncertainty, unstable employment, and rural depopulation all translate into difficulties for schools, particularly those whose students are drawn from rural towns and villages.

Governments have turned to various forms of expert advice and enacted a range of political-democratic processes to help navigate the educational landscape in these new times. Since the mid-1960s, two education royal commissions, two referenda, and numerous educational task forces and special panels have provided direction to political leaders, many of these studies recommending fundamental structural and curricular reforms. For example, Newfoundland and Labrador's school system was reengineered following the Warren Commission in 1967, the Crocker Task Force in 1989, the Williams Royal Commission in 1992, and the 2004 budget of the then newly-elected Conservative government. All of this leads to the impression that educational reform has been a recurring theme in the post-Confederation history of education in Newfoundland and Labrador.

In this chapter, we argue that, within the Canadian context, one of the most fundamental restructuring exercises took place in Newfoundland and Labrador, where, by constitutional amendment, the 150-year-old denominationally-based school system was replaced in 1997 by a public system of education. We use the metaphor of a "perfect storm" of policy influences to contend that denominational reform was inevitable. We begin the discussion with an examination of the origins of the denominational system of education. This is followed by a review of the etiology of denominational reform; in particular, an examination of six policy drivers that we suggest facilitated this profound reorganization. We conclude by offering a conceptualization for educational reform following on the work of Kingdon (1995).

The denominational education system

Philip Warren in Chapter Two gives a careful and thorough account of the history of denominational education in Newfoundland and we will not repeat it here. However, the discussion in this chapter requires that we include some brief historical background as to why ownership of education fell to the Christian churches and not the government. Several factors paved the way for the establishment of separate, denominational school systems in Newfoundland. These factors are deeply rooted in the cultural, socio-economic, and secular heritage of the province's two main immigrant groups—the Irish Roman Catholics and the English Protestants—who collectively composed virtually the entire population of "planters" in Newfoundland at the beginning of the eighteenth century. The Irish residents outnumbered those of English descent, but they were poor, having fled difficult conditions in Ireland into the servitude of the English merchant class. As Rowe (1964) notes, "the majority of the early Irish immigrants had no resources and the conditions under which they reached Newfoundland were often such as to preclude the possibility of their return" (p. 17). Rowe's account of the relationship between the English and the Irish lays the foundation for understanding why the denominational system, once established, became one of the most robust in the Commonwealth:

> The Irish brought with them their fear and detestation of English "tyranny." The English settlers maintained their fear of "Popery," and without making very much effort to get at the root of the problem, regarded the Irish element as unstable, quarrelsome and thriftless. [Sir Humphrey] Gilbert had decreed that the practices of the Church of England were to obtain in Newfoundland...; consequently the early Irish immigrants enjoyed no religious or political rights.... Priests were forbidden to come to the Island, and those who did..., were warned of severe penalties, including deportation, if apprehended. (p. 17)

Shortly after the establishment of civil governance, the first Education Act was introduced in 1836. According to Rowe (1964), the government preferred a non-denominational system of elementary schools and provided £2,100 to assist organizations in their efforts to set up and sustain such schools. But the original attempts to introduce non-denominational education were met with general discontent. Disputes over which text of the Bible would be adopted, political and denominational maneuvering, and general religious intolerance effectively killed this first attempt by government to regulate education (McCann, 1988a). The second Education Act of 1843 divided public funding for education between the Roman Catholic and Protestant churches, effectively inscribing in the Newfoundland way of life a denominational system that lasted for more than a century and a half.

The controversy did not end with the separation of Protestant and Roman Catholic children. From 1843 forward, there was conflict among Protestant denominations regarding the allotment of the educational grant (McCann, 1988a). In the 1860s, both residents and politicians complained of "widespread illiteracy, uneducated teachers and deprivation arising from grants apportioned per head of denominational population rather than on the basis of need" (p. 47). According to Rowe (1964), "[h]aving tried all reasonable alternatives, many in the government felt the only workable system was complete denominational separation" (p. 90). This paved the way for the Education Acts of 1874 and 1876 which provided for further sub-division of the educational grant: the Protestant allocation would be shared among the Church of England and Methodist churches. The Education Act of 1892 recognized the Salvation Army, thus creating four separate government-funded education systems.

The churches' authority over education in Newfoundland was further solidified in 1949. As part of the Terms of Union with Canada, Newfoundland negotiated a term to replace section 93 of the British North America Act, which relates to education (Appendix A). Term 17 of the Newfoundland Act entrenched the rights of the denominational authorities in the administration of education, including the funding of schools. In effect, Term 17 guaranteed funding for denominational schools to the churches on a proportional basis. While the major Protestant churches did amalgamate into the Integrated School System following the recommendations of the 1967 Royal Commission on Education and Youth, the Warren Commission, as it has become known, also recommended the establishment of the Pentecostal Assemblies School System, and by extension the Seventh-Day Adventist School Board. For the next twenty-five years the Government of Newfoundland and Labrador funded three[1] separate school systems and numerous duplicate school boards and schools.

Drivers of education (denominational) reform

Economics, geography and the "achievement problem"

As we move into the second decade of the twenty-first century, Newfoundland and Labrador can be seen to have made impressive gains in general literacy levels, post-secondary completion rates, levels of educational attainment, and student performance on national and international standardized tests (Statistics Canada, 2004, 2007a). In fact, general participation rates for K-12 and university education now exceed the Canadian average. The province's position on some key achievement indicators, however, still remains slightly below the Canadian average and below the position of several other Canadian provinces. As Press, Galway, and Collins (2003) note, against international standards, Newfoundland and Labrador students are achieving relatively strong performance; but in comparison to Canada, one of the top-achieving countries in the world, that province, like the other Atlantic provinces, still falls short. That is not to say that progress has been slow—quite the contrary. In fact, relative to educational standards in 1949, Newfoundland and Labrador has been closing the longstanding educational gap between that province and its sister provinces. Education outcome indicators, notably international measures of student achievement and education attainment, show Newfoundland and Labrador learners in a favourable position, relative to their international counterparts (Council of Ministers of Education, Canada, 2005). For example, the OECD's Program of International Student Assessment (PISA) assesses students in three curriculum areas: mathematics, reading, and science. The 2003 assessment placed Newfoundland and Labrador well above the international average in all areas, while performance in reading and science was comparable to the Canadian average (Council of Ministers of Education, Canada, 2005).

However, the prospects for high levels of student achievement during the 1970s and 1980s did not look as bright. Student performance on the Canadian Tests of Basic Skills (CTBS), a battery of standardized tests that was administered on an annual basis beginning in 1974, was dismal. Between 1974 and 1978, the composite percentile rank for the province in Grades 4, 6, and 8 never rose above 26. In 1974, the Grade 8 composite percentile rank was 18, indicating that provincial student performance was lower than 82 per cent of a representative Canadian sample of Grade 8 students (Table 1).

Table 1: Newfoundland percentile ranks on CTBS sub-tests, 1974–1978

Sub-Test	Year and Grade				
	1974 (Grade 8)	1975 (Grade 4)	1976 (Grade 6)	1977 (Grade 8)	1978 (Grade 4)
Vocabulary	11	16	16	18	23
Reading	13	23	22	21	28
Language	18	22	23	25	29
Mathematics	19	24	27	26	25
Composite	18	20	21	25	26

Source: Crocker and Riggs (1979)

The issue of low student achievement in Newfoundland is rooted in its difficult history. Rowe (1964) theorizes the problem as follows:

The nature of the fisheries encouraged a large degree of dispersal of population, [and] the dispersal to remote and isolated areas was accentuated by...repressive policies.... By forcing residents to depend entirely on a precarious fishery, which even in the best of years could give only the minimum means of subsistence, they had contributed greatly to the lowering of the economic status of the population and nullified, in part at any rate, the laudable efforts made later to establish educational and cultural organizations. (p. 11)

Newfoundland and Labrador has always relied on traditional, primary resource-based industries such as mining, agriculture, and most importantly, the fishery—the so-called "lifeblood" of the province. Since the sixteenth century, fishers have settled in coastal bays and inlets along the East Coast—places that would provide shelter and proximity to the rich fish stocks they sought. Numerous geographically dispersed communities grew up along the coastlines, resulting in a population base that was located in virtually all corners of the region. From the perspective of the construction and maintenance of required roads and infrastructure, provision of education, health care, and delivery of other social programs, this configuration evolved into a logistical and financial nightmare. For example, outside the capital region, Newfoundland and Labrador has some 400 towns and communities over which is spread a population of only about 340,000 people (Statistics Canada, 2001).

Until the 1970s, many children in Atlantic Canada—and in Newfoundland particularly—did not finish secondary school, and few completed post-secondary education, opting instead to work in the fishery, on farms, or in the (mainly coal and iron ore) mines. Relative to other education systems across Canada, education in Newfoundland and Labrador could quite legitimately have been described as primitive. The Department of Education was not established until 1920, at which time the student population of over 55,000 was spread over 1107 mostly one-room schools. The student-teacher ratio stood at 37:1, the entire budget for education in the province was about $400,000, and a quarter the teaching force was ungraded (Government of Newfoundland and Labrador, 1967, 1968). As one Department of Education report from that period lamented:

In my visits to schools I have often met good meaning and zealous young girls in charge, who while doing their best, yet not having sufficient knowledge of teaching or those taught, were hindering, rather than helping. (Government of Newfoundland and Labrador, 1967, p. 21)

The Education Act of 1920 created the Department of Education, authorized the establishment of the Normal School (Teachers' College), and more than doubled the education grant of 1916 to $815,810 (Rowe, 1964). Although these early efforts signalled promise, the funding level was paltry in comparison to the need. Most students left school before Grade 8. According to the 1967 Warren Commission, early reports prepared by the newly-established Department of Education noted that very few children continued past elementary school and placed the proportion of students that reached Grade 9 at 6.4 per cent. Moreover, after the surrender of responsible government in 1933–1934, the annual education budget, which had slowly risen to $1 million, was reduced by half (Rowe, 1964), and over the entire 15-year period of the Commission of Government, total educational spending amounted to less than $32 million (Callahan, 2003).

There were, however, some notable gains during the period of Commission of Government. By 1944, the education grant reached $3 million and the School Attendance Act of 1943 established that attendance for all children aged 7 to 14 would be both free of fees and compulsory (Rowe, 1964). But it would not be until Confederation with Canada that the province began to experience meaningful change in school attendance. The introduction of family allowances, linked to school attendance, became an incentive for parents to send their children to school, and they came in significantly greater numbers, and for longer periods (Rowe, 1964). The Warren Commission (Government of Newfoundland and Labrador, 1967, 1968) later reported that student attendance had increased from 76.4 per cent in 1947–1948 to 92.4 per cent by 1964.

While the "achievements" of the Commission of Government arguably represented progress in keeping students in school longer, they must be placed in context. At the end of the period, annual per-student spending on education was less than $50. No comparable Canadian figure could be found for 1944; however, the average annual educational spending in Canada in 1950, a few years later, was approximately $143 per student (Statistics Canada, 1999). Although obviously not a balanced appraisal of the achievements of Commission of Government, Joseph R. Smallwood's (1967) summary of how the system was managed during those years in is, nevertheless instructive, at least in providing a snapshot of the Newfoundland education system as the province entered Confederation:

Apart from St. John's, Grand Falls, Corner Brook and perhaps a dozen other larger centres of population, there was no essential difference between the type of education enjoyed by children at all levels and that which had been available seventy years before. The schools were small, ranging from one up to six or seven classrooms. They were wooden buildings, primitive in construction and appearance, heated by wood or coal stoves, improperly ventilated, lacking auditorium, gymnasium, library and laboratory facilities. Most of them lacked running water either for drinking or sanitation, the only concession to the latter being decrepit and obnoxious outhouses. Vast stretches of the Province lacked electricity and where lighting was provided kerosene was the medium. In the smaller of the schools teachers generally lacked training, apart perhaps from what training they might have got in one or two summer sessions at St. John's. Even in the larger schools the majority of the teachers had not spent more than one year at University. Out of the 2,375 teachers in 1949 only fifty-seven had degrees and these, of course, were for the most part in St. John's and the larger centres. School transportation as such was non-existent. Out of 1187 schools 778 were "sole-charge," that is, one-room schools, and of these 778 teachers over 700 had not spent even one year at University. The median salary to teachers in 1948 was $981. (p. 114)

After Confederation, the new provincial government had a difficult time making up for lost ground. In 1964, there were 1266 schools governed by 270 separate denominational or amalgamated boards. Seventy-five per cent of the school boards were each responsible for fewer than 500 students—evidence of a grossly inefficient and duplicative education system (Graesser, 1990). In an optimistic era of space travel and emerging new forms of telecommunications, the quality of education in Newfoundland continued to be low by national standards. The province's university had opened its main campus in 1961, only three years earlier, teacher qualifications were still poor, and K-12 infrastructure was in dire need of upgrading and reorganization. The 1967 Warren Commission revealed that in the 1960s, many schools still had outdoor washroom facilities or no washrooms at all, few had gymnasiums, libraries, or science laboratories, most teachers had not completed university degrees, and few rural students made it to high school.

The province responded to Warren's report with an aggressive program of school construction and modernization (Callahan, 2003). Buoyed by access to transfers from the federal government, the education budget in Newfoundland increased 800 per cent over the first two decades following Confederation (Callahan, 2003) and, as the end of the 1970s approached, it reached almost $300 million (Crocker & Riggs, 1979). By that time, however, inflation had become a serious problem, and the province's education system—still segregated into three denominational systems—was struggling to keep pace with enrolment increases associated with an unprecedented post-war baby boom, rising teacher salaries, increased pupil transportation costs, and an expensive and geographically-isolated triplicate infrastructure. By 1977, there had been marginal gains on some indicators, but, as reported by Crocker and Riggs (1979), the dropout rate in Newfoundland[2] was still 34 per cent as compared to the Canadian average of 21 per cent. To add insult to injury, at the time of the Crocker-Riggs Task Force in 1979, Newfoundland was still operating a K-11 system; the rate would have been be much higher—as high as 46 per cent—if the planned implementation of Grade 12 had been completed.

The next 10 years saw considerable political and economic upheaval in Canada's youngest province. As McCann (2002) notes, government concern over mathematics and science achievement, and a perceived mismatch between what schools had to offer and the demands of an emerging post-industrial society, led to a series of government-commissioned policy studies. In his Task Force Report on Mathematics and Science Education, Crocker (1989) complained of a "crisis of low expectations" and called for sweeping curricular changes—especially in mathematics and science—combined with measures to increase participation in advanced mathematics. Other recommendations focused on increasing instructional time, improving classroom and laboratory facilities, enhancing teacher qualifications and instructional practices, and overhauling the province's assessment programs. By this time, the Newfoundland and Labrador Teachers' Association had already weighed in. In their 1986 report, *Exploring New Pathways*, the teachers argued the system was isolationist, over-administered and underfunded.

Demography and enrolment

With two-thirds of its current population (approximately 510,000) residing in smaller, rural, and remote communities, demographically, Newfoundland and Labrador is small; however, its geography covers an expanse of more than 400,000 square kilometers (Statistics Canada, 2006). It has a land mass three times the size of the other three Atlantic provinces combined, but with a population almost four times smaller. Many K-12 schools now have fewer than five students in each kindergarten cohort and virtually all have some multi-graded classes, particularly at the K-9 level. A major challenge facing Newfoundland and Labrador is significant population decline.

The province's population grew at record rates from 1949 to the mid-1960s, peaked in the late 1980s, and began to decline in absolute terms in the mid-1990s. As noted by Galway (2004), demographic factors, such as changing fertility rates, out-migration, and an ageing population, have had profound impact on the school-aged population. Newfoundland and Labrador has experienced some 35 years of declining birth rates, net out-migration, and enrolment decline. The province's fertility rate, defined as the number of children that an "average" woman could be expected to have over her entire childbearing lifetime, was once the highest in the country. It is now the lowest—indeed it is one of the lowest in the world. The fertility rate, declined from 4.58 in 1966 to 1.4 in 1990 and stood at 1.3 in 2005 (Statistics Canada, 2008). Since 1951, Newfoundland and Labrador's median age has increased by more than 20 years and now stands at 41.7 (Statistics Canada 2007b). Statistics Canada anticipates that the Newfoundland and Labrador population will continue to age more rapidly than that of Canada.

From the perspective of population, Canada has benefited from international immigration flows. Because immigrants were comparatively young, by and large, these flows had a positive impact on the country's demography, including births, the natural increase, and age structure. However, most immigrants have tended to settle in other provinces, particularly in central and western Canada, rather than in Newfoundland. Interprovincial migration flows, however, were quite a different story. For at least five decades net-migration has been negative, as the number of people leaving has outnumbered the number moving to the province. This is not new. Before 1949, it was common for young people to move to the USA or Canada for seasonal or year-round work and this continued after Confederation. Since the 1960s, when the number of post-secondary graduates began to increase, and well into the 1990s net out-migration averaged about 3,500 people annually before trending downward. In the last five years net out-migration ranged from about 2000 to more than 4000 (Government of Newfoundland and Labrador, 2009).

During the post-World War II period, before Newfoundland could adequately adapt to a massive increase in the number of school-aged children, educational demographers were already predicting a reversal in enrolment trends. These trends had been forecast in several pre-1980 reports. In fact, as early as 1967 the Warren Commission published birth rates from 1949–1965 which clearly showed that natural population increase was on the decline. But, like opinion polls and economic forecasts, one of the remarkable things about population projections is that when they are positive they give people hope, and when they are negative, people still cling to the possibility that they might be wrong. Whether for political reasons, or simply wishful thinking, the Commission failed to acknowledge or comprehend the importance of this reversal in the direction of birth rates. Instead, it projected that enrolment would reach 240,000 by 1991. The actual enrolment peaked at 162,818 students in 1971, only four years after the publication of the Commission's report. Over the next 20 years the number of school-aged children dropped a startling 23 per cent to approximately 125,000—about half of what the Commission had forecast (Figure 1).

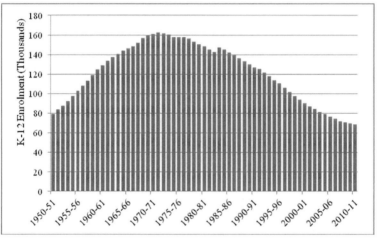

Figure 1: Student enrolment, Newfoundland and Labrador, 1950/51–2010/11

By 1976, according to Jackson (1979), the total fertility rate in Newfoundland was at a respectable 2.4, but already, family size had begun to decline. Crocker and Riggs (1979) accurately predicted that enrolment would drop to below 120,000 by 1993, but even their pessimistic outlook suggested a long period of enrolment stability in the 120,000 student range throughout the 1990s. As the 1980s progressed, the gravity of the enrolment crisis had become clear. Press (1986) wrote a Department of Education demographic projections report which set the predicted enrolment for 1995-1996 at just over 114,000, and predicted no change in the direction of this trend. Among the findings of that report was the revelation that there would be significant decreases in high school enrolment throughout the 1990s and continued annual total enrolment loss into the new century.

Corporate managerialism and the educational reform movement

The 1990s in Canada has been described as the longest decade (Banting, Sharpe, & St-Hilaire, 2001); it was a decade of commissioned studies, large-scale program reviews, accountability frameworks, performance indicator systems, internal and external scans, and strategic plans, all of which fed significant restructuring and reorganization. Many of these adjustments and reinventions—packaged under the broad banner of "restructuring"—were heralded as a means of keeping education current, relevant, and responsive as policy-makers tried to negotiate the new educational arrangements (Levin, 1998, 2003; Levin & Riffel, 1997). These included: sweeping educational accountability reforms; the proliferation of private postsecondary institutions; widespread school-based technology initiatives; wholesale curriculum renewal; modifications to the entire apparatus around special education; and a host of other fundamental changes in the approach to teaching and learning (Levin & Riffel, 1997). No matter how they have been packaged, the principle of efficiency has been a fundamental driver of many of these restructuring efforts.

The modern theory of political governance emerged in Germany after World War II, at a time when governments aspired explicitly to steer their nations' social and economic development in the direction of their defined goals through robust regulatory means. In the post-war period, governments managed their economies based on Keynesian economic policies which are widely believed to have led to excessive public debt (Trinczek & West, 1999). Subsequently, market principles were adopted by many governments throughout the world as an alternative to regulation and a means to debt reduction. Mayntz (1998) observes that "market principles became the backbone of the political ideology of neoliberalism emerging in the 1970s, promoting deregulation and privatization as means to stimulate economic growth and to increase economic efficiency" (p. 3). As new sets of governance arrangements matured there emerged a press for smaller, more effective, and efficient government operations and public service delivery mechanisms.

The ideological shift to a corporate managerialist (also known as New Public Management) orientation involved distinctive private-sector-driven principles, themes, styles, and patterns of public service management, such as those which have become evident in the past two decades, notably in Australia, New Zealand, Sweden, the USA, and Canada (Barzelay, 2001). These include a press for greater productivity, privatization, a stronger service orientation, decentralization, and divestiture from national to state/provincial governments, and the accountability movement (Kettl, 2000). Galway (Chapter Five) describes how these changes in public service ideology affected the education system in Canada. Faced with budget shortfalls, school boards and post-secondary institutions scrambled to adjust their operations and to demonstrate, through a range of externally-mandated public accountability measures, efficiency and effectiveness.

It was at the beginning of this period that the Conservative government, under Brian Peckford, fell to defeat in 1989. When the Clyde Wells government came to power, inflation in Canada was running at about 4-5 per cent annually (Statistics Canada, 2006). The new Liberal government was facing a crushing provincial debt, a near-extinct fishery, and reduced federal government transfers. In keeping with the more conservative political climate of the 1990s and the precarious fiscal position of the province, Wells embarked on a neoliberal program that included the sale of government-owned corporations, budget cutbacks, and wage freezes within education and the civil service. The most notable policy action, however, was the establishment of a Royal Commission of Inquiry into the Delivery of Programs and Services in Primary, Elementary and Secondary Education. McCann (2002) has written about the events leading up to the Williams Commission and summarizes the Government's motivation as follows:

> Aware of the depression of the economy...and of a critical public and institutional opinion which demanded change and improvement in both the economy and the educational system, the government felt the need for planning documents which would chart the path for the last decade of the century. The [Williams] Education Commission was the first, mandated in August 1990 and reporting in March 1992, with the ostensible purpose of seeking ways of making better use of resources in a period of "fiscal restraint" and declining school enrolment.... (¶ 15)

By the end of the 1980s, with the decline of the fishery, high rural unemployment, a trend towards urbanization, a startling drop in the birth rate, and increased mobility among the educated, rural schools were becoming depopulated. By the time the Williams Royal Commission reported, there were more than 130 schools with enrolments of fewer than 100 students (Government of Newfoundland and Labrador, 1992b). Consistent with corporate managerial principles, the K-12 education budget, which had risen to $602 million in 1993–1994, was reduced to under $536 million by 1995–1996. Meanwhile, public expectations for education were escalating and, notwithstanding the system's long history, support for the continued funding of a three-track denominationally-based system seemed unlikely. As it became clear that the Williams Commission would recommend the dismantling of the denominational system in its current form, the churches and their supporters argued that a non-denominational education system would remove Christianity from the classroom. For its part, the government and its supporters made the argument that the existing model promoted waste and inefficiency, lacked effectiveness, and infringed on individual rights. It was the inefficiency and duplication of the denominational system that emerged as the central theme of the 1992 Royal Commission report and it was a key impetus for change.

Social and religious change

According to Nolasco Mulcahy (1988), the key educational issues for Christians have traditionally centred on what should be taught and who should educate. In the traditional Christian view of education there is a very clear differentiation between church and state. The role of the state is purported to be the promotion and protection of the common good, the protection of children in cases of neglect or abuse, and other activities commensurate with the common good. The role of the church is to work in a compatible manner with the state, but to serve eternal and spiritual interests and to provide moral teaching. Thus, there emerges the notion of a co-dependency relationship. The state requires citizens to act according to a moral code, yet has no means of teaching moral integrity. The church is relied upon to instill desirable and commensurate values in its citizenry (lawfulness, selflessness, and respect for authority). The pre-Confederation Newfoundland education system exemplified this relationship; the system was, essentially, an arms-length partnership between the churches and the state whereby the government provided funding, but the churches operated the schools, virtually independently (Graesser, 1997). The fact that the Government of New-foundland did not create a Department of Education until 1920 suggests that the governments of the day were passive funding agents, content to let the churches determine how education would be delivered. But not every-one was happy with the way the system had evolved. By 1903, funding for education had increased to $144,702, but there were signs that a rigidly-im-posed denominational school system was creating practical and economic problems for the government. About three-quarters of this amount was being expended on the general grant, with only one-quarter reserved for teach-ers' salaries. The first challenge to a totally denominationally-separate sys-tem came in the form of the 1903 Education Act, which approved the for-mation of "amalgamated schools in sparsely-populated settlements where the number of children did not warrant the building of separate schools for denominations" (McCann, 1988b, p. 62). Sir Robert Bond was an advo-cate of the change and argued that "if grants were split between two or three denominations in a small outport, the result was inferior schools and 'starvation wages' for the teachers" (p. 62). There were other attempts to consolidate; for example, the 1927 Act made provision for common schools in districts that coincided geographically, and some amalgamation of Pro-testant schools took place. Rowe (1964) points out, for example, that in the industrial towns, notably Corner Brook and Grand Falls, common Protestant schools were established, but the government of the day stipu-lated this could only occur with the express approval of the denominations and the Council of Higher Education.

Before 1970, in Newfoundland, most people held a strong attach-ment to the Christian churches. But the 1970s and 1980s were marked by increasing secularization and, according to Harte (1993), a rejection of the education and church-based authorities. McCann (2002) associates changes in religiosity with urbanization, globalization, and general social change:

> It is no exaggeration to say that the outlook and way of life of the pre-Confederation era—localised, frugal, god-fearing, so-cially conservative—has all but disappeared in the urban cen-tres, and has also undergone some changes in the rural out-ports. Further indicators of the advance of modernity are the number of divorces: 6,195 in 1986, compared with a mere 47 in 1945, and the growth of single-parent families to nearly 16,000, 11% of all families. The burgeoning of activity in art, music, lit-

erature and drama in the last two decades, and the formation of social action groups—the women's movement, organisations for peace and social justice, the environmental movement, white-collar unionism, and ad hoc protest factions of various kinds, most virtually unknown before the '70s, is testimony to the transformation of Newfoundland society. (¶ 7)

McCann goes on to note that this change was also expressed in a more critical attitude toward the church and the denominational educational system. Graesser (1988b) reported that in 1976, 50 per cent of people favoured a single public educational system. By 1979, this figure had increased to 56 per cent, and by 1991—during the period of the Williams Commission— more than two-thirds of the public indicated they were in favour of a non-denominational system of public education. As Harte (1993) observed, these secularized views were typical of Western society; however, in Newfoundland there were additional factors. Contributing to a loss of faith in the denominational system was the devastating news of the Mount Cashel scandal, which, in 1989, led to the conviction of several priests and Christian brothers for sexually molesting young boys in their care (Bergman & Stokes-Sullivan, 1997).

Political climate

Although Warren addresses the political context of denominational reform more fully in Chapter Two, a brief discussion of the political climate in Newfoundland and Labrador in the years leading up to the reform events of the 1990s is central to the argument we are advancing in this chapter. Warren (personal communication, 2003) said that if the political mood had been right, he would have recommended full amalgamation of schools in the Royal Commission Report of 1967. But, as it was, even the modest recommendations for amalgamation of the Protestant schools, and reorganization of the Department of Education—which had hitherto been structured along denominational lines—had the effect of generating a minority report that was appended to the Commission's findings. The report, written by the Roman Catholic representatives on the Commission, took issue with some recommendations that were perceived as opening the door to a secularized system:

> On the surface this proposed set-up may appear to safeguard the traditional rights of parents to have their children taught in

denominational schools under Christian influence. However
the dangers are obvious. In this rapidly changing world the influence of traditions is fading. While the Commission clearly
believes it has provided safeguards for the traditional rights of
the Churches, we, the undersigned, believe that if these rights
are not continued in law, then they can, and most likely will, be
overthrown. (Government of Newfoundland and Labrador,
1967, p. 195)

Thus, the politics of the denominational system in the late 1960s
were essentially the same as they had been since the 1800s: the denominational system represented a political compromise between two classes of
people who still did not seem to trust one another. Rowe's admonition of
1952 was indeed prophetic:

The real enemies to an efficient education system in Newfoundland appear to be the same as existed a century ago—isolation,
small villages and hamlets, dependence on a precarious occupation, and the general poverty of the Province.... Changes, to be really effective among a people whose philosophy and outlook have
been so peculiarly nurtured and molded by centuries of history,
economics, and geography, must be evolutionary rather than revolutionary, especially where such changes are likely to impinge
upon religious scruples or prejudices. (p. 140)

In fact, had the churches been able to resolve their differences, there might
have evolved a system of education in Newfoundland that was not denominational, but Christian in character. Given that almost 97 per cent of people in Newfoundland and Labrador still identify themselves as Christians,[3]
it is plausible that this system would still be in effect today.

But political climates change. McCann (1988a) suggests that the societal values of people in Newfoundland in the 1970s and 1980s were shifting away from a religious-communal orientation. Changing ways of life and
a generally less insular world-view led to a more individualist orientation.
This seems to have been expressed in public concern over several high-profile cases in which the rights of the denominations took precedence over
the rights of individuals. Graesser (1990) documented several situations in
which the legal framework for the denominational system conflicted with
teachers' rights or the rights of citizens as parents and taxpayers. For years,
teachers had expressed concern that certain school boards kept general

surveillance over them to ensure they maintained a suitable religious and moral lifestyle. One example profiled by Graesser occurred in 1984, when the St. John's Roman Catholic School Board dismissed a teacher because he had converted to the Salvation Army faith. A Supreme Court of Newfoundland decision upheld the right of the school board, which argued that religious affiliation was a legitimate condition of employment, and as such, the dismissal was not a violation of the Charter of Rights and Freedoms. A second example involved the Avalon Consolidated School Board, which refused registration of a child into their French-immersion program, based on the fact that neither of the child's parents were members of one of the denominations served by the Board.

In the years preceding the establishment of the Williams Commission, enough of these cases had come to the fore that there seemed to be a general public view emerging that the denominational system was archaic and intransigent. Although there was still considerable vocal opposition to such a move, particularly within the Roman Catholic and Pentecostal churches, by the late 1980s the notion of changing the faltering church-run system seemed possible—perhaps even politically popular.

The perfect storm: Conceptualizing educational (denominational) reform

Bezeau (2002) described the shift to a public school system in Newfoundland and Labrador as moving from the most denominational school system in Canada to one of the least denominational systems. We use the metaphor of a "perfect storm" to suggest that because of the temporal convergence of so many significant policy drivers—social, religious, economic, political-democratic, and pragmatic—the reform of the denominational system of education in Newfoundland was inevitable. These factors, combined with the actions of certain policy entrepreneurs, notably Premiers Clyde Wells and Brian Tobin, finally reformed a system steeped in a tradition of religious segregation.

Our conceptualization for educational reform in the Newfoundland context draws on the work of Kingdon (1995), who explains policy formation in terms of agenda setting and decision making under conditions of ambiguity. Unlike theories that base their principles on the existence of a set of stable social parameters or equilibrium, multiple streams (MS) theory takes a discursive perspective on policy systems; it defines them as constantly evolving without necessarily settling into stasis. According to the three-stream model (problems, policies, and politics), policy issues (problems) come to light either through identification by officials and policy advisors, research and indicators, catastrophic events or feedback on existing policies and programs. In the context of the Newfoundland education system, the "problems" stream emerged in the form of a radically contracting enrolment base, continued low achievement in the face of an increasingly global economy, fiscal shortfalls, poor quality infrastructure, and a general loss of faith in the denominational structure.

The "policies" stream identifies policy issues from ideas and concepts generated by political ideology or by formal policy actors such as networks of academics, the justice system, legislators and bureaucrats with common interests, commissions, or the recommendations of major studies. Policy proposals generated by this stream rarely survive to policy implementation unless they are buttressed, through the identification of the same policy issue at about the same critical moment in time, by another stream—a process described by Kingdon (1995) as coupling. By 1992, when the Williams Commission reported, the proposal to consolidate three separate school systems into a single public system had gained widespread approval. The government, the teachers' union, certain academic voices, the business sector, and a large segment of the population of parents were all calling for change, and it seemed that the only way to resolve some of the persistent problems affecting the system would be through major restructuring.

The "politics" stream refers to the establishment of policy issues by national or regional mood, special-interest group agendas, and turnover of elected and non-elected public officials. The attractiveness of policy options emerging from any one, or from a combination of one or more of these streams, is thought to be dependent on the robustness of the mood, the power, and resources of the special-interest group and the degree of change within the policy arena. Coupling occurs when the streams come together; that is, when two or more streams simultaneously highlight the same problem, more or less agree on a desired policy option, and when that option is favoured by policy-makers and the public. It is during this time that the opportunity to effect policy change is greatest and when a "policy window" is said to be open. This may occur through serendipity; more likely, however, policy entrepreneurs make these linkages. Kingdon (1995) suggests that even when such favourable conditions exist, the intervention of a policy entrepreneur is required to ensure the opportunity to initiate action is not lost. Policy entrepreneurs may also work deliberately to connect streams or to "interpret" the messages emerging from different streams as being connected and to bring these connections to the fore.

It seems clear that the political landscape, in the 1990s, was safe enough for policy entrepreneurs, such as Clyde Wells and Brian Tobin, to bring forward an educational policy option that would hitherto have been unacceptable to a majority of the public. By the mid-1990s the *zeitgeist* in Newfoundland had shifted—almost five decades since Confederation, the province was emerging from its insularity. Socio-religious changes in the population were driving demands for greater efficiency and higher educational standards, and many people were not confident that denominationally-based school boards would be able bring about the kinds of changes deemed necessary.

Conclusions

In many ways, this "perfect storm" presented a policy window that enabled governments to make sweeping, revolutionary changes to the structure of the province's education system. The analogy of the perfect storm might suggest that the changes were uncontested or that the transition to a new educational era was an easy one—such was not the case. Although the drivers of education reform articulated here portray a compelling argument for change, there were resisters to the reform movement, and there are those who continue to argue that the reform of the denominational school system was an unnecessary exercise (see, for example, Fagan, Chapter Six).

Often, during times of radical reform, conflicting ideologies manifest themselves in resistance to change. Not unexpectedly, resistance to the establishment of a public system of education emerged from some citizens, the religious community, and the overseers of the former system—the denominational education councils. What should not be overlooked in any examination of this period is that the Williams Commission *did not recommend* a wholesale move to a public system of education. With respect to the denominational issue, the report recommended that children would generally attend the nearest school and religion would not be a basis for assignment. But, "where numbers warrant, children [would] be provided with opportunities for religious activities and instruction in their own faith" (Government of Newfoundland and Labrador, 1992b, p. 23), while the school system would be sensitive and responsive to children of all faiths (Graesser, 1997). In fact, Recommendation 1 of the Commission's report specifically recognizes the "desire of the majority to retain a school system based on Judeo-Christian principles" (Government of Newfoundland and Labrador, 1992b, p. 23).

Kim (1997) notes that the first provincial referendum on educational reform, held in September, 1995, was conducted "for the purpose of preparing a way to a single system of education by redesignating denominational schools to inter- or non-denominational schools" (¶ 10). The results were thought to be equivocal—only 52 per cent of the population voted and, of this group, only a slim majority voted to accept a non-denominational school system. Graesser (1997) has argued that the churches actively campaigned for the "No" vote, and used the emotive argument that the change would lead to the exclusion of all religious exercises, including the Christian celebrations of Christmas and Easter. DeMont and Stokes-Sullivan (1997) reported in *Maclean's* that Premier Wells stated that "the 'No' side ran an organized campaign for a longer period than you would run in a general election...so you have to take into account the fact that in all probability virtually every last 'No' vote was gotten out" (p. 25). This certainly seems to have been the case. Under the Wells government there appears to have been no aggressive "Yes" campaign associated with the first referendum. Using the fiscal analysis prepared by the Williams Commission, the government instead made a financial and quality argument claiming that reform could save up to $21.3 million (depending on which option was selected) by eliminating duplication, which could be applied to improvements in instruction. According to this line of argument, the poor performance of students in standardized tests could only be redressed with a more efficient delivery system.

Following the first referendum, the Government of Newfoundland and Labrador initially approached the change through non-constitutional negotiations with denominational leaders. But, by 1997, no compromise had been reached with the churches, and the government, now under the leadership of Premier Tobin, was pursuing educational reform through a constitutional amendment to Term 17 of its Terms of Union. The original amendment which was authorized by the House of Commons and proclaimed by the Governor General on April 21, 1997, represented a compromise. According to the statement made by the Honourable Stéphane Dion to the House of Commons on October, 1997, when the Bill to amend Term 17 was introduced, the original plan would not have eliminated all single denominational schools:

> The amendment was designed to provide the Newfoundland House of Assembly with additional powers to organize and administer public education through a system of "interdenominational" schools, while retaining the rights of Roman Catholics

and Pentecostals to "unidenominational" schools under certain conditions. These conditions were to be set out in provincial legislation that was equally applicable to all schools, either unidenominational or interdenominational. (Government of Canada, 2008)

However, the first attempt legislatively to implement the new Term 17 under a revised Schools Act was successfully challenged in the Newfoundland Supreme Court, and Roman Catholic and Pentecostal churches were granted a temporary injunction. This effectively placed the entire educational reform process in limbo. An appeal was filed by the provincial government, but by then the Tobin government had decided to switch gears and aggressively pursue a different policy option to a fully non-denominational system. Premier Tobin announced in a province-wide telecast that he would hold a referendum on September 2, 1997, to secure a mandate to amend Term 17 once again. In his address, he charged that the discussions with the denominational authorities had been a "never ending debate," with the provincial government, school boards, the teachers' association, parents, and students on one side, and the churches on the other. This time there was far less resistance; the 1997 referendum resulted in 73 per cent of voters opting to revise Term 17. The scope of the subsequent system reform was unprecedented; in the name of efficiency and modernization, more than 150 schools were closed between 1997 and 2000.

Chapter Two

The Politics of Educational Change: Reforming Denominational Education

Philip Warren

There are significant challenges associated with analyzing the politics of educational decision making and policy determination. One is finding a model or research framework that helps to organize the data and provide a focus for the analysis. Perhaps the best-known such model is that developed by political scientist David Easton (1965). In his book A *Systems Analysis of Political Life*, Easton declared that the political system included all actions, activities, and relationships concerned with the "authoritative" allocation of values. His model portrayed the political system as responding to the various environmental inputs or demands generated in society that could change the system.

Several modifications have been made to the Easton model. In the early 1980s, Dubnik and Bardes (1983) provided a more specific classification of the societal or environmental forces brought to bear on political actors and institutions. Their classification included: physical forces, such as climate or terrain features; socio economic forces, such as per capita income or education level of the population; psychological forces, such as the ideological climate and public attitudes; and historical forces, including customs and traditions.

Twenty years ago, Newfoundland educator Austin Harte (1989: 29–36) used the work of Dubnik and Bardes to analyze denominational joint-service agreements in Newfoundland education. He added political forces to the list. Harte also referenced the works of Holmes (1984, 1986). Holmes claimed that reforms occurred when traditional values were in conflict with the forces of modernization, reflected in the growth of secularization, the decline in the traditional power and authority of school decision-makers and the school, and the emphasis on process rather than product in schooling. He described Newfoundland in the 1980s as a classic case of ideological confrontation: a struggle between the forces of tradition and modernization.

In analyzing the politics of change in Newfoundland's denominational system during the 1990s, the present discussion drew on each of these models. They helped to identify several interrelated forces that contributed to the eventual elimination of the system, including: the work of the Royal Commission on Education (Government of Newfoundland and Labrador, 1992b), the single most important factor; demographic and economic changes; the growth of secularization and the declining credibility and influence of the churches; the influence of special-interest groups and the media; and sustained political leadership. The discussion of these forces will be prefaced with a brief history of the system. The chapter will conclude with a summary of some of the challenges that now face elementary and secondary education in the second decade of the twenty-first century.

A brief history of the denominational education system

As Galway and Dibbon have argued in Chapter One, Newfoundland's denominational school system had deep roots in the province's past. Many claimed that the system was an inevitable consequence of our early political history, our economic circumstances, and our ethnic and religious backgrounds. Because early policies restricted the growth of permanent settlement, settlers spread out around the coastline for more room to fish and more freedom. Because they came primarily from England and Ireland, with strong personal characteristics and values, they tended to segregate themselves geographically. The Irish, largely Roman Catholic, settled large stretches of the coastline. In the same way, other stretches were settled primarily by people of English descent, adhering to a branch of the Protestant faith.

The only organizations providing even a modicum of education in Newfoundland's early years were the churches and their agencies, such as the British-based Society for the Propagation of the Bible, the Benevolent Irish Society, and the Newfoundland School Society. It was not until 1836, three years after the colony received representative government, that the state provided grants to assist in the provision of education. Even though these grants were meagre, they did demonstrate the state's willingness to accept a degree of responsibility for education.

The Act of 1836 intended the school system to be a non-sectarian one, similar to the Irish non-denominational state system. But that legislation immediately ran into difficulty—not unexpected, given the racial, religious, and political forces at work at the time. Conflict resulted from the decision of some school boards to restrict Bible reading in the schools to the "Authorized Version." Attempts to find a compromise failed. The only solution was to divide the grant between the two confessional groups and let Catholics and Protestants have separate boards to run their schools. This happened in 1843. It was primarily the work of Church of England Bishop Feild that led to the further subdivision of the system. The bishop, who served in Newfoundland from 1844 to 1876, was known for his unbending principles and commitment to church doctrine and ritual. He saw the Anglican Church as a divinely-appointed order, with responsibility for the care and nurture of its children. He had little sympathy for other Protestants, particularly Evangelicals, who brought more emotion and a simpler interpretation of the Bible to the practice of their religion. Feild argued, therefore, that Anglicans should be accorded the same privileges as Roman Catholics, operating their own schools and instructing their own children in their own beliefs. He contended, as well, that if the grants were divided to give Anglicans their share, the Anglican communion would take a greater interest in education. In the Act of 1874, therefore, Protestant grants were apportioned among the several Protestant denominations (Church of England, Wesleyan, the Congregational Church, and the Free Church of Scotland), according to population. The 1874 Act also made provision for the appointment of three inspectors: Church of England, Roman Catholic, and Wesleyan. In the legislation of 1876, these inspectors were renamed "Denominational Superintendents," responsible for advancing the educational interests of their own denominations, including the construction of schools. These superintendents remained dominant in education until their positions were eliminated in 1969.

The 1874 and 1876 Acts laid the foundation for a denominational structure which remained largely unchanged for nearly a century. While politicians sometimes criticized the system, in the end governments found it politically wise to uphold the denominational principle and focus on changes within the system, such as the establishment of the interdenominational Council of Higher Education in 1892. That Council was granted the responsibility to control examinations and award diplomas and scholarships for students of all denominations. In 1892, as well, the system was expanded by an Act recognizing the rights of a fourth denominational group—the Salvation Army. In 1912, the Seventh-Day Adventists were formally recognized.

Several scholars have documented the changes that occurred in the system during the first half of the twentieth century. McCann (1988b) and Rowe (1964), for example, have provided us with an understanding of the numerous legislative battles and compromises which helped the system's development during that period and sanctioned its survival. A Bill by the Bond Government in 1903 authorized the establishment of "amalgamated" schools in sparsely populated areas where the number of children did not warrant the construction of separate denominational ones. At the time, this was a minor accommodation within the denominational principle. It took over 20 years before the 1903 provisions were liberalized to include the larger amalgamated schools established primarily in new industrial towns. A single Department of Education and an interdenominational Normal School for the training of teachers were established in 1920. In 1925, Memorial University College was opened as a secular institution. Several church officials, particularly the Roman Catholic, Church of England, and Methodist superintendents of education, provided visionary leadership in the establishment of these non-denominational post-secondary institutions.

The Commission of Government, established in 1934 following the Amulree Report (1933) on the financial state of Newfoundland, saw the improvement of education as one of its most important challenges. The English members of the Commission, led by Thomas Lodge, Acting Commissioner for Education, were critical of the denominational structure of education, particularly the division of funds on a denominational basis and the operation of many small, ineffective denominational schools. Lodge's proposals were seen as a frontal attack on the power of the churches in education (Neary, 1996). Conceding that the churches had certain rights in education, he knew that Roman Catholics would react strongly to his position. But he did not expect the objections he received from the Protestant population, particularly from Church of England authorities.

Clearly, the Commission was not prepared for the hostility with which the two churches greeted the reforms. Both Roman Catholic Archbishop Roche and Anglican Bishop White, representing two-thirds of the population, condemned the abolition of the post of superintendent as striking at the very principle upon which the denominational system was built. They thought a state system would destroy the religious atmosphere of their schools and threaten the millions of dollars the churches had invested in education. Because of the hostility, compromises were reached and the Commission's position moved from reforming the denominational system to introducing other measures, including the reorganization of the Bureau of Education, which had replaced the Department (Andrews, 1985a, 1985b; McCann, 1988b).

The Commission of Government also established the Council of Education, with authority for all educational policy. With the Education Commissioner as chair, membership included the three executive officers representing the Roman Catholic, Church of England, and Methodist denominations. This gave the churches a tremendous amount of power. Indeed, when the Commission of Government concluded its term, the power of these denominations may have been greater than at any time in Newfoundland's history. The denominational system had outlived the Commission.

During the Confederation with Canada debates of the late 1940s, the future of the denominational system again became a major political issue. These debates took place in the National Convention, elected to consider the financial situation of the country and to make recommendations concerning possible forms of government that could be put before the people in a national referendum. One member, Joseph R. Smallwood, masterminded much of the discussion of education to avoid the controversy surrounding the denominational issue. An avowed confederate, Mr. Smallwood was eager to remove denominational education as an issue in the referendum debates, believing that it had the potential to derail the prospect of Confederation if the religious denominations actively opposed it (Smallwood, 1973). Consequently, after a bitter political fight, Term 17 was included in the Terms of Union of Newfoundland with Canada, largely in response to the Roman Catholic Church's position on education (Appendix A). The Term guaranteed the following rights, many of which had been held for the previous 75 years: (1) the right to denominationally-based school boards, (2) the right of denominational boards to appoint and dismiss teachers, (3) the right to public funds for the recognized denominations on a non-discriminatory basis, and (4) the right to establish denominational colleges (Penney, 1988).

When Newfoundland joined Canada, it had the most denominational school system in the country. Five separate church systems—Roman Catholic, Anglican, United Church, Salvation Army, and Seventh-Day

Adventist—existed, the first four of these with formal representation in the newly-formed Department of Education. In addition, there was a relatively small Amalgamated system, largely non-Catholic, and several Pentecostal schools. The Pentecostal system was officially recognized and granted formal representation in the Department in 1954. Later, the Amalgamated system was also granted formal recognition in the Department.

After Confederation, the system again became the subject of growing criticism. Rapidly increasing enrolments, fiscal restraint, and demands for improved programs, facilities, and services highlighted the problems of duplication inherent in the system. One result was a demand for the integration of educational services. In the late 1960s, to enhance educational accessibility, efficiency, quality, and equality, the Anglicans, United Church, Salvation Army, and Presbyterians fully integrated their educational systems. Anglican Bishop Robert Seaborn provided strong leadership in the integration movement. The resulting "Integrated System" served nearly 60 per cent of the province's enrolment. Andrews (1985b) has provided an excellent account of this development.

Structural reforms, including the reorganization of the Department of Education along functional rather than religious lines, the elimination of many of the province's small denominational school boards (the province had 270 school boards in 1964), and the further consolidation of schools (the province had 1266 schools in 1964), resulted from the work of the 1967 (Warren) Royal Commission on Education and Youth (Government of Newfoundland and Labrador, 1967, 1968). Although the reorganization of the Department did not require a constitutional amendment, it did require the cooperation and goodwill of all the denominations, including the Roman Catholic Church.

Archbishop P. J. Skinner played an important role in the reforms of the late 1960s, demonstrating a more open attitude towards non-Catholic schools than many of his predecessors (Dunn, 1991). As a result of the Second Vatican Council, the archbishop knew that there were many Roman Catholics in the province who supported the changes. In a March 12, 1968, Memorandum to Successors, the archbishop wrote as follows: "Standing firm on the letter of our constitutional rights we might win a legal battle, but lose a war. The results would be far worse in the not distant future" (as cited in Dunn, 1991, p. 174).

During the 1970s and 1980s, there were few changes in the system. In an attempt to increase interest and participation in educational decision-making at the local level, Education Minister Lynn Verge (1979–1985) changed the composition of school boards and election procedures. She increased the number of elected trustees from one-third to two-thirds, and scheduled elections to coincide with municipal ones. This diminished to some extent the power of denominational authorities in the nomination and appointment of trustees. Efforts were also made during the 1980s to improve the system by increasing the number of shared or joint services and schools among Integrated, Roman Catholic, and Pentecostal authorities, a policy based on the principle that cooperation should preserve and respect the identity of each denomination but not prejudice the ultimate right of each denomination to operate its own schools (Coffin, 1977; Harte, 1989).

Considerable controversy concerning the denominational system resulted from the Canadian government's 1982 repatriation of the Canadian Constitution and the inclusion of a Charter of Rights and Freedoms. During the debates, the Newfoundland government supported the churches when they pointed out the potential threat to the system arising from the Charter and an amending formula which could override Newfoundland's Terms of Union. The result was the inclusion of Section 29 in the Charter, further protecting denominational rights. For example, Magsino (1988) pointed out that the right of a Catholic school board to dismiss Catholic teachers for marrying in a civil ceremony or in a non-Catholic church, or marrying a divorced person, had to be maintained as permissible conduct for a Roman Catholic school board. In 1987, another constitutional amendment was approved by the federal parliament, entrenching for Pentecostal Assemblies the same educational rights that the other denominations acquired in 1949.

The early 1990s saw the beginning of the end of the denominational system. The remainder of this chapter will focus on some of the forces that contributed to this dramatic policy change, beginning with the work of the 1992 Williams Royal Commission (Government of Newfoundland and Labrador, 1992b).

The 1992 Royal Commission on Education

A review of the denominational system was inevitable when the provincial government changed in 1989, for several reasons. As noted earlier, the system had again come under increasing criticism. Declining enrolments, fiscal restraint, and demands for improved programs, facilities, and services had highlighted the problems of duplication inherent in the system. The economic downturn and large budgetary deficits made it necessary to review government spending to ensure greater efficiency in all services, including education. There were also reports that, on standardized tests, students were performing at levels below their counterparts in other jurisdictions. Some claimed that education had become a major impediment to our competitiveness in the information-based economy, nationally and internationally, and a threat to our place in the world and our standard of living. Questions about the denial of human rights in the system were also raised, in the context of the Charter of Rights and Freedoms. Such developments brought unprecedented pressure on policy-makers and politicians to improve educational performance and reform our system.

Calls for a review of the denominational system had earlier been made by various groups. In 1986, the Newfoundland and Labrador Teachers' Association (NLTA) made such a proposal, as did the Royal Commission on Employment and Unemployment (Government of Newfoundland and Labrador, 1986a). Both groups pointed out that few changes had been made in the system since the implementation of some of the recommendations of the earlier Royal Commission on Education and Youth (Government of Newfoundland and Labrador, 1967, 1968).

And, then, there was the composition of the newly elected Liberal caucus, which included several educators, some of whom had been political activists. Two were past presidents of the NLTA, one a reform-minded school board chair, and still another, the chair of the 1967 Royal Commission on Education and Youth. The premier, Clyde Wells, had himself had called for a reform of the denominational system earlier in his political career. By initiating a comprehensive review of the educational system, these and other caucus members believed that the new government would be demonstrating its commitment to providing strong leadership in challenging times.

Before proposing the establishment of the Royal Commission, as Minister of Education I considered other mechanisms for reform. I examined the progress of the interdenominational sharing movement, and considered the establishment of a special joint church/state committee to actively promote such sharing, but soon concluded that this movement had run its course. I even considered recommending unilateral legislative action by the government, but realized the political and legal risks associated with such action. In the end, therefore, I recommended to Cabinet the appointment of the Commission. As the chair of the 1967 Royal Commission, I believed that this mechanism was uniquely capable of contributing to educational reform.

As a policy instrument, it seemed that a Royal Commission could have many potential benefits. It could recruit well-qualified, prestigious, and independent members, representing several disciplines and special-interest groups; it could access professional and technical expertise and data, internal and external; it could use a consultative decision-making process that conformed to the public's ideal of how decisions should be made; it could package its findings in a well-written and well-illustrated report; because it was external to government, it could be critical of the government and the churches, without suffering political consequences; and, because it was highly visible and commanded a wide audience for its proceedings and reports, it had the capacity to persuade others, politicians as well as the public, to support its findings and adopt its recommendations. The use of the word "royal" gave the Commission greater prestige and wider powers to investigate than other special committees and agencies.[1]

Of course, I was aware of the potential criticisms associated with the use of the Commission as a mechanism for change, particularly if its terms of reference included a review of the denominational system. These criticisms included the following: it could reawaken the divisive religious battles of the past; it could be time-consuming and costly; it could be seen as a political move to delay action or to relieve pressure; the people appointed as commissioners could be seen as supporters of the government, recommending what the government wished; and, because the Commission had no responsibility for implementing its recommendations, it could disregard the financial implications and political challenges in submitting its report.

The Williams Commission was appointed on August 7, 1990. Members were selected because they were highly qualified, broadly experienced, well-known, respected, and independent. Although they were selected from diverse backgrounds, they were not appointed to represent any one particular interest. Dr. Len Williams, a Memorial University professor, was a widely-known and respected educator, both provincially and nationally. Regina Warren, assistant superintendent with the Humber-St. Barbe Roman Catholic School Board, had provided outstanding service at the classroom, school, and school district levels, and Trudy Pound-Curtis, comptroller at Memorial University, was highly respected in the financial community. She had also served with distinction as the executive-secretary of the St. John's School Tax Authority.

The public response to the Commission's appointment was positive. In 36 public hearings all across the province, there were hundreds of presentations. In all, 1041 written and oral submissions were received. Also received were 129 petitions signed by thousands of citizens. Eighty-six per cent of the submissions referenced the denominational system, many supporting it. The Commission conducted or commissioned major studies of specific aspects of the system, including a cost-analysis and a public opinion poll of the attitudes of the population. It also visited schools, conducted focus groups, held private meetings, and travelled outside the province to consult and solicit views and opinions.[2]

At some public hearings, there was strong support for the denominational system. Certain themes were repeated: that the system was enshrined in Term 17 of the Terms of Union of Newfoundland with Canada; that other parts of Canada looked with envy at our unique partnership between church and state; that the amount of duplication in Newfoundland education was exaggerated; that if the government could justify the creation of francophone and native schools, then there was a right to denominational schools; that the problems of the denominational system resulted largely from the fact that the system was underfunded; that the problems of duplication could be minimized through interdenominational sharing; that under the Universal Declaration of Human Rights, parents had the prior right to choose the kind of education that should be given to their children; and that public schools, like those in the USA, were "Godless" schools, denying use of such activities as repeating the Lord's Prayer.

Critics of the denominational system consistently pointed to the duplication of schools and the wastage of precious resources. They also claimed that the system was divisive and an impediment to social cohesion; that the system did not respond to the children and parents of other religions and cultures; and there was a glaring lack of parental and public involvement because of church domination.

In its Report (Government of Newfoundland and Labrador, 1992b), the Williams Commission made 211 recommendations, calling for fundamental reform of all aspects of education. Although only 10 or 11 of the recommendations directly affected the denominational character of the system, these became the focus of much of the ensuing debate. The Commission acknowledged, however, that the denominational proposals were so fundamental that they could conflict with some of the constitutional guarantees contained in the Terms of Union. The Commission concluded that it could not "accept that the wording of these rights and privileges established decades ago were intended to paralyze the system in perpetuity, and stifle the ability of the system to respond effectively to change" (pp. 2–3).

The Commission recommended a single interdenominational system, retaining, it believed, many of the benefits of "denominationalism." It saw the new system as the most cost-efficient and effective way of dealing with the demographic changes and educational challenges confronting the schools. The Commission also recommended that the 27 denominational school boards be replaced by nine publicly-elected boards, and the three Denominational Education Councils be dissolved. A School Planning and Construction Board would be responsible for the allocation of funds for school construction, such funds to be distributed on the basis of province-wide priorities. The principle of neighbourhood schools would be the primary element of new admission policies.

The Commission hastened to add that, where numbers warranted, children should be provided with opportunities for religious activities and instruction in their own faith. It also recommended that the school system should be more sensitive and responsive to children of all religious groups. With regard to the role of the churches, the Commission concluded that their primary role should be the development and provision of religious education programs and the provision of pastoral care to students, fostering their spiritual growth; assisting with spiritual and religious activities in schools; providing skilled pastoral counselling in the areas of individual, group, and family therapy; and providing ethical consultation.

In what may have been wishful thinking, the Commission pointed out that just as, in 1969, five churches joined together voluntarily to form a single Integrated System, now, in 1992, it was possible for all churches to "disengage further and create a new system which will preserve the valued Christian character of schooling, and at the same time recognize the educational, economic and social advantages of participating in a co-operative approach to schooling" (Government of Newfoundland and Labrador, 1992b, p. 5). The Commission concluded that implementing the recommended system with the maximum consolidation could result in savings of over $21 million a year, a figure widely disputed by the churches. Unlike the Commission Report of 1967, which included a minority report submitted by the three Roman Catholic members, the 1992 Report was unanimously supported by all three members.

In retrospect, it could be argued that one of the most important contributions of the 1992 Royal Commission was that it provided, at a very important point in time, a vehicle for the public discussion of educational issues. In the process, the Commission captured a surprising amount of public attention and provoked the liveliest debate in years. School boards, teachers, students, parents, and the general public were truly engaged. The Commission conducted a considerable amount of research and travelled widely to examine developments elsewhere. In addition to its recommendations on the denominational system, it made recommendations on improving the operation of school boards, the curriculum, instructional time, teacher education, the education of children with exceptional learning needs, and even the way we fund education. Unfortunately, the implementation of many of these latter recommendations was overshadowed by the debate on reforming the system.

For six years following the release of the Royal Commission Report, there was extensive lobbying by many special-interest groups, long periods of negotiations, and periods of stalemate between the government and the churches, many political threats and counter-threats, two provincial referenda (in 1995 and 1997), two provincial elections (in 1993 and 1996), the appointment of the chair of the Royal Commission as deputy minister of education, a change of premiers from Premier Wells to Premier Tobin (in the winter of 1996), failed attempts by Premier Tobin and his minister of education to negotiate a "framework agreement" to resolve the issue, the collapse of the "common front" among the religious denominations, the passage of several pieces of legislation concerning the denominational system by the House of Assembly, two constitutional changes approved by the Parliament of Canada, and several important court cases, the final being in 2002. In the end, however, the denominational system was abolished.

Demographic and urbanization

In Chapter One, Galway and Dibbon provided an overview of the radical shifts in Newfoundland's demography in the post-Confederation years and I will not replicate their discussion of those trends here. But it bears repeating that the radical declines in student population greatly contributed to demands for the consolidation of school, as did the need—evident in student achievement data—to offer improved educational programs. The cost-efficiency of the denominational system was severely questioned; particularly where denominations operated separate schools in the same geographical area and streamlining of the denominational system offered a means to redistribute educational funding. The ageing of the Newfoundland population resulted in an increase in the number of people without children in school, with fewer contacts with the educational system. An ageing population is more likely to be concerned with other social services, particularly health and programs for seniors. Because of the general funding crises that existed in the province during the 1980s, many argued that a more efficient educational system could result in some re-direction of educational funds to these other services, or, at least, better use of the scarce financial resources that were available for education.

Associated with these demographic trends were urbanization and industrialization. In larger communities, other institutions take over functions that were once primarily the responsibility of the church. Urban dwellers enter into new relationships in every sphere of their lives and shed older ones. Improved communication and increased education allow people to become aware of religious viewpoints very different from their own, and of people who have no religious affiliation at all. They become aware of choice, and of the fact that value systems are often relative. These things tend to erode the power of the church as the regulator or interpreter of social life, as they erode the authority of the family. Indicators of industrialization include occupational changes, an increased division of labour, rising incomes, a move away from a resource-based economy, the greater use of technology, and an emphasis on increased productivity. All of these require an improved educational system at the elementary and secondary as well as the post-secondary levels. They, too, were forces that contributed to demands for educational reform in Newfoundland during the 1990s.

The growth of secularization

The reform of the denominational system in the 1990s was also influenced by a major ideological transition in the province—the growth of secularization. Social scientists generally define secularization as the process by which traditional religion and religious rituals lose their hold over society as a whole, and other institutions assume the functions of religion (Bibby, 1993).

During the 40 years following Confederation, Newfoundland's society became increasingly more secular. While at the end of the twentieth century many of the province's citizens considered themselves religious, and identified with a particular denomination or religion, the extent to which religion influenced their lives had declined. This was reflected in the decline in church attendance in most denominations, the difficulty of raising funds for church use, the shortage of students for the priesthood and the ministry, the increasing number of interdenominational marriages, and the unwillingness of an increasing number of people to see the church as the pre-eminent ethical and moral authority in their daily lives. The tendency was to consider the church as just another institution in an increasingly pluralistic society, whose role was largely confined to serving the spiritual needs of fewer and fewer people.

The credibility of the churches declined for many reasons, in addition to growing urbanization and industrialization. Included were the controversies surrounding abortion, pre-marital sex, homosexuality, the role of women in the churches, the establishment in the province of civil marriage and divorce courts, and, of course, the highly publicized sexual abuse cases involving Roman Catholic priests and other clergy. The reports of two commissions of enquiry, the Winter Commission (Roman Catholic Archdiocese of St. John's, 1990) and the Hughes Commission (Government of Newfoundland and Labrador, 1991), criticized the Roman Catholic hierarchy for acquiescing in the sexual abuse of children. The Winter Commission said that the denominational system may have tended to compound paternalistic and patriarchal attitudes, and that the church's administrative role in education was threatening if not oppressive.

These controversies, among others, clearly reduced the influence of the churches in a province in which, until then, they had retained power almost unknown elsewhere in Canada. With the decreasing power of the churches in education came an increase in the influence of the state. This transfer of authority and power happened in health and social services, as well as education.

In addition, there was the growth of mass education. The extension of formal education to a larger proportion of the Newfoundland population for longer periods of time increased literacy and prepared more people for productive lives in a more modern society. Mass literacy and the knowledge and skills of higher education are the foundation of the modern economy and essential for future prosperity. While Newfoundland continued to face many challenges in the development of mass literacy and the preparation of post-secondary graduates, a great deal had been accomplished over the previous three or four decades.

Associated with the growth of formal education came an increase in the self-confidence of many of our young people. They became more knowledgeable about international developments and more open to the outside world than their ancestors. They aspired to break out of the syndrome of hardship and deprivation that characterized much of our early history. In education, they demanded improvements in the quality of education, greater cost-effectiveness, and greater accountability, academic as well as financial.

While the province became increasingly more secular during the 1970s and 1980s, the denominations retained a great deal of power and influence in education, exercised through their Denominational Education Councils (DECs). These Councils had very specific legislated powers, negotiated as part of the reforms of the late 1960s. Included were the following: (1) making recommendations to the Cabinet on the establishment and alteration of school district boundaries, (2) making recommendations to the minister of education concerning the selection and appointment of school board members, (3) approving the constitutions of school boards to be forwarded to the minister for approval, (4) examining all proposed education legislation and regulations and making recommendations for changes, (5) administering and allocating capital grants from the government for school construction, (6) making recommendations to the minister of education regarding the selection, training and initial certification of teachers, (7) developing and administering religious education programs for the schools, and (8) advising the government on all educational policy which might affect the rights of the churches.

The retention of these powers was influenced by the fact that all three Councils— Integrated, Roman Catholic, and Pentecostal—worked closely together. They often spoke with a single voice and presented a "common front." With their executive officers and staff, they had easy access to politicians and senior government officials, both formal and informal; they served on high-level educational committees and agencies, such as the General Advisory Committee to the Minister of Education; and they attended many, if not all, educational workshops and conferences. They had the opportunity, the power, and the knowledge to respond directly to any challenges and criticisms of the system. And they did. As one political scientist concluded, they acted as "gatekeepers," removing the denominational issue from the public policy agenda whenever possible (Graesser, 1990).

When the Royal Commission was appointed in 1990, the Councils were placed on the same playing field as other partners, and forced to get involved in the public debate, both jointly and separately. The Commission's terms of reference did not provide parameters for the discussion of the denominational issue, as the terms of the 1960s Commission did. The earlier Commission was directed to examine all aspects of education and make recommendations having due regard to the constitutional rights of the churches. In the terms of reference of the 1990 Commission, the denominational system was identified as a central issue for examination, a decision that was opposed by the denominations.

In separate briefs, the Councils presented differing approaches to denominational reform. The Integrated Council (IEC) recommended a single interdenominational school system, to include the Roman Catholics, Pentecostals, and Seventh-Day Adventists. That position, which could be seen as an extension of Integration, reflected the views of the vast majority of the province's Anglican, United Church, Salvation Army, and Presbyterian adherents. Roman Catholic and Pentecostal authorities, on the other hand, recommended the retention of the enshrined denominational system, with provisions for greater interdenominational cooperation and sharing.

When the Report of the Williams Commission was released in 1992, the three DECs unanimously opposed the denominational recommendations, which they said would lead to the end of the system. Cracks within the common front began to appear, however, when Integrated school boards responded to the Report. Speaking to a reporter from the *Evening Telegram* (Consolidated school board, 1992), James Oakley, the chair of the largest Integrated school board in the province, said that his Board believed that all children should attend schools under the jurisdiction of a single school board, with provision for religious education and religious activities. Representatives of other Integrated school boards from across the province also supported that position. This put significant pressure on Integrated leaders.

The DECs again presented a common front when the first referendum was called in June, 1995. At a joint news conference, the executive officers stated that if the government's proposals were approved in the referendum and subsequently implemented, the denominational system would be abolished and a secular one established. Early in the campaign, Integrated authorities cooperated with Roman Catholics and Pentecostals to oppose the government's action. Many Integrated supporters found this disconcerting, because their leaders had earlier recommended a single interdenominational system. United Church adherents were particularly concerned because their denomination had long advocated the single-system model.

It did not take long, however, for fractures in the united front to reappear. Integrated authorities refused to join the Roman Catholic and Pentecostals in the formal "No" campaign. As the referendum date approached, the government made efforts to address the concerns of the Integrated group about the wording of the proposed amendment, the mood of Integrated church leaders as a whole changed, moving closer to accepting the government's position. That mood-change reflected the views of many of their adherents. Near the end of the campaign, Bishop Donald Harvey, a spokesperson for the Integrated System, came close to supporting the government by saying: "I don't think Wells is trying to pull a fast one. I don't think he has any double agenda, no hidden agenda or anything else" (Jackson, 1995, p. 1).

Bishop Harvey also sent a pastoral letter to members of the Anglican Diocese of Eastern Newfoundland and Labrador before the referendum. The bishop said that many people had written him stating that they were "confused, dismayed, and exasperated" over what was happening in the province under the broad topic of education reform. Almost all, he said, had pleaded for something to be done to "clear up the mess" and give priority to the educational needs of our children. He added that he believed this referendum (as costly as it would be) could be an instrument for doing just that. He went on to say: "the question is clear, concise and certainly very much to the point. This time we all should know exactly what it means. It is comforting to me to realize that it basically sums up the position taken by our church from the beginning of the debate five years ago. We consistently have asked for a single school system, neighborhood schools, employment of teachers on merit and ability, and the constitutional provision for Religious Education and Observances. I believe that an affirmative answer to the Referendum question will provide all of these objectives" (Harvey, 1995, p. 1).

That statement and others by leaders of the Integrated group marked the beginning of a breakdown of the common front.[3] The breakdown was a deciding factor in the outcome of the 1995 Referendum, when the vote was 53 per cent "Yes" and 47 per cent "No." Fagan (2004) acknowledged that the change of position by the Integrated leaders publicly undermined the "No" position and made the "Yes" victory possible. Undoubtedly, if the Government had lost the referendum, the reform agenda would have been set back for years. Divisions between and within the denominations, therefore, hastened the end of the denominational system.

The impact of special-interest groups and the media

Many special-interest groups supported the school reform movement in the late 1980s and the 1990s. One such group was the Newfoundland and Labrador Teachers' Association (NLTA), which had acquired the right to collective bargaining during the early 1970s. Collective bargaining granted teachers and their Association more presence and power, not only in matters of teacher welfare, but also in education generally.

With the publication of the document *Exploring New Pathways* (NLTA, 1986a) the Association launched the first major criticism of the denominational system since the 1967 Royal Commission Report. Roger Grimes, who was elected to the provincial legislature in 1989 and later became minister of education and premier, was the president of the Association at that time. The criticism by the Association was based largely on efficiency and economic grounds, rather than ideological ones. In 1990, the NLTA convened a provincial conference, also entitled *Exploring New Pathways*, to examine all aspects of the denominational issue. Cody (1994) stated that the conference became a focal point in the denominational debate.

The NLTA's support of government in the 1990s, particularly during the second referendum, was important not only because of the Association's influence in the wider community, but also because it was made up of teachers of all denominations. While Pentecostal teachers had a separate voice within the NLTA, and sometimes disagreed with its stand on denominational issues, such was not the case for other teachers, including Roman Catholics. Many such teachers believed that, in their campaigns, the denominations should have focused more directly on the rights of all children in the province to quality education, rather than on their constitutional rights to denominational control.

Another association that became increasingly involved in the debates of the 1980s and 1990s was the Newfoundland and Labrador Human Rights Association. During and after the entrenchment of the Charter of Rights and Freedoms, that Association strongly criticized the denominational system for limiting: (1) the lifestyle rights of teachers, (2) the rights of "non-adherents" of the system, including non-Christians, and (3) the rights of "non-adherent" parents to run for election to school boards that educated their children. The Association's presentations to the Royal Commission, their comments on the public opinion polls, and their reactions to arbitration and court decisions affecting the rights of school boards, teachers, parents, and students, were widely publicized and accepted. Although there were few documented cases, for example, where teachers were dismissed for religious and personal lifestyle reasons, the possibility of this happening in an era of human rights offended many citizens, including Roman Catholics.

The business community and various coalitions of parents also played an important role in supporting reform. The St. John's Board of Trade, for example, echoed the views of the Royal Commission on Employment and

Unemployment (House, 1986), linking education with economic growth and calling for changes to denominational education. The Newfoundland and Labrador Home and School Federation and the Education First Group, a diverse coalition containing persons of all religious and political persuasions, were very influential during the referendum campaigns. Change which tapped into that kind of public support was likely to be successful.

And, then, there was the influence of the media. For three or four decades after Confederation, few journalists openly criticized the denominational system, and those who did received little visible public support. That changed over time, for obvious reasons, including the sexual abuse cases involving members of the clergy. The media reported extensively on these cases, undoubtedly fuelling the anti-church sentiment. They also gave extensive coverage to the hearings and recommendations of the Winter, Hughes, and Williams Commissions, the negotiations following Williams, the two referenda, and the court cases, often supporting the Government's position and criticizing the churches (Cody, 1994). Through newspapers, radio, television, and films, therefore, the media became a powerful influence on how people saw the denominational issue and how they responded. They helped to set the reform agenda in education, greatly influencing policies, politics, and values.

Many supporters of denominational education believe to this day that they were unfairly treated at that time by certain journalists and media outlets. Fagan (2004, pp. 105–106) concluded that, during the campaign, Gerald Fallon, the executive director of the Catholic Education Council, was targeted by some of the "worst journalism that Newfoundland and Labrador had witnessed for a long time, much of it written by the Evening Telegram's regular columnists Ray Guy, Peter Fenwick and Peter Boswell."

Public opinion surveys also contributed to the open public debate concerning denominational education and the reforms that resulted (Bulcock, 1990; Crocker, 1990; Graesser, 1988a, 1988b; Warren, 1973b). While findings were sometimes ambiguous, and even contradictory, they demonstrated growing support among the public for a single, interdenominational system, and almost unanimous support for interdenominational sharing, provided religious education was included. The polls demonstrated that more and more people were critical of the traditional system because, they believed, it resulted in too many small schools, the duplication of facilities and programs, excessive school busing, the discrimination of non-Christians and non-religious, and the discrimination of teachers who could be hired or fired on the basis of religious affiliation. Publicity surrounding these polls helped to create doubts regarding the denominational system and legitimize and give confidence to the Royal Commission's findings and conclusions (Cody, 1994).

Publications such as *The Vexed Question: Denominational Education in a Secular Age* (1988), edited by William McKim, an outspoken critic of the denominational system, and *Unholy Orders* (1990) by well-known author Michael Harris, also contributed to the momentum for reform, as did the production of several films and television programs concerning sexual abuse and the churches in the province. These helped to weaken the moral authority of the churches and strengthen the view that, by reforming the school system, the government was doing the right thing.

Political leadership

Early Newfoundland political and church leaders were careful not to incur the disfavour of one another. A rule-of-thumb for many politicians was that messing with the churches was political suicide, because the churches had the power to mobilize public opinion against them. Consequently, over the years, the churches acquired considerable power, influencing not only education but almost every aspect of government—cabinet-making, civil service positions, patronage contracts, judicial appointments, knighthoods, and Rhodes Scholarships (Gwyn, 1968). With this went an agreement to keep religion out of political debate.

In return for these rewards, consciously or otherwise, the churches were very hesitant to criticize the government. Many of them remained silent on social problems, when one might have expected them to give leadership in an attempt to improve the lot of their people (Pottle, 1979). Even the Methodists in Newfoundland were more reluctant to agitate for social change than their colleagues in mainland Canada. As Pottle (1979, p. 53) pointed out, a "concordat" existed between the churches and the state, "virtually guaranteeing a condition of perpetual peace in which both parties found their respective terms and ambitions fulfilled." Anglican Bishop Meaden expressed this view when, in 1960, he said: "I am satisfied that everything that lies within the power of both the church and the state is being done to improve education in Newfoundland.... If there are any areas in which the state is not doing its best to improve then lot of Newfoundlanders, the Church of England does not publicize them" (Canadian Church Historical Society, 1960, p. 8).

In some respects, the early churches in Newfoundland were as powerful as the government, and church politics as influential as state politics. As

Dunn (1991) points out, several early bishops, consummate politicians in both church and public affairs, were consulted by politicians on all kinds of policy decisions. They used politics and politicians to promote the status and rights of their adherents. And politicians used the churches in the electoral process. In other words, the churches and politicians had what could be called a symbiotic relationship: they needed each other (Ponder, 1987).

While Premier Smallwood strongly believed in the importance of education, and considered his educational achievements an important part of his legacy, he left denominational reform to the churches. By staunchly defending the system in the 1960s, he was seen as a reactionary, at a time when the public, particularly younger people, preferred change. Improved educational opportunities had created a more thoughtful and critical population that wanted greater change and involvement. They had more confidence and hope than any other citizens in our history, and made it clear that they were not prepared to be governed as generations were in the past.

Premier Smallwood could have taken the recommendations of the 1967 Royal Commission and run with them, demonstrating real vigour and renewal. But he did not. In fact, he described the Commission as a "runaway" commission, exceeding its mandate. He even tried to undermine the Commission's recommendations for reforming the system. As someone once said, in times of stress, Mr. Smallwood's natural conservatism led him to resist aspects of that very quiet revolution that he had initiated.

Premier Brian Peckford was also eager to modernize education, but within the existing denominational structure. A reformer with a nationalistic bent, advocating more industrialization and greater provincial control of our natural resources, he refused, however, to stir the waters around the denominational issue. His government fully supported the system during the constitutional debates of the early 1980s when the churches feared that the enshrinement of the Charter of Rights and Freedoms threatened the system. With his support, the churches were successful in having Section 29 added to the Charter, guaranteeing that nothing in the Charter would negatively impact their rights. Through such actions, he earned the trust and respect of the religious leaders.

Graesser (1990) discussed with Premier Peckford his conservative tendencies concerning the denominational system. Graesser quotes the premier as follows: "Our overriding philosophical bent (in policy initiatives) was that on social and cultural matters, where there are deep-seated values, a gradualist, consultative approach was best, whereas in economic and constitutional matters we took a more aggressive categorical approach" (pp. 26–27). Mr. Peckford acknowledged that he was aware of the considerable body of public opinion favouring a more active approach to educational issues, but felt that "historical and cultural realities could not be disregarded." Perhaps, the premier was also concerned about the capacity of the churches to mobilize popular opposition to politicians who threatened the system, particularly in central parts of the province where his government was strong.

During the Peckford era, the denominational system received a boost with the visit of Pope John Paul II in September, 1984. In his address at the Basilica in St. John's, the Pope focused on the role of Catholic schools and Catholic educators in the attainment of the goals of Catholic education, encouraging teachers and parents to lead by example and to reflect God's presence in the world. More specifically, he said: "Teachers and parents must strive for a mature spirituality in their own lives; a strength and relevance of faith which can withstand the assault of conflicting values upon the home and the school. If the teaching of the Gospel is visible in your daily lives, it will have visible influence upon the young whom you teach" (John Paul II, 1984, pp. 18–19).

One of Mr. Peckford's education ministers, Lynn Verge, was more open than the premier to reform of the system. In fact, my judgment is that Ms. Verge strongly supported many aspects of a reform agenda while she was a member of the legislature. She promoted equality for all, particularly women. She believed in the importance of involving all stakeholders in educational decision-making. As noted earlier, she was the minister when the province increased the proportion of elected school board members from one-third to two-thirds, with elections scheduled to coincide with municipal elections so as to increase public interest and participation. Undoubtedly, she would have preferred 100 per cent elected, but, at that time, had to compromise with the churches.

Premier Clyde Wells, Premier Brian Tobin, and Prime Minister Jean Chrétien were the politicians who provided sustained leadership in the reform of the system. Without their commitment and determination, and the support of their governments, reform would have failed. Their actions are described here in considerable detail to demonstrate that commitment and determination, as well as the political sensitivity of the denominational issue, even in the 1990s.

As a rationalist in policy development, Premier Wells, like former Prime Minister Trudeau, believed that the state should aggressively promote economic and social justice. He saw a modernized school system as the key to our future in a knowledge-based economy. That philosophy was reflected in his government's Strategic Economic Plan. To achieve the new order, the premier and his government believed that the school system had to be made more efficient, more cost-effective, and more responsive to the needs of children and the province.

While Mr. Wells and his government preferred the single, unified, interdenominational system proposed by the Williams Commission, that proposal was totally rejected by the churches, particularly the Roman Catholic, Pentecostal, and Seventh-Day Adventist denominations. After months of negotiation and stalemate, the premier developed what he considered a compromise Term 17 amendment, between what the Commission recommended and what the denominations were demanding. The amendment provided for separate denominational schools where it could be demonstrated that such schools had sufficient numbers of students to provide quality education. Under the proposal, the province would have both uni- and interdenominational schools, operated by common school boards.

On June 1, 1995, Premier Wells announced that Newfoundlanders would go to the polls on September 5 in a referendum on the issue. Although such a course of action was not legally required, he wanted an expression of the will of the people before asking the House of Assembly and Parliament to approve an amended version of Term 17. He believed that the House and Parliament would listen carefully if the majority of the people voted in favour. To do otherwise, he believed, would invite criticism that the government was behaving "undemocratically."

Several issues emerged as a priority during the referendum campaign. The priority concern for the government was the duplication and wastage of funds associated with operating four separate school systems. It argued that the inefficient use of scarce financial resources could not be justified in a time of declining enrolments, increasing demands for quality education for all students, and fiscal restraint. The priority issue for the churches was the abolition of the denominational system and the elimination of religious education, religious practices, and the religious atmosphere that they believed should permeate education. This, the churches identified as their constitutional right. For many citizens, the priority issues were the inefficiencies of the system, particularly small schools and excessive school busing, the absence of neighbourhood schools, and, for an increasing number, the elimination of discrimination and intolerance that they believed was inherent in the system.

Although the government did not organize an "election-type" campaign, it did promote its position through frequent statements to the press, advertising, and the distribution of a question-and-answer document and a brochure to households. Opposing the proposed reform was a powerful coalition of two denominational groups—Roman Catholics and Pentecostals. The coalition hired an experienced political organizer and staff to conduct a focused and aggressive campaign. It did polling, prepared brochures and information kits, arranged advertisement campaigns for the media, called open-line shows, lobbied politicians, involved religious leaders at all levels, trained volunteers, identified supporters, and arranged to get their vote out. Near the end of the campaign, there were indications that the denominations were gaining momentum.

On September 5, the Newfoundland electorate voted 54 per cent "Yes" and 46 per cent "No," with a 52 per cent turnout. When the vote was broken down regionally, major differences emerged. For example, the "Yes" vote exceeded 65 per cent in 12 of the 52 provincial electoral districts, dominated by Integrated supporters. The "Yes" side lost decisively in seven rural districts where the Roman Catholics (in the case of five districts) and the Pentecostals (in the remaining two) were strong. The real surprise on referendum day was the results in the six St. John's districts, where an estimated 60 per cent of the electorate were Roman Catholic. In these districts combined, the "Yes" vote of 56 per cent was higher than the provincial average (Government of Newfoundland and Labrador, 1995a).

Both the "Yes" and the "No" sides claimed victory after the campaign. The churches had received a higher vote than anticipated. The government claimed that the "Yes" side had done well, seeing that it had not mounted an aggressive campaign, as the churches did. When the House of Assembly opened in the fall, the government proceeded immediately by tabling a resolution to amend Term 17. After a debate that split both political parties, the resolution was passed on October 31. Premier Wells requested the prime minister to proceed expeditiously with passage by Parliament. Mr. Chrétien indicated that he would, but it took months for that to happen.

Just before Christmas, 1995, Premier Wells announced his retirement from politics, and within weeks, Brian Tobin had replaced him as premier. After a successful provincial election, when the premier indicated that he would subsequently consult with all parties in an attempt to resolve the denominational issue, Mr. Tobin and his new minister of education, Roger Grimes, held a series of meetings with the churches and arrived at what they called a "Framework Agreement" that could make the Wells amendment unnecessary. But that agreement fell apart when the church leaders in Integration and IEC officials met with their school boards to discuss it. Many Integrated school board officials were very critical of the agreement, claiming that it was a return to the status quo. When their church leaders failed to aggressively defend it, it was obvious that the proposal would not fly. Growing anger in the public led to the organization of a "Yes Means Yes" Committee to lobby the government to reject the Framework Agreement and get on with the reform.

Even before the resolution approving the amendment reached the House of Commons, strong lobbying was underway, particularly by Roman Catholics in the province and across Canada. Lobbying continued, emphasizing that: (1) the amendment abolished the rights of minority groups in Newfoundland and Labrador, and (2) passage by the federal government would set a precedent for the treatment of minority education rights elsewhere in Canada.

The motion to approve the amendment was not introduced in the House of Commons until May 31, 1996, and a free vote taken on June 3. The vote was 170 members in favour and 46 against, including 35 Liberals and 2 Progressive Conservatives. The Bloc Québécois voted largely in favour because they wanted to set a precedent of basing constitutional change on a referendum vote, arguing that secession should get the same speedy treatment from Ottawa should the Québécois vote "Yes" on separation in the future, even by a small majority. The Reform Party supported the use of the referendum for policy-making on controversial issues and, therefore, voted in favour, as did the New Democratic Party (NDP).

The battle for approval in the Senate turned out to be even fiercer than that in the Commons. The Senate's Legal and Constitutional Affairs Committee held televised public hearings on the amendment, in Ottawa and St. John's. The Senate could approve the amendment, reject it, or amend it, but it could not kill the Bill. Within six months, the Bill had to be returned to the House of Commons for another vote.

The Senate Committee received presentations from groups and individuals across the country, as well as the province. The issues were vigorously debated, particularly the minority rights question. Although the Senate Committee approved the original amendment, the Senate itself passed an amended version, incorporating some of the changes proposed by those opposing reform. On December 4, the amended resolution was introduced in the House of Commons and defeated, and the original resolution passed by a vote of 172 to 42, almost the same as the June 3 vote in the House of Commons.

A day after the House of Commons passed the amendment, on December 6, 1996, Newfoundland and Labrador's minister of education, Roger Grimes, issued a statement noting that this was an historical moment for education in the province. He added that the Newfoundland legislature, by virtue of this amendment, would now have control over the way schools were organized and administered. The minister could hardly have envisaged what would happen over the next year.

The Department of Education then began the implementation of the amended version of Term 17, a complex model that required a high level of goodwill on the part of all. After months of controversy surrounding the designation of schools as being denominational or interdenominational, and some progress, the Roman Catholic and Pentecostal authorities sought a court injunction to halt the process. Judge Leo Barry's decision (*Hogan v. Newfoundland (School Boards for Ten Districts)*, 1997a) approving the injunction requested by the Roman Catholic and Pentecostal authorities, threw the school reform movement into turmoil, halting moves to close or restructure many denominational schools, including Roman Catholic and Pentecostal ones.

While supporters of the two churches saw the court decision as a victory for denominational rights, others believed that the result was uncertainty, confusion, and even chaos. Several schools had already been closed, students had been relocated, and teachers reassigned or even declared redundant. And this delay was only the beginning, because in the fall the court case testing the validity of both the provincial legislation and the constitutional amendment enacted the previous year would be heard. Reform would be deferred even further, with what the government described as significant financial and educational costs.

The essence of political leadership is in knowing when to think and act quickly and when to back away. Building on what Premier Wells had accomplished, Premier Tobin, riding a wave of popularity, acted quickly and decisively to complete the reform process. Sensing that the political mood of the province had changed, on July 31, 1997, he announced that the public would vote in another referendum on Tuesday, September 2, this time on a fully public system, with provision for religious education. More specifically, he said the government would seek a mandate from the people to end the separation of children, to end the denominational system, to eliminate Term 17 as it was drafted, and to create a new single school system where all children, regardless of their religion, attended the same schools.

For the previous five years, the premier claimed the government, school boards, the NLTA, the churches, parents, and students had all been engaged in what seemed to be a never-ending debate about how to reconcile the need for reform with the rights of the denominations in education, resulting in ever more confusion and conflict. The time had come, he said, to recognize that we could not maintain our commitment to achieving the reform necessary to shape our future if we continued to tie it to the denominational system of education that shaped our past. He described Premier Wells's compromise proposal an honourable attempt at reform, which did not work. The churches, he said, exercised their remaining constitutional rights in a manner that frustrated reform.

While not being critical of Wells, Tobin sought to distance himself from the first referendum campaign. He campaigned aggressively on what was seen as a clear and straightforward question, and he focused not only on the inefficiency and ineffectiveness of the system, but also the philosophical arguments on which it was based, particularly that Christians belonging to different denominations should be educated in separate schools. He claimed that the real issue was the correction of a "moral wrong" inherent in the system. By using this argument, he shifted the campaign from primarily economic grounds to the greater welfare of all students and society generally.

Both politicians and special-interest groups in the community soon spoke in support of the government's new proposal. A citizen's group from all political and religious backgrounds, Education First, became actively involved, and contributed a great deal to the campaign. Unlike 1995, the premier had the support of all members of his caucus, including well-known Roman Catholics and a senior cabinet minister of the Pentecostal faith. He also had the support of the Opposition in the House of Assembly, whose leader, Loyola Sullivan, represented a district with a high percentage of Roman Catholic constituents. The leader of the NDP, Jack Harris, whose party traditionally favoured one single school system for all faiths, enthusiastically supported the premier.

The main issues for the opposing churches in the campaign, Roman Catholic, Pentecostal, and Seventh-Day Adventists, were again the abolition of constitutional rights, the denial of parental rights to choose the education of their children, and the emergence of "Godless" schools. Other issues were that: the government should have returned to the bargaining table after the Justice Barry decision to negotiate a settlement; the proposed amendment did not adequately protect religious education and observances; the referendum was poorly timed and the wording of the proposed amendment held until just before the vote; funding was not made available to the "No" side, which was blatantly unfair; and, based on past performance, the premier and the government could not be trusted to carry through on their commitments.

While the Roman Catholic bishops took the lead in opposing the government, the 1997 campaign did not compare in organization, funding, or enthusiasm with that of 1995. The Catholic Education Council had been abolished, and its executive director, Gerald Fallon, who provided strong leadership in 1995, had retired. The Council's replacement, the Catholic Education Committee, did not have the same power and financial resources. Many citizens who had vigorously supported their cause in the first referendum appeared tired of the fight. Some were frustrated with what had happened after the first referendum and had changed their position, now supporting a single system. Fewer well-known organizations and individuals were prepared to become actively involved in opposing the government.

The Roman Catholic campaign was primarily local, at the parish level. The Alliance for Choice in Education, a volunteer organization made up largely of supporters of Catholic education, got involved in St. John's to inform Roman Catholic citizens of the issues and to encourage them to get out and vote "No." Pentecostal Parent Action Committees, with the same mandate, also organized in selected areas of the province. Both denominational groups prepared press releases and paid for advertisements. In letters to the editor and newspaper columns, Pentecostal supporters were more passionate than Roman Catholics. When Anglican Bishop Harvey, one of the Integrated leaders, stated that he was voting "Yes" because in some ways the new plan was an extension of Integration, the common front among the denominations had finally disappeared.

On voting day, the government was successful, with 73 per cent voting in favour (Government of Newfoundland and Labrador, 1997a). Following the referendum, the premier immediately began the constitutional amending process, with the added confidence provided by the strong base of public support. The House of Assembly was called into session to debate the new Term 17, and on September 5, it unanimously passed a resolution approving the amendment. That afternoon the premier wrote Prime Minister Chrétien informing him of that fact. The premier urged the federal government to approve the amendment in sufficient time to permit the orderly organization and operation of schools for the 1998–1999 school year.

The proposed amendment was referred to a Special Joint Committee of Parliament, made up of seven senators and 16 members of parliament.

The Committee was instructed to report back not later than December 5. Over a two-week period in November, it heard from a wide variety of witnesses, most of whom were from Newfoundland and Labrador. Minority and denominational rights again became the focus of presentations. In addition to arguing that constitutional minority rights in education were being abolished as a result of the actions of the provincial government, representatives of Roman Catholic groups and organizations stated that before minority rights could be abolished or amended, the consent of that minority should be obtained. They saw the referendum as an exercise where minority rights were subject to the will of the majority.

Supporters of the new Term 17 responded in several ways. First, they argued that the vote affected the rights of groups making up nearly 95 per cent of the residents of the province. While the Integrated Group as a whole made up over half of the population, it included persons of Anglican, United Church, Salvation Army, and Presbyterian faiths, denominations who had never given up their individual constitutional rights. Because the Roman Catholics had approximately 37 per cent of the population, the Pentecostal Assemblies 6 per cent, and the Seventh-Day Adventists less than 1 per cent, supporters of reform argued that these denominations were not minorities, because the rest of the population was not a single entity. This, supporters stated, was not a case of a majority voting on rights that belonged only to a minority: all groups were minorities. The real minority, supporters of reform contended, was the 5 per cent of the residents who were non-Christian. This interpretation of the minority rights issue, espoused earlier by Premier Wells and reiterated in some of the Supreme Court decisions, was totally rejected by the Roman Catholic, Pentecostal, and Seventh-Day Adventist authorities and their legal counsel.

Supporters of the constitutional amendment also claimed that if one accepted the view that, once given, rights could never be revoked or changed, democracy would never be possible. They expressed the view that no right was ever absolute, that the exercise of any one right must always be balanced against the effect of that exercise on the rights of others. This principle, it was suggested, had been consistently reaffirmed by the Supreme Court of Canada in the context of the Charter of Rights and Freedoms.

Thirdly, supporters of the government argued that the presence of amending formulas in the Constitution implied that rights could be changed. As political scientist Peter Boswell pointed out, a right, whether constitutionally guaranteed or not, could properly be diminished or eliminated by due process, using the amending formula included in the legislation (Boswell, 1997). He added that this was why Canada's parliamentary system operated on the principle that no current parliament could bind a future parliament, and why constitutions had amending formulas. Religious rights, as well as other freedom rights, equality rights, or language rights, could, therefore, be changed in accordance with the amending formula, in this case with the approval of the House of Assembly and the federal Parliament. The amending formula was designed not to prevent constitutional change but to ensure, by making the process more difficult than the passage of an ordinary bill, that rights were given "due regard and protection."

During the Joint House of Commons/Senate Committee hearings, many passionate statements were made on both sides of this issue. One of the most emotional in favour of reform was made by the NLTA, representing all teachers of the province. The NLTA concluded its presentation as follows:

> We are a proud people. We want to be self reliant and strong. As teachers in this province, we want our time and talent to provide a world-class education system for our students. It is a testament to human ingenuity and endurance that teachers operating within the present system can succeed in delivering a reasonable quality of education. We urge the Committee to remove the present barrier and allow us to deliver the very best in education. Our teachers and students deserve no less; the people of this province expect no less. (NLTA, 1997b, p. 5)

On December 9, 1997, the House of Commons voted overwhelmingly in favour of the amendment, 212 to 52. The following week, the Senate voted 45 to 26 in favour, in contrast with 1996 when senators voted to amend the resolution. The political fight in Ottawa was finally over. On December 12, Bill 41 was introduced in the Newfoundland House of Assembly amending the Schools Act and the Education Act to reflect the new Term 17.

January 8, 1998, was described by the provincial government as an historic day in the province. On that day, the new Term 17, establishing a single school system, was signed into law in Ottawa. Taking part in the signing were Governor General Romeo LeBlanc, Prime Minister Chrétien, and Premier Tobin on behalf of the province. The premier had this to say:

> Finally, we can move forward and end the separation of our children along denominational lines, and create a new single

school system where all children, regardless of their religion, can attend the same school.... We can now concentrate on improving educational opportunities for our children. We have focused far too long on the issue of governance, power and control. It is time to direct all of our energies, our imagination and commitment to providing the best possible education system available within our financial means to the children of Newfoundland and Labrador. (Government of Newfoundland and Labrador, 1998a)

Subsequent to that signing, the Roman Catholic authorities continued their fight in the courts. In September, 1997, a group of Roman Catholic adherents had filed an action in the Newfoundland Supreme Court challenging the validity of the 1997 referendum and the results (*Hogan v. Newfoundland (School Boards for Ten Districts)*, 1997b). Several unsuccessful actions in the Court followed. The legal battle finally ended on November 9, 2001, when leave to appeal the Newfoundland Appellate Court's decision to the Supreme Court of Canada was denied. All legal avenues had been exhausted.

While the above discussion has focused primarily on the determined leadership of a small number of provincial and federal politicians, the leadership of church officials and others who both supported and opposed the reforms should also be acknowledged. In his publication *Trial*, Fagan (2004) described the role of the Roman Catholic bishops and Catholic Education Council officials who led the opposition, particularly Gerald Fallon, the CEC executive director. According to Fagan, from 1989 to 1997, Fallon was the passionate voice of Catholic education in Newfoundland and Labrador, indeed across Canada, a role which earned him respect from all quarters. The role of Integrated, Pentecostal Assemblies, and Seventh-Day Adventist church leaders and their officials remains to be told.

Conclusions

The second half of the twentieth century was a period of profound changes in Newfoundland and Labrador. Society became less "traditional" and more "modern." There were massive improvements in transportation and communication, and moves away from an economy based largely on the exportation of natural resources to include more manufacturing and greater use of technology. The province became much more urbanized, not only in the distribution of population, but also in terms of culture and values. Values became more universal and secular and less denominationally-based, reflecting a reduction in the power and authority of the churches. Values were also impacted by the slow but steady growth of the feminist movement, and the modest increase of the multicultural community. Over the five decades, Newfoundland, like Quebec earlier on and Ireland more recently (Foster, 2008), experienced a quiet revolution in which citizens became more educated, innovative, pluralistic, and egalitarian.

The governance of the province's educational system also went through a modernization process. Before Confederation, when there was a conflict between the forces of traditionalism and modernism in education, traditionalism generally won. Whenever church control of the system was threatened, the denominations fought back politically and ended up with the same or only slightly less power than before. Such was the case during the Commission of Government period and the Confederation with Canada debates.

During the 1960s, there was a slight change in the balance of power between the two sets of forces. It might be said that, at that time, the forces of traditionalism and modernism in education fought to a draw. Although there were moves towards a streamlined denominational system (for example, the integration of the educational services of the major Protestant denominations, the establishment of a non-denominational Department of Education, and the consolidation of small denominational school boards and schools), the churches were able to acquire significant powers through the establishment of the DECs and the Denominational Policy Commission.

Another wave of educational reform occurred in the 1980s and 1990s, when modernization forces became even more influential. That period saw an increase in the level of general education among the population; a progression away from narrow sectarianism in education towards greater secularism; the growth of greater religious tolerance in education, resulting from, among other things, greater understanding of other denominations and religions; an openness on the part of many citizens to the idea of a common school system; and the acceptance of interdenominational sharing and joint services in education by Roman Catholics and adherents of the Pentecostal Assemblies. Some would describe the educational reforms of that period as a win for the forces of modernism.

From the time of the release of the Royal Commission Report in 1992 until the system was eliminated in 1998, there were occasions when the government could have ended the political debate by agreeing with church demands. But it did not. It continued in its efforts to reform the system.

There were occasions, as well, when the churches could have negotiated a deal, retaining some form of interdenominational education. Certainly, Premier Wells sought a compromise with the churches. And Premier Tobin did as well, until July, 1997, when Mr. Justice Leo Barry granted the court injunction halting implementation of the Wells amendment. It became obvious, then, that no compromise was possible: that the Roman Catholic, Pentecostal, and Seventh-Day Adventists authorities were demanding the retention of their 1949 rights—the right to operate separate denominational schools, controlled largely by their own school boards, staffed primarily by teachers and administrators of their own faith, and attended by students accepted in accordance with their own admission policies. That was totally unacceptable to the government and most of the population.

In opposing the government's proposals, church authorities asserted that they were standing on principle. They may have also believed that their influence and their constitutional guarantees would ultimately result in the retention of the system: that political leaders would either change their position or the courts would rule in their favour. Neither, indeed, happened. These authorities and their advisors underestimated the determination of government leaders. They also misread the public mood, not realizing that many citizens of all denominations no longer supported the system, and were prepared to vote accordingly. And, they failed to acknowledge the possibility that the courts would rule against them and support the Government's proposals. This, the courts finally did.

Earlier in this chapter I gave a brief introduction to the influence of special-interest groups in the reform process, and particularly the impact of the NLTA in the denominational debate. In the chapter following, Edward Hancock, who has had a long-standing, close affiliation with the NLTA, examines in greater depth the significant role of NLTA in the reform process.

Chapter Three

A Call for Reform–Teachers and Denominational Schools

Edward Hancock

For more than 100 years, the Newfoundland and Labrador Teachers' As-sociation (NLTA), formerly named the Newfoundland Teachers' Asso-ciation (NTA), has been promoting the interests of education. The NLTA was formed in 1890 and its original Constitution states that it *shall have for its object the protection of teachers and the advancement of the interest of educa-tion generally* (Cuff, 1985). With this dual mandate, the NLTA has been di-rectly involved in, and its members have been affected by, all education reform measures undertaken in the province. A cursory examination of the history of the NLTA in Newfoundland and Labrador would show that the province's teachers and their Association have been key players in most, if not all, of the major developments of the province's education system. Throughout its history, the NLTA has taken its educative mandate as seri-ously as its protectionist mandate and has consistently sought to promote progress towards the best and most effective education system attainable.

The call for change

Much has been written and said about the province's denominational school system as it existed up to the mid-1990s. For 100 years the NLTA worked within the denominational structure of the school system. How-ever, from its inception, the NLTA was formed as, and has remained, an interdenominational organization. As Cuff (1985) notes, even at the inaugural meeting of the Association in November, 1890, teachers "represented all denominations, which shows that, from the beginning, the NTA was conceived as an interdenominational body" (p. 4). This interdenominational character has stood the test of time. When, in the early- to mid-1980s, an analysis of the province's school system led the NLTA to the conclusion that radical change was needed in the structure and administration of education in the province, its interdenominational nature was a major factor in permitting it to undertake a critical analysis of the system.

The decades following Confederation saw major improvements in the province's education system, including improvements in such areas as school facilities, teacher qualifications, curriculum, and pupil transportation. However, pressures on the system also increased. There was a dramatic rise in the province's student population (which peaked in 1971–1972), placing great pressure on school facilities. The province's citizens demanded improvements in education services and programs. Rightly, the public expected that students in the province's education system province should have access to educational opportunities equal to those of students throughout Canada.

Chapters One and Two describe several inter-related forces that influenced and drove the reforms of the province's denominational education system, which Warren (2008) has described as a time when the province experienced one of the most significant educational changes in its history. One of the key occurrences in moving towards that reform, and a pivotal event which focused attention and debate on the need for change, was the publication by the NLTA of its brief to government, titled *Exploring New Pathways* (NTA, 1986a). The *Brief* focused on three major areas of concern to the NLTA and the teachers of the province:

(1) Action for Today: Requested legislative changes to the NLTA Act, the Teachers' Pensions Act, and the Teachers' Collective Bargaining Act.
(2) Teachers for Tomorrow: Teacher training in Newfoundland and Labrador.
(3) Pathways from Isolation: The delivery system for education in Newfoundland and Labrador.

It was the third section of the *Brief* which provoked the greatest response and eventually had a major impact on the province's education system. This section focused on a critical evaluation of the province's denominational school system and identified what the NLTA considered be a serious and extensive flaw, that being isolation by denomination. The *Brief* argued that this flaw "is now seriously reducing the quality of education which this province is capable of delivering" (p. 17). Presented to the Social Policy Committee of Cabinet on May 28, 1986, this *Brief* is considered by many to be a seminal event leading to the reform of the denominational education system.

The NLTA's concerns related to the delivery of educational opportunities within the denominational system. An overview of the content and direction of the *Brief* is summarized well in a December, 1986, *Newsletter* (NTA, 1986b) sent to all teachers from then President Roger Grimes, who would later be elected and become minister of education:

> We gave information showing that the per pupil expenditure on education in Newfoundland is still far below the Canadian average and amongst the lowest in Canada. We indicated that practices such as duplication of certain services and overlapping of school board jurisdictions were causing an inefficient and wasteful use of the current dollars that were being spent on education in our province.

> We deliberately highlighted some examples of areas of waste and duplication to encourage the Social Policy Committee of Cabinet to give serious consideration to the only recommendation that we made arising from this section of the Brief. That recommendation was that the provincial government should establish a Royal Commission with the broad mandate of examining the administrative and economic disadvantages of the current denominational system and provide recommendations for improvement.

> The Executive made this statement in the Brief since it is clear, in our opinion, that such a comprehensive study of the delivery system of education in our province is long overdue, realizing that the last time such an overall review of our system was conducted was through the Warren Commission in 1968, almost 20 years ago.

> We indicated clearly in the oral presentation of the Brief to the Social Policy Committee of Cabinet that our references to waste and inefficiency did not indicate the feeling on behalf of teachers that too much money was being spent on education,

but that the money being spent could probably be used in more efficient ways to enhance educational opportunities for students and that, in fact, more money was required if a system was to move close to average Canadian standards.

There was considerable public reaction to the *Brief* following its release and the accompanying public statement issued by the NLTA. Some people interpreted the Association's comments on waste and inefficiency, and its call for a Royal Commission, as an indication that the NLTA wished to abolish the denominational system. The NLTA took pains to note that its objective was the improvement of the system and its educational offerings for students, and not the abolition of denominational involvement in education.

The fall of 1986 saw further activity in response to the NLTA *Brief*. In a press conference called by the minister of education in October, the government took exception to the NLTA's estimates concerning waste in the system while admitting that some waste did exist. The conclusion of the government, as stated by the minister, was that there was insufficient documented evidence of inefficiency and duplication of effort in the system to warrant the establishment of a Royal Commission at that time. The NLTA was disappointed by the response. Shortly thereafter, representatives of the Denominational Education Councils (DECs) held a joint press conference in which they concurred with the government's conclusion. Again, there were some suggestions that the NLTA *Brief* was misleading and motivated by a desire to discredit the denominational system and see it abolished. The NLTA issued a statement in reaction to the responses from the minister and the DEC representatives, reiterating its belief that there continued to be waste, inefficiency, and duplication of effort in the system and that a comprehensive study was warranted.

Some of the reactions to the NLTA *Brief* questioned the Association's motives in its direct criticism of the denominational system. Wayne Russell was executive director of the NLTA from 1984 to 1997 and worked closely in 1985–1986 with then NLTA President Roger Grimes in the preparation and presentation of the *Brief*. In an interview, Russell (personal communication, November 2008) expressed adamantly that the single major issue in recommending a Royal Commission on Education was the NLTA's concern for the quality of education in the province relative to Canadian standards. Although the province had a highly trained teaching force and its educational effort (education spending as a proportion of a jurisdiction's per capita GDP) at the time was the highest in Canada, the

NLTA argued that inefficiencies and duplication of the denominational system were preventing the province from raising the quality of education to Canadian standards. The denominational system created barriers to the appropriate deployment of teachers and administrators, and had a major influence on who was selected for the leadership positions at the district level. In the interview, Russell charged that the large number of school districts with overlapping jurisdictions was an obvious duplication of effort and inefficient use of resources and that the NLTA's case was entirely based on economic and not ideological considerations. That is, the NLTA's aim was not to see the system dismantled but to improve its efficiency and effectiveness. These comments concerning the NLTA's position are consistent with comments expressed by Russell (1991) in an article appearing originally in *The Morning Watch* in 1989. That article states:

> We did not consider the option of dismantling the denomination (*sic*) system and replacing it with a single public education system. We were aware of the provisions in Term 17, and the principle of denominational education where it is a marriage of the support of the church with the value of education is supported by the Association. It was also recognized that the inefficiencies were not so much associated with denominational education as they were with the structure utilized. The problem, as seen by the NTA, is isolation by denomination, that is, each denomination operating independent of the other. The solution we believed was to reorganize along cooperative lines. (pp. 101–102)

This position also concurs with the NLTA's policy on the denominational education system as it was stated at the time. As quoted in *Exploring New Pathways* (NTA, 1986a), that policy stated (in part) as follows:

> The Newfoundland Teachers' Association is explicit in its concern for the quality of education and the welfare of teachers. This must be our concern no matter in what type of education system we function. Our response to denominational education must be from this perspective. The NTA is not attempting to weaken or destroy denominational education. (p. 15)

The NLTA made its arguments knowing full well that the creation of an interdenominational system would lead to a major consolidation of schools and school districts with potential impact on teacher numbers and possible teacher layoffs. Moreover, the NLTA was aware that a natural enrolment decline, brought on by a staggering decline in birth rates, would lead to further losses of teachers. The NLTA argued that a reduction in the number of schools and the number of boards would not have a huge additional impact on the number of teachers, and that revamping the system would provide an opportunity for maintaining and improving upon current resources (human and financial) and using them in a more effective fashion. Russell (personal communication, 2008) suggested it was a time when, within the NLTA, the concern for the system, the quality of education, and teachers' professional well-being superseded concerns related to ongoing teacher welfare.

Following the release of *Exploring New Pathways* (NTA, 1986a) and the reaction from the government and the DECs in the fall of 1986, the NLTA continued its efforts to have government undertake a detailed examination of the system. In 1987, the NLTA initiated a media and speaking campaign aimed at improving the funding for education. Media coverage and public discussion of this topic increased greatly. In response, the government established a Task Force on Educational Finance in September 1988. In its input to this Task Force, the NLTA (1989a) raised several concerns regarding the duplication and inefficiency of the denominational system and expressed its hope that some of these concerns would be addressed with specific recommendations from the Task Force.

In June 1989, the report of the Task Force on Educational Finance (Roebothan, 1989) was released and its sole recommendation on interdenominational sharing was that the DECs establish a joint committee system to identify further possibilities for promoting interdenominational cooperation in education. In its reaction to the report of the Task Force, the NLTA expressed its disappointment with the Task Force's approach to this matter and reiterated the concerns which had been raised in its *Brief* to the Task Force. These fell under the following key areas: (1) the overlapping jurisdiction of school boards; (2) administration of the education system; (3) duplication of school facilities; and (4) proliferation of small schools. The NLTA again used this opportunity to press its case, noting that:

> The difficulties identified here are inherent in the denominational system as it is currently administered in Newfoundland and Labrador. The Newfoundland Teachers' Association believes strongly that the provincial government and the Department of Education must take the leadership in overcoming these problems. The people of this province have on many oc-

casions strongly voiced their willingness to support increased inter-denominational cooperation. The provincial government must act on this initiative. (NLTA, 1989b, p. 19)

Russell (1991) commented on the effect the NLTA *Brief* had on the delivery system. He noted that several things had happened in keeping with the general premise of the NLTA *Brief*, but that it would be somewhat presumptuous to conclude that they are a direct result of the *Brief*. However, he noted that "it is clear that the Brief has had an impact" (p. 102) and he provided several examples of what had occurred since the release of the *Brief*. This list included:

❖ An open and frank discussion among educators of the denominational system and in particular, the inefficiencies of the isolated structure;

❖ A number of major studies released following the *Brief* also considered and made recommendations on the denominational system;

❖ Some examples of denominational cooperation;

❖ A pause in the division of schools by denomination.

He concluded by noting that, while these were positive changes, the question is whether they were "tinkering" to bring the system through this period of time when there were serious questions about its effectiveness or whether they indicated a positive direction for the future (p. 104).

In the spring of 1989 the Liberal party defeated the Progressive Conservatives, who had been in power since 1972, and Clyde Wells became premier. The immediate past president of the NLTA, Roger Grimes, was elected as a Liberal MHA, as was the current NLTA president, Patricia Cowan, who resigned early to run in the 1989 provincial election. Cowan was appointed to cabinet as minister of labour while Grimes was appointed parliamentary assistant to the premier (but soon to be appointed to cabinet and occupy a number of significant portfolios under Wells and his successor, Brian Tobin). Dr. Philip Warren, author of the 1967 Report of the Royal Commission on Education and Youth, who was also elected, was appointed minister of education in the Wells cabinet. Wells, Warren, Grimes, and, later, Tobin would all play significant roles in directing the path of education reform in the 1990s.

After the Wells administration took office, the NLTA turned its attention to continuing the discussion of the duplication and inefficiencies which existed in the denominational system. In August 1989, the NLTA amended its policy on the denominational system to bring it more in line with its position expressed in the 1986 *Brief* and its input to the Task Force on Educational Finance. The amended policy made specific reference to support for denominational cooperation and the belief that the Term 17 rights of denominational authorities should not restrict educational opportunities or undermine the quality of education. In the fall of 1989, the NLTA began planning a public forum on the denominational system. As indicated in letters of invitation from the NLTA, the purpose of the forum was to examine closely the efficiency and effectiveness of the current delivery system and to present alternatives for discussion. The forum provided for a broad spectrum of input on several issues concerning the denominational system. Several prominent educators and scholars were invited to conduct presentations and panels were put in place to react to them.

Nearly 200 people attended the forum, including representatives from government, education, labour, business, various religious affiliations, other professions, special-interest groups, and students. In his opening address to the forum, then NLTA President Keith Coombs (1990) noted:

> In approaching this analysis, we would best be served by approaching the topic with a free and open mind. We should leave our biases and preconceived attitudes outside the forum's walls. We should be willing to debate and speak openly on each of the issues that we will face.

In August 1990, just six months after the public forum, government announced the appointment of a Royal Commission of Inquiry into the Delivery of Programs and Services in Primary, Elementary, and Secondary Education. The establishment of such a Royal Commission was the single recommendation on the denominational system made in the NTA's 1986 Brief *Exploring New Pathways*. Chaired by Dr. Leonard Williams (also a former president of the NLTA), the mandate of the Commission was to investigate, report on, and make recommendations regarding all aspects of the organization and administration of the province's school system. More specifically, the Commission was set a number of tasks, most of which had implications for the denominational system. These included: examining the organizational and administrative structures for delivering school programs; examining the possibilities for further district and school consolidation; examining the extent of duplication resulting from the denominational system and the costs associated therewith; examining the effectiveness of existing cooperative efforts within and across school districts and suggesting new initiatives; identifying any existing barriers to the effective, efficient, and equitable delivery of programs and services and proposing corrective measures and incentives; and considering the matter of accessibility for those who may not now be adequately served (Government of Newfoundland and Labrador, 1992b, p. 5).

Teacher representations to the Royal Commission of Inquiry

With the implementation of the major recommendation from its 1986 *Brief*, the NLTA turned its attention to providing input to the Commission. On November 9, 1990, less than two weeks before the Association's 100th anniversary, the NLTA made an introductory presentation to the Commission, the purpose of which was "to suggest those questions and issues which should be considered by the Commission" (NLTA, 1990, p. 1). In that presentation, the NLTA noted that the core of what needed to be studied was the effective, efficient, and equitable delivery of programs and services. It further suggested that the Commission remain aware that the target for its work was "Canadian standards," with the child at the centre of its deliberations.

The NLTA established a committee to prepare a brief to the Williams Commission. Although the brief was later endorsed by the Association's 57 branches and 26 special-interest councils, it did engender some internal debate within the membership. In a March 1992 Presidential Update to the membership (NLTA, 1992a), then President Morley Reid acknowledged this when he stated:

> Your Association...fully realized that our recommendation would not have unanimous support within our membership. Even realizing that we were going to meet with some objection, despite the consensus at the meeting of branch and special interest council representatives, the provincial executive felt that NLTA should recommend the unified system because it was the right system for this province.

That newsletter further went on to elaborate on the Association's position, stating that:

> The role the churches had in the past was not the one they should have in the future. Churches should continue to have

responsibilities in determining the kind of moral and religious education that would be offered in our schools,...providing chaplaincy services,...promoting customs, traditions and observance of religious holidays. However, it was felt that all students, regardless of religious faiths, should attend school under the one roof.

In October 1991, the NLTA submitted its formal brief to the Williams Commission entitled *Building a Vision for the Future* (NLTA, 1991). The brief contained the following two key recommendations:

(1) That the province move immediately to a unified system of education which integrates the officially recognized denominations and other religious groups; and

(2) That a province-wide referendum be held to determine whether there is support to move to a single public school system involving the officially recognized denominations and other religious groups in authorizing and mandating religious instruction in schools.

Although there was obviously some internal debate, the NLTA did not incur any significant damage from division within the membership and reiterated its position in a response to the Commission's report in December 1992 (NLTA, 1992b). In fact, just one year after the Commission's report was released, the NLTA, with the full support of its members, found itself at odds with the provincial government regarding attempts to reduce the costs of public services and, in particular, compensation costs to public sector employees.

The Williams Commission recommended a new model for the school system, which would be a modification of the existing denominational system, to retain denominational characteristics but to include those groups/individuals not presently served in the governance of schools. This system would involve the formal integration of all faiths into a single school system, but retain significant input on the part of the denominations. Furthermore, the Commission recommended that, where numbers warrant, children should be provided with opportunities for religious activities and instruction in their own faith, and that the school system be sensitive and responsive to children of all religious groups. The Commission also recommended the creation of nine new interdenominational school districts—the first significant overhaul of the province's school system in 25 years.

The turbulent post-Commission years

The NLTA reacted quickly to the Commission's report, indicating in a letter to the minister of education in June 1992, that the basic thrust of the report was acceptable. In a more detailed response, submitted in December of the same year, the NLTA (1992b) made the point that it supported a major restructuring of the system:

> The province is ready for change, and its citizens will accept change. We know the opposition, and we know the legal complications. The question now is whether the will exists within government to bring about these changes. We believe it does, and we strongly urge that the correct decisions be made and a process begun.

The story of the events of the ensuing five years is available from government documents and other sources, and has been told from various viewpoints. Warren (Chapter Two) and Fagan (Chapter Six) offer useful, albeit somewhat divergent, perspectives of the events of the post-Commission period, and I will not add to those accounts here. The result was that after nearly three years of discussions and negotiations between government and denominational representatives, no agreement was reached on a restructured school system. Following the second referendum in September, 1997, the provincial government moved to petition the federal government to amend Term 17 with the effect of removing all denominational authority for education, providing exclusive authority to the legislature. The amendment also provided for courses in religion which are not specific to a religious domination and for religious observances to be permitted where requested by parents.

The NLTA maintained its position on the unified system throughout these events. Following the release of the Williams Commission report in 1992, the NLTA anticipated that government and church leaders would quickly complete the details for its implementation. This did not occur. The NLTA then supported the first referendum in 1995. As stated by the Association in a position paper (1997a), "it did so reluctantly since it recognized that a referendum was, at best, a blunt instrument with which to change the school system. It believed that the referendum was necessary because all restructuring of the school system had deadlocked." Although the NLTA considered the first amendment to Term 17 in 1995–1996, and the new Schools Act which followed, a "workable compromise," it found it

impossible to reconcile the rights of the denominations for uni-denominational schools under the revised legislation with the redundancy and reas-
signment rights of teachers under the collective agreement. As the
NLTA's same 1997 position paper expressed it, the continued disagree-
ment between government and the Roman Catholic and Pentecostal authorities following the first amendment to Term 17 led to "confusion,
frustration and, finally, chaos."

In NLTA's view, the confusion relating to teacher reassignments involving interdenominational and uni-denominational schools in the spring
of 1997 was followed by chaos when the July 1997 court injunction was issued in favour of the Roman Catholic and Pentecostal authorities. School
closures and reconfigurations were reversed, decisions relating to their as-
signments for September 1997 were in doubt, and teachers were in turmoil.
Thus, when the second referendum was announced by the premier in July
1997, the NLTA again "reluctantly" gave its support. However, it expressed anger and frustration over the power struggle between church leaders and government. Ironically, by the fall of 1997, partly because of the
intractability of the leaders of two of the denominations, the outcome that
the NLTA had been wrongly accused of advocating for—a complete dismantling of the denominational system—had essentially come to pass. The
frustration felt by NLTA leaders towards the end of the process is perhaps
best summed up by an excerpt from its position paper released prior to the
1997 referendum:

> While reason should have prevailed, the leaders of government
> and churches would not allow it to happen. The people of
> Newfoundland and Labrador must now speak clearly. Students
> should come first. (NLTA, 1997a)

Conclusions

This chapter has presented an insider's perspective on the part played by
the NLTA in influencing the events leading to educational reform in Newfoundland. My view, that the NLTA played a significant role, is one that
has been shared by others. In his report on the costs of the denominational
system (on behalf of the Williams Commission), Press (1992) stated that
the NLTA was "first off the mark" in its criticism of the inefficiencies of the
denominational system and in trying to quantify those additional costs (p.
10). Meanwhile, Warren (personal communication, November 2008)
noted that the publication of *Exploring New Pathways* in 1986 represented

the first major criticism of the denominational system since the 1967 Royal Commission Report. Regardless of one's particular perspective, it would be hard to deny that the NLTA *Brief* was a landmark document in the reform of the denominational system. Considering the record of its involvement in the events of the ensuing decade, it would be equally hard to deny the NLTA as a key player in shaping Newfoundland and Labrador's public education system.

We move now to a fuller exploration of two significant ideological changes in the delivery of education. In Chapter One, Galway and Dibbon introduced the notion that the push for efficiency in educational governance (and the way other public services were delivered) was a key impetus for change. Gerald Galway develops this idea further in Chapter Five with his analysis of the economics of educational reform. In the next chapter, Phillip McCann provides his account of how, beginning in the 1980s, government, industry, and the public began to reconceptualize education as a driver of economic prosperity. As McCann explains, this shift to a neoliberal, competitive orientation was part of a broad set of ideological changes that were transnational in nature and had profound implications for schools.

Chapter Four

From Christian Humanism to Neoliberalism–A Decade of Transition, 1985–1995

Phillip McCann

The argument presented in this chapter is that, between the mid-1980s and the mid-1990s, the ideology of the political class in Newfoundland and Labrador changed from liberal humanism with Christian overtones to neoliberalism, reflecting changes on the international scene, and that this transformation had important effects on the theory and practice of education.

Neoliberalism, global competitiveness and education

What is neoliberalism? The economic historian David Harvey (2005) defines it as the liberation of "individual entrepreneurial freedoms and skills within a framework characterized by strong property rights, free markets and free trade" (p. 2), which swept away the liberal democratic welfare regimes of the post-war period. Neoliberalism promotes rolling back the state, deregulation of economic controls, privatization of public industries and services, the growth of a service sector at the expense of industry, the outsourcing of jobs to developing countries, and the restriction of welfare facilities and trade union rights. From the late 1970s onwards, these doctrines and practices influenced the policies of international agencies, think-tanks, and governments of every type from social democratic to the extreme right (Harvey, 2005).

The roots of neoliberalism go back to the 1930s, when a group of economists, inspired by the Austrian aristocrat Friedrich von Hayek, came together in Paris in 1938 to re-invent liberalism. Hayek's (1944) *The Road to Serfdom*, augmented by the theories of Milton Friedman (1962a), laid the foundation of post-war neoliberalism. But the turning point is seen by economists as the late 1970s, with the OPEC oil crisis followed by the election of the neoliberals Ronald Reagan in the USA and Margaret Thatcher in the UK (Harvey, 2005).

The educational component of neoliberalism is underpinned by the theory of human capital advocated by the US economist Theodore Schultz (1961). The theory assumes that the amount of a country's general education, together with the production of knowledge, makes a significant contribution to national economic growth. Education is thus seen as investment rather than consumption, and an essential element in economic productivity; human beings must become "income-producing agents of the economy," and the curriculum needs to be restructured along scientific-technological lines to create the most effectively productive workforce (Salamon, 1991; Schultz, 1961).

Two decades later this theory received the endorsement of the Reagan government with the publication of a document issued by the National Commission on Excellence in Education (1983) entitled *A Nation at Risk*, which argued that the education system was being undermined by "a rising tide of mediocrity," which was putting the nation in jeopardy. Radical reforms were necessary if the USA was to maintain, and improve on its "competitive edge" in world markets. Education, therefore, should be aligned to the imperatives of the market economy: that deficiencies in schools rather than structural defects in the national economy were the root cause of the nation's weakness; that business and corporations had a right to help determine educational policy; that the curriculum should emphasize scientific, technical, and vocational subjects, including a large input of computer studies, and that more rigorous standards had to be enforced, and tested regularly. Numerous other reports on the state of education followed, generally emphasizing the need to upgrade "human resources" to meet the needs of high-tech industry that was seen as vital to the competitive market economy (Martin, 1990).

As in the USA, so in Canada. In the late 1980s and early 1990s, the Canadian government sponsored a series of reports from agencies and task forces which essentially followed the line of *A Nation at Risk*. The titles tell the story: *Focus 2000: Report of the Task Force on Education and Training*, by the Canadian Chamber of Commerce (1989); *Reaching for Tomorrow: Science and*

Technology Policy in Canada issued by the now-defunct Science Council of Canada (1991); *A Lot to Learn: Education and Training in Canada*, a statement by the Economic Council of Canada (1992); *Inventing Our Future: An Action Plan for Canada's Prosperity*, from the government-sponsored Steering Group on Prosperity (1992), and *A Knowledge-Based Canada: The New National Dream*, from the Information Technology Association of Canada (1992). Flexible training, generic skills, technological and computer literacy, life-long learning, underpinned by a scientific and technological curriculum, were thus to be the guidelines to Canada's future prosperity.

Embedded in these Canadian and US reports were references to "a global, knowledge-intensive economy"; "international commerce"; "the information age"; "industrial competitiveness on a global scale," and so on, which assumed the existence of a global economy underpinning the ideology of neoliberalism.

Globalization has been given many definitions. Hobsbawm (2008) described it as a transformation of the world into a single unit of interconnected activities unhampered by local boundaries. The dominant features of this world-wide development have been elaborated by the eminent Spanish sociologist and leading authority on globalization, Manuel Castells (2000b), as the invention of the computer and the micro-chip, the growth of a large labour force engaged in knowledge and information processing, the emergence of a network society, the rise of Asia-Pacific economies, and electronically-linked global financial markets—all aspects of a rejuvenated, flexible capitalism. Wealth, Castells contends, is now generated by innovative productivity, activated by informational technology, new forms of management, and the flexibility of labour. This is capitalism adapted to the Information Age or, in Castells' words, "informational capitalism" (p. 369).

It is interesting to note that the late Canadian economist J. K. Galbraith (2004) drew attention to the fact that the word "capitalism" has virtually dropped out of the Western political vocabulary, to be replaced by "the market system" (p. 6). It would be hard to find a more meaningless designation, declared Galbraith; that, he added, was the reason for the choice (p. 17).

Newfoundland and Labrador: The transition to neoliberalism

By the mid-1980s the new developments in international trade and finance, and the accompanying growth of neoliberal policies, had begun to make themselves felt in Newfoundland and Labrador. New thinking on the economy first appeared in the Report of the Royal Commission on Employ-ment and Unemployment (Government of Newfoundland and Labrador, 1986b), a major agency established by the Conservative Peckford govern-ment in 1985. The long post-war boom in the construction and resource industries was over and unemployment had become a chronic problem. Be-tween 1974 and 1985 the percentage of the labour force out of work rose from 13 per cent to 21.3 per cent; if "discouraged workers" were included, the rate had reached 26.3 per cent.

The members of the Royal Commission on Employment and Unem-ployment under the chairmanship of Douglas House, a professor of sociol-ogy at Memorial University, set about finding a cure for unemployment "regardless of political philosophy or ideology" (House, 1999, p. 6). This was true in the conventional political sense, but it left them free to adopt many of the prevailing ideas of the so-called "new economic order" that were swirling around the media, academia, and certain political circles.

The Report of the Commission was a thorough and detailed investi-gation of the whole socio-economic landscape of the province. It began with the premise that there was "something fundamentally wrong" in New-foundland—too much poverty, unemployment, and dependence on gov-ernment, too little initiative and too little education, and an overall feeling of pessimism about economic prospects. The way forward from this de-pressing situation was to put aside any idea of a return to a "mythical past" of independent, subsistence-based fishing outports, or to "lost industrial dreams," and boldly go forward into "a post-industrial society." The pro-jected new society would have balanced industrial and non-industrial sec-tors, and urban and rural communities. The latter would be "modern, sophisticated rural villages with literate, well-educated, well-trained peo-ple," who would enjoy new systems of transport and communications, com-puter technology, advanced service industries, up-to-date forms of enter-prise, a revamped social security system and active social participation (House, 1999).

The education of the people able to meet the challenges of the post-industrial world was elaborated in a companion volume, *Education for Self-Reliance* (Government of Newfoundland and Labrador, 1986b). It comprised lessons in entrepreneurship, economic development as an objec-tive of the University, post-secondary education which emphasized generic skills, the achievement of basic computer literacy at all levels, and the gen-eral recognition of the positive relationship between the level of the educa-tion and the degree of economic development.

A recurring theme in both Reports was the importance of business enterprise in the revitalization of the economy, a key element in neoliberal economics. "In a capitalist society such as Newfoundland," *Building On Our Strengths* emphasizes, "the business sector, both small and large, is generally the main well-spring of entrepreneurship," though other sources are also important, "but to succeed they must be entrepreneurial" (Government of Newfoundland and Labrador, 1986a, p. 32). "Enterprise" is a word with a halo, and it helped to illuminate an attractive picture of a post-industrial future; the Reports appeared to offer a way to prosperity which embraced neoliberal ideas without subverting the economy or unduly upsetting tradition.

This vision of a new order proved too dazzling for some politicians to accept. House called them the Old Guard, a powerful group of senior civil servants whose mind-set was formed in the post-Confederation "old economy," dependent as it was on natural resource exports and government transfers, which laid the foundation of a welfare state (House, 1999, p. 11). Their reception of the Reports was negative, and the Peckford government did little to implement them (House, 1999). House was, however, able to bring off what he called a major victory for the Commission's ideas by persuading Clyde Wells, who became premier in the 1989 election, to issue a document called *Change and Challenge: A Strategic Economic Plan for Newfoundland and Labrador* (Government of Newfoundland and Labrador, 1992a). Wells was described by House as a "lawyer who embodied the values of the official class" (p. 281), which he elsewhere described as consisting of the "economic and political elite of Newfoundland society, plus the top tier of professionals" (House, 1983, pp. 145–146). Wells had, at this time, close ties to the St. John's Board of Trade, which advocated several of the ideas found in the Commission's Reports and *Change and Challenge* (St. John's Board of Trade, 1990–1993).

Although the main focus of *Change and Challenge* (Government of Newfoundland and Labrador, 1992a) centred on the revitalization of the economy, education occupied an important place as "the key to economic development." The theme of the document, as the title stated, was "change"—change in education, the income security system, taxation and, significantly, a change within people. Each segment of the plan was seen as part of an integrated whole. The revamped education system would train a flexible workforce with an entrepreneurial outlook suitable to the new economy, to which business will be attracted by favourable tax rates. A reformed income security and unemployment insurance system would reduce people's alleged dependence on government assistance and foster an independent, competitive spirit. These transformations would require a partnership among government, business, labour, academia, and the community groups. Economic salvation for Newfoundland (and indeed for Canada) lay, it was argued, in the creation of a positive economic and social climate, in which the private sector of the economy—seen as "the engine of growth" and to be armed with a "competitive edge"—could respond to new opportunities in the global market place. To achieve this goal, education had to be subordinated to the demands of production. The workforce would be educated, or trained, to become more skilled, adaptable, and flexible, and the whole educational system imbued with the spirit of entrepreneurship as the means to the formation of an "enterprise culture" (Government of Newfoundland and Labrador, 1992b).

Subsequent government publications—*Meeting the Challenge* (Government of Newfoundland and Labrador, 1994a), *Adjusting the Course* (Government of Newfoundland and Labrador, 1993, 1994b), and *At the Crossroads* (Economic Recovery Commission, 1994)—confirmed and elaborated the message of *Change and Challenge*, with emphasis on a scientific-technological curriculum, assessed by tests and "performance indicators" linked to national and international standards.

The question of education was further pursued in a Royal Commission, entitled *Our Children, Our Future* (Government of Newfoundland and Labrador, 1992b), the Report of which was issued almost simultaneously with *Change and Challenge*. It was chaired by an educationalist, Dr. Leonard Williams, and thus largely followed the humanist tradition, although it was not untouched by prevailing neoliberal ideas. Its basic standpoints were the statements that the school system is designed for academic education, and that the curriculum reinforces social values, stimulates new thinking, prepares students to become participants in society, and helps them gain a critical awareness of their heritage, traditions and environment (Government of Newfoundland and Labrador, 1992b). A section on "Changing Economic Conditions" included, however, some of the key ideas of *Building On Our Strengths* (Government of Newfoundland and Labrador, 1986a): the advocacy of new forms of education linked to the economy and providing skills by which "students could function in information-based industries and those linked to international markets," undergirded by new forms of accountability (p. 379).

As Warren (Chapter Two) has indicated, the Commission was cautious on the issue of the denominational school system, advocating the creation of new structures while retaining some element of church involvement. But answers to a questionnaire showed which way the public wind was blowing: between 80 per cent and 90 per cent believed schools should teach all religions, and two-thirds of denominational supporters and 96 per cent of non-supporters favoured schools open to all children (Government of Newfoundland and Labrador, 1992b).

I have suggested elsewhere that public attitudes to the denominational system, and to much else, were connected to social changes that took place in the post-Confederation era, among them increased urbanization (long known as inimical to religious belief) (Cox, 1966), rising educational levels, the growth of a service sector in the economy, and the beginnings of consumerism (McCann, 2002). Broadly speaking we may say that, if in 1949 Newfoundlanders could be considered localized, frugal, God-fearing, and socially conservative, by the 1990s they had become urbanized, more secular-minded, better educated members of the consumer society.

No doubt this modernization of public attitudes also paved the way for the reception of many of the new ideas of the Economic Recovery Commission. Despite the less than whole-hearted support of certain politicians for the project, before the beginning of the millennium Newfoundland and Labrador had become linked to the global economy. Telecommunications were booming, the business and investment climate had improved, new economic zones were in operation, entrepreneurship, self-employment and small businesses had become respectable, and private and public post-secondary institutes offered an array of training programs in education related to the neoliberal new economy (House, 1999).

In education particularly, the new development contrasted starkly with the educational and religious outlook of the period between Confederation and the mid-1980s, which I have called Christian humanism. It can be traced back to the establishment of the interdenominational Council for Higher Education in 1893. The Council initiated an extensive examination system in a wide range of literary, historical, geographical, and scientific subjects, instilling in the minds of generations of young people the range and worth of a humanistic curriculum.

Subsequent statements on education by, for instance, the Commission on the Curriculum (Commission of Enquiry, 1934), by various educators in the late 1930s, and in reports and commissions of the early Confederation era, underlined the value of this type of education. The Smallwood government had given an official stamp to this tradition in 1959 with the publication of the *Aims of Public Education for Newfoundland* (see Appendix B). There could scarcely be a greater contrast between this tract and the educational aims of *Building on Our Strengths* (Government of Newfoundland and Labrador, 1986a), *Education for Self-Reliance* (Government of Newfoundland and Labrador, 1986b), and *Change and Challenge* (Government of Newfoundland and Labrador, 1992a). These Reports envisaged education as an investment in human resources, which would lead to the creation of human capital and a subsequent increase in economic productivity, whereas the *Aims* regarded education as a personal and public good (Government of Newfoundland and Labrador, 1986b).

The opening paragraph, however, struck a religious note—that individual development can best be achieved in "a Christian democratic society" in which each person adheres to a religious faith as taught by a church, the source of moral values. This was consistent with the outlook of the period, although it is likely to come under criticism in an increasingly multicultural and secular society. The remainder of the pamphlet reflected a humanistic position, best seen in the statement that the primary aim of education should be the best and fullest development of the individual so as to live "sanely, happily and satisfyingly in harmony with themselves and their individual circumstances." Education would also enable people to develop their critical faculties, to appreciate their human heritage and the natural environment, and to operate as skilled members of society, with a sense of their rights and responsibilities as citizens.

The *Aims of Education* document was used in schools and university courses and exercised a wide influence until the mid-1980s, as republication of the original pamphlet in 1964, 1965, and 1984 testified. Of almost equal significance was the Royal Commission on Education of 1967–1968 chaired by Dr. Philip Warren. This highlighted the role of education in personal fulfilment and equitable social development, while stressing the importance of "the value system that...may be found in Christianity" (Government of Newfoundland and Labrador, 1967, p. 1). One of the last statements of the humanist tradition was made by the authors of a provincial *Task Force on Education* (Government of Newfoundland and Labrador, 1979, p. 25), to whom it was "self-evident" that the fundamental goal of education was "to help each person achieve his (*sic*) fullest development both as an individual and as a member of society." A set of guiding principles included the development of the intellectual, social-cultural, moral-religions and physical attributes of all individuals, geared to the unique characteristics and traditions of the province (Government of Newfoundland and Labrador, 1979).

Conclusion

The years 1985–1995 can thus be seen as a decade of transition, marking the end of one era and the beginning of another. *The Year Book of Education* (Young & Levin, 2000) for the year 2000 summed up the position at the millennium, and though the focus is on Canada as a whole, the analysis also applied to Newfoundland and Labrador:

> Echoing, in part, broader international trends, school reform in the 1990s in Canada has seen an increasingly managerialist focus on curriculum standardization, testing, accountability and control, a centralizing reduction in the number and authority of local school boards, along with some attention to giving parents a greater say in which schools their children will attend and in select aspects of local school governance. Associated with these developments has been a stalling or reorientation of many of the egalitarian initiatives in education that had begun to take root in the 1970s and 1980s. (p. 50)

I have not ventured to express an opinion on the relative worth of either the humanist or the neoliberal position. My purpose has been to show, as far as the evidence goes, that in Newfoundland and Labrador in the 1980s and 1990s, a transition from one to the other took place. I leave it to another time to pronounce on whether this is or is not an advantageous development.

Chapter Five

The Economics of Educational Reform

Gerald Galway

Demographic change, cultural, geographic, and linguistic challenges, fiscal pressures, the maintenance of high student performance standards, and increased public and employer expectations—these are some of the contextual problems facing provincial education policy-makers today. In negotiating these competing demands, educational decision makers pay considerable attention to political pressures—media reports, advocacy, and public opinion—but they are also influenced by a host of related factors outside the immediate and localized sphere of politics and pedagogy (Galway, 2006). One of the most salient of these policy drivers is the demand for efficiency and fiscal accountability.

Over the past two decades in Canada, as governments have struggled with the problem of adequate funding for social institutions, competition and other market-based principles have emerged as an alternative to government regulation and a means of expenditure reduction. As Phillip McCann (Chapter Four) has argued, within this global-competitive orientation, education systems were targeted as one social sector where efficiencies could be gained. Using the Newfoundland experience as a point of reference, this chapter reviews the economic arguments for educational reform made by governments and their agents and explores how the language of competitiveness, efficiency, and accountability dominated public discourse in the 1990s and became a principal driver of the reform movement.

Education and the Canadian economy

Canada's economy is primarily driven by industrial and technology-based sectors supplemented by traditional resource-based industry and agriculture (Dea, Kustec, Lapointe, & Lawlis, 2000; Harder, 2001). Relative to other Organization for Economic Co-operation and Development (OECD) countries, Canada has traditionally performed well on most international economic, labour market, and human development indicators (Harder, 2001; OECD, 2001; Robitaille, Taylor, Orpwood & Donn, 1998; Statistics Canada and Human Resources Development Canada, 2001) and been a strong performer in GDP growth among G7 countries (Atlantic Provinces' Economic Council, 2003). According to the World Economic Forum's Growth Competitiveness Index (GCI), Canada ranked tenth out of 130 nations in 2007–2008. In 2009 an international monetary fund report predicted Canada would again lead G7 nations in economic growth. To some extent, these positive indicators may explain why this country was at least partly inoculated against the transnational economic downturn of 2008–2009.

While Canada's corporate tax rates are in the middle of the G7 range, the country's overall personal tax regime is considerably more burdensome than the G7 average. Government revenue from personal income taxes is proportionately higher than those of its main trading partners—in fact, it is the highest of all OECD countries (Laurin, 2007). In Canada, the highest marginal tax rate is about 50 per cent, and this applies to all Canadians making in excess of about $60,000 per year. By contrast, in the USA the highest marginal tax rate is 44 per cent which applies when income is in excess of about $400,000. Economists explain Canada's high tax levels within the context of the policy choices of governments. Brown (2000) maintains that it is the standard of living and not the personal income tax rate that is the more relevant indicator of prosperity, and ultimately of societal well-being. Essentially, high taxation pays for pan-Canadian social programs, universal medical care, and public schooling, subsidized post-secondary education, and social welfare—programs that either do not exist in many other OECD countries, or, if they do exist, are considerably less robust (World Health Organization, 2001). For example, while US marginal tax rates are low by Canadian standards, there is no universal public-health care program and about 14 per cent of Americans are not covered by any form of health insurance (OECD, 2004).

According to a strict economic model, the primary factors that influence the economies of the provinces include population size, density, and educational level, value of natural resources, climate, geography, and proximity to the USA and other markets (Lipsey, Reagan, & Courant, 1997). Economists claim that these primary factors, interacting with government economic policy, determine employment, productivity, and the overall strength of provincial economies. Ontario, Alberta, British Columbia, and to a lesser extent, Manitoba and Saskatchewan have economic advantages in terms of infrastructure, population density, proximity to markets, high employment, and a strong revenue base (from agriculture, energy resources, manufacturing, mineral production, forestry, and cattle production) (Statistics Canada, 2003). Several of these factors are not common to Quebec and the Atlantic provinces; their economies have been generally less robust, with higher unemployment and more dependency on federal transfers (Dea et al., 2000). Although new oil and gas revenues have buoyed economic forecasts for the provinces of Newfoundland and Labrador and Nova Scotia, all of the other Atlantic Provinces have traditionally struggled to reach a standard of living comparable to the so-called "have" provinces.

Ross, Roberts, and Scott (2000) suggest that government transfers alone are not sufficient to overcome the disadvantages associated with low incomes and high unemployment. Nowhere has that been more evident than in Newfoundland and Labrador. Unemployment rates in the Atlantic Provinces typically range from four to six percentage points above the national average while average family incomes are well below the national average—more than 20 per cent lower in Newfoundland and Labrador (Statistics Canada, 2009a).

Canadian investment in education

At the macro level, Canada's investment in education is very strong. In 2001–2002, total public expenditure on education in Canada was $68.6 billion, making it the highest area of public expenditure after health (Canadian Education Statistics Council, 2003). By 2005–2006, provincial, territorial, federal, and local governments were spending $75.7 billion on all levels of education, which represents 16.1 per cent of total public expenditures (Council of Ministers of Education, 2008). Considering both private and public spending on education, Canada's investment in education has been high by international standards, although recent figures show that its ranking among G7 nations has slipped to third (OECD, 2008).

Notwithstanding Canada's favourable ranking on most international indicators of economic performance, there is significant disparity among the economies of its ten provinces and three territories. While pan-Canadian equity has been a laudable goal, in effect, governments have largely failed in their attempts to equalize economic and social standards across provinces and territories. There is considerable variation in relative educational funding levels across provinces and this disparity—expressed in terms of per-student expenditures—seems to be driven both by government ideology (what provinces are willing to invest) and capacity to fund education. Not all provinces have the ability to finance education at the same level, even though all would likely assert that their education systems are adequate, in relation to their ability to afford education.

Table 2 below provides comparative data on educational spending, by province. In terms of their actual per-student public school expenditure, the four Atlantic Provinces were ranked 7th, 8th, 9th, and 10th. The table also provides a key indicator of educational effort: *per-student expenditure as a percentage of GDP per-capita.* Here we see an interesting difference; with the exception of Newfoundland and Labrador (which showed the third highest *actual* increase in per-student expenditures), the other three Atlantic Provinces are ranked 1st, 2nd, and 5th in terms of educational effort. These figures accentuate differences in educational investment across provinces, but they also show that, generally, the Atlantic Provinces have placed a high priority on education, relative to their economic capacity. From the perspective of actual expenditures, however, funding has historically trailed the central and western provinces, making any opportunity to achieve efficiencies through structural reforms all the more attractive to governments.

Table 2: Comparative education finance statistics, by province, 2004–2005

Province	Public School Expenditure per Student	Rank	% Increase from 1998–99	GDP per capita	Public School Expenditure per Student as a % of GDP per capita	Rank
NL	$8,075	8	39.1	$37,566	21.5%	9
PEI	$7,583	10	38.1	$29,173	26.0%	3
NS	$7,728	9	36	$31,871	24.2%	5
NB	$8,653	7	33.2	$30,549	28.3%	1
PQ	$8,663	6	29.9	$35,118	24.7%	4
ON	$9,267	3	22.6	$41,702	22.2%	8
MB	$9,394	1	30.9	$34,174	27.5%	2
SK	$9,031	4	46.1	$40,228	22.4%	7
AB	$9,346	2	40	$58,397	16.0%	10
BC	$8,960	5	20.4	$37,421	23.9%	6

Source: Statistics Canada (2007c, 2009b, 2009c)

The accountability movement

Most authors (e.g., Aucoin, 1995; Levin, 2003; Ungerleider, 2003) agree that the educational accountability movement began to emerge in the late 1980s and early 1990s; however, the discourse of educational efficiency has had a much longer history. In Raymond Callahan's 1962 book, *Education and the Cult of Efficiency*, he argued that the objectives of efficiency and cost-effectiveness were evident in how early-twentieth-century schools were administered, and that these objectives were often achieved at the expense of high quality teaching and learning. Callahan observed that the way schools were conceptualized followed a business model; they were seen less as places where children could be provided a high quality education and more as institutions to be managed efficiently. Economists began to develop educational units such as the "student-hour" and calculate comparative indicators for different subject disciplines, such as the *cost per student-hour*. Cost differentials between subjects, for example, mathematics *versus* history, were considered to be problems to be corrected. Educational finance began to be thought of in terms of the "price" or "cost of service" rather than as an investment in future social and economic stability.

Interest in educational efficiency was rekindled in the 1950s when Milton Friedman, an American economist and public intellectual, began a movement to advocate for school choice. Friedman (1962b) argued that public school systems propagated stagnancy and ineffectiveness because schools were not organized according to the principles of the free market economy. These and other similar claims fuelled the development of the school voucher system in the USA—Callahan (1962) called this kind of preoccupation with the economics of education the "cult of efficiency." Although there is evidence of this "bean counter" approach to educational funding in Canada (e.g., most provincial grants are still fundamentally enrolment-based, even though the resource needs of schools are quite different across school communities), the notion of education as an investment in social and economic well-being is a more common way of conceptualizing education today.

After World War II, the poor state of the economy dominated public discourse. Like the approach advocated by many of those countries severely affected by the 2009 global economic downturn, governments in the post-war period, managed their economies using Keynesian economic policies. But, this approach, whereby governments try to stimulate employment and kick-start their lagging economies by infusing public money, has a troublesome side-effect: it leads to budget deficits and excessive public debt. These spending policies are widely believed to have contributed to the difficult economic times of the 1980s and early 1990s when the prime interest rate reached 21.5 per cent in the USA[1] and government deficits in Canadian provinces mushroomed. Macklem, Rose, and Tetlow (1995) point out that Canada's debt-to-GDP ratio[2] rose sharply in the last third of the twentieth century. In the late 1960s the level of consolidated public sector net debt was 12.5 per cent of GDP. By 1991 this country's inflation rate was at 5.9 per cent and by 1995 the debt-to-GDP ratio peaked at a staggering 71 per cent before trending downwards toward the end of the decade (Government of Canada, 2001). During this period, as demands for more efficient use of public money grew, some governments began to change the way they thought about education and other public services. As new sets of neoliberal governance arrangements matured, there emerged a press for smaller, more effective, and efficient public service delivery mechanisms— a new, "corporate" approach to public management.

Four significant political and socio-economic events are thought to have been the dominant precursors to this shift in governance orientation (Aucoin, 1995; Barzelay, 2001; Kettl, 2000; Pusey, 1991). First, social and economic systems underwent radical reform. The word "globalization" emerged around the mid-1980s as a collective term to replace earlier terms in common usage such as "transnationization" and "internationalization" (Hoogvelt, 1997), and according to Armstrong (2000), is associated with the proliferation of rapid exchanges across borders. But many scholars (e.g., Appadurai, 1996; Castells, 1997, 2000a; Dale, 1999; Giddens, 1990, 1991, 1994, 2003; Henry, Lingard, Rizvi, and Taylor, 1999) ascribe a broader set of meanings to the term. Giddens (1990) defines it as "the intensification of world-wide social relations which link distant localities in such a way that local happenings are shaped by events occurring many miles away and vice versa" (p. 64). The fall of communist governments forced a new democratic order in eastern European countries that required new relationships with citizens. Worldwide, many nations underwent major upheavals of their existing social structures such as apartheid and traditional conceptualizations of gender roles. At the same time traditional family structures underwent unprecedented change; after the initial post-war "baby-boom," birth rates declined, there were more divorces, more single-parent families, and significantly more females in the workplace. This was also the beginning of a technological revolution—a period when advances in personal and business technologies and telecommunications turned workplaces and lifestyles upside down.

Second, developing nations were overwhelmed with demands to modernize their economies, especially with an emerging global e-commerce trade and the infiltration of products and services by transnational corporations. Deregulation and privatization strategies promised to create jobs and stimulate economic growth, and while they have had questionable results, they remain important instruments of new governance orientations. Third, Western countries faced significant demands from a skeptical public to increase public services while, paradoxically, being more efficient and trimming the size of government institutions. Finally, special-interest groups began to evolve into well-organized and influential power bases which were able to exert a level of pressure on the public-sector policy agenda, once unimaginable. In education, for example, advocacy groups have placed difficult demands on schools and have become increasingly litigious. Based on a study of legal challenges to education policy decisions, Dolmage (1992) has argued that, increasingly, advocacy groups are attempting to force education policy change through legal challenges to ministry and school board decisions.

Advocates claim that these new corporate managerial arrangements were fundamentally driven by a desire to reconnect government with a disillusioned citizenry through visibly better productivity and the push for cost savings and a new service orientation. This involved infusing market-based, competition-driven strategies into public institutions while eliminating traditional authoritarian rules-based processes. Examples include devolution or quasi-privatization of public institutions/services and crown corporations such as airlines, utilities, schools, and post-secondary education, and allowing greater autonomy in front-line spending and decision making, with concomitant accountability mechanisms (Barzelay, 2001; Kettl, 2000).

Corporate managerialism, however, has been widely criticized on the grounds that the goals and mandates of public institutions are not always consistent with the principles of competition and the free market (Dehli, 1996; Yeatman, 1998). Critics have charged that the shift to a corporate orientation was politically motivated. They suggest it represented a narrow approach to the provision of public services driven by corporate interests and not by any form of inclusive policy process which had, as its goal, better service to citizens (Avis, 2000; McWilliam, 2000).

Education and corporate managerialism

The corporate managerial wave is thought to have been resisted by conservatives under the Mulroney government, and, according to Aucoin (1995), never got implemented to the same extent as similar initiatives in other Commonwealth countries. However, education systems were the notable exception; echoes of the new philosophy began permeating school systems in the late 1980s. New corporate governance ideologies coupled with broad expectations for education systems, especially notions of competitiveness, innovativeness, and economic performance, contributed to radical reform and accountability trends evident in this country's education systems. In his 2003 book *Failing our Kids: How We are Ruining our Public Schools*, Charles Ungerleider says that Canadians, fearful of warnings about rapid social and technological change, lacklustre economic competitiveness, and the effects of globalization, have been placing untenable demands on the education system, while at the same time losing confidence in schools as social institutions. He argues that Canadians, "anxious about the state of the country's economy and the security of their own employment" (p. 17), have allowed market forces to dominate the discourse around what is an appropriate ideology and vision for education:

> We have learned that our talents, abilities, and efforts enable us to transcend our social and economic locations. We are less confined by our social and economic origins than in the past. But the value of talents, abilities, and efforts has become largely market-driven. Economic considerations have come to dominate decision-making to the exclusion of other standards. (p. 11)

Calls for education systems to demonstrate accountability and international competitiveness seem to have been at their peak in the 1990s. Early in the decade we began to see considerable development work on educational indicator systems, at both the provincial and pan-Canadian level. These systems began churning out a series of operational efficiency and effectiveness measures, and improvement on these measures quickly became strategic goals of ministries of education and school boards. Since 1990, Ungerleider (2003) notes, all jurisdictions in Canada reduced educational expenditures. However, provinces also stepped up their efforts to quantify student learning by collectively participating in international assessment programs such as the Trends in Mathematics and Science Study (TIMSS) and the Program of International Student Assessment (PISA), introducing national standardized tests (the School Achievement Indicators Program—SAIP), and developing provincial criterion-referenced testing programs (Young, Levin, & Wallin, 2007). While the quantification of student outcomes is useful evidence of accountability domestically, from the perspective of national and international competitiveness, it is also symbolic. The effectiveness of education systems tends to be linked to perceptions about the competitive strength of regions and nations, regional and national identity, and a host of interconnected social and economic arrangements; thus, the local and the global are interconnected (Blackmore, 1999a).

As part of the shift towards accountability, education ministries looked for opportunities to sever ineffective or underutilized programs through program review/renewal exercises. As a former senior official in a provincial ministry of education, I participated in several program reviews during my 16 years in government, as did many of my colleagues across the country. These became part and parcel of a slate of organizational efficiency and effectiveness initiatives, including school improvement programs and various "total quality management" schemes in which citizens were reconceptualized as customers and students as clients who consumed education and other government services. This ideological shift is also evident at the school district level. Many school boards are now required by law to generate strategic/business plans, annual reports, and audited financial statements that are tabled in provincial legislatures. Increasingly, such plans include proposals to increase revenues, such as the sale of educational programs and services or the generation of revenue through international student tuition. For example, in reference to the education system in Ontario, Dehli (1996) notes:

> The Minister refers to education as a business, students as clients, and parents and employers as consumers. Schools and the Ministry itself are expected to produce mission statements, as well as business plans and performance indicators.... (p. 366)

According to Lawton (1996), provincial governments in Canada exist in a symbiotic relationship with their school boards whereby governments have been able to capitalize on local solutions to educational problems by applying (and sometimes mandating) best practice in one school board to others under their jurisdiction. Until the early 1990s, there was little evidence of policies or review processes that would signal much in the way of centralized intervention in local school governance. As Lawton (1996) notes, the powers of provincial governments over school boards, as written in legislation, are almost absolute; however, until recently, they have rarely been used. In fact, he suggests that provincial departments of education have been just as likely to take policy direction from school boards as they have been to provide such direction to the boards.

If such were the case in the past, it is no longer. Provincial relationships with school boards over the past 20 years have focused on greater efficiency and "quality assurance." According to a report of the Canadian School Boards Association (CSBA), as early as 1995 provinces were concerned about reforms in six key areas: school board consolidation and boundary changes; changes in roles and responsibilities of school boards; creation of school/parent councils; school choice and charter schools; service delivery through cooperative ventures; and the imposition of measures to promote greater accountability (CSBA, 1995). In the intervening period, school boards do not appear to have regained the autonomy they used to enjoy. David Dibbon and his colleagues (Chapter Eleven) point to several examples in which provincial governments have intervened directly into school board operations. They report on several recent high-profile examples where political actors within provincial governments publicly criticized or overturned the policies and decisions of school boards and postsecondary institutions. In such situations, the political and ideological interests of elected governments may run counter to the perceived mandates of school boards. These realities raise questions about whether there has been a tacit change in the governance roles of elected trustees and their senior administrators and whether these roles need to be re-examined.

Complementing these structural reform initiatives has been a series of centralizing measures, initiated by provinces, such as province-wide testing, stronger provincial control over curriculum, and funding that is specifically targeted to particular programs and which can be spent only in those areas. Lawton (1997) speculates that a shift to full centralization is possible in Canada, whereby the provinces would operate schools directly. There may be some truth to this assertion, particularly in the small population provinces. Recent trends in educational governance arrangements in Canada have been towards a reduction in the number of school boards—largely driven by fiscal restraint, restructuring, and enrolment decline. Wagner (1997) summarizes the first wave of school board downsizing as follows:

> Despite the complexity of these existing [education] systems, the last two years have seen school board numbers decline dramatically. Alberta reduced school boards from 181 to 67; Ontario is in the process of shrinking 129 boards into 72; Nova Scotia moved 22 local school boards to 6 regional boards. In British Columbia amalgamation created 59 school boards from 75; P.E.I. now has three instead of five school boards. New-

foundland will replace denominational school boards with interdenominational ones and reduce the numbers from 27 to 10. Quebec is moving from 156 to 71. New Brunswick has eliminated local school boards from their governance structure, replacing them with two provincial-level elected boards which include parents. (p. 2)

Still, accountability as we know it in Canada is very different from Callahan's (1962) account of early-twentieth-century US schools. Few parents would agree that our school boards should be populated primarily with business leaders and efficiency experts or that schooling should be guided by the principles of "scientific management," as if student learning could be compared to the production of widgets. Today's educational accountability is not as much about counting pencils as it is about performativity—being able to demonstrate to the public that citizens are getting good value for the money governments invest on their behalf. As the former minister of education for Newfoundland and Labrador, Philip Warren (Chapter Two) was fond of saying: we are constantly striving to get "more scholar for the dollar." For governments, part of that process involves positioning themselves as being responsive to public demand for effectiveness and efficiency.

School system consolidation: Economic and social arguments

Claims and counter-claims about optimal school and district size, cost, and quality have been an enduring feature of educational debate in Canada. Many, if not most, issues in education relate to the perceived adequacy of resources. Parents in struggling rural areas have the same expectations of the education system as their counterparts in urban centres; however, the collapse of rural industries and the associated population loss means that their communities, in many instances, are no longer economically viable. Public funding necessary to keep services at an acceptable standard in schools with dwindling enrolments may now need to be deployed elsewhere, in larger centres or to other sectors, in particular, health and public works. The same demographic changes—urbanization and ageing populations—that threaten the demise of the rural lifestyle are placing relatively greater demand on health services and requiring higher spending on urban infrastructure.

Structural reform, whereby schools are closed and consolidated and school districts are expanded or eliminated, has been one of the principal policy levers by which provinces have been able to reduce operational costs and demonstrate fiscal prudence. The principle here is *economy of scale*: larger (centralized) schools administered by fewer school districts covering a greater geographic zone equates to a more cost-effective (and potentially a higher quality) system. Larger schools tend to be less expensive to operate; there is more efficient use of space and teacher resources can be optimized. Operational costs for such items as teaching and support services, information and communication technology, energy, food services, and maintenance tend to be lower because, in larger schools, there are more students per unit of almost any resource. Larger schools also permit greater flexibility in staffing and programming, and can usually sustain a more complete range of support services. For example, individually, three small schools might not be in a position to offer advanced mathematics or music, but, reconfigured as one larger school, such programs become viable.

Hintz (2002) says that the orientation towards mass delivery of education actually began in the USA more than a 100 years ago as industry was becoming oriented towards mass production:

> Using a similar line of reasoning, state governments and education experts called for more efficiency and expertise in education. These reformers advocated giving control of schools to education experts, removing it from communities and smaller local school boards. Bigger schools and districts were said to attract higher quality and more specialized staff while money would be saved as bigger units replaced smaller, more costly ones. (¶ 21)

While most observers would likely agree that consolidation results in less duplication and more effective and efficient use of resources, not everyone accepts that structural reform necessarily results in a higher quality educational experience. In a review of the literature on rural school consolidation, Bard, Gardener, and Wieland (2006) concluded that much of the consolidation taking place in US states was driven by financial considerations without enough attention to the impact on "student achievement, self-concept, participation in extra-curricular activities, dropout rates, and on the community itself" (p. 44). Following decades of school and school district consolidation in the USA, there have been recent attempts to reverse the trend through special funding initiatives (Jones, Toma, & Zimmer, 2008).

The claim that "bigger, is not necessarily better" has been one of the central arguments of those who favour smaller, community-based schools. There is ample evidence in the recent literature to lend support to this position. Jacobowitz, Weinstein, Maguire, Luekens, and Fruchter (2007) conducted a study examining student and teacher demographic characteristics, student outcomes, and organizational and instructional practices that contribute to positive learning environments. Their data, collected over a 10-year period from 67 New York high schools, suggests that, notwithstanding the fact that small high schools (500 or fewer students) tend to attract less qualified teachers and serve student populations with greater needs than large high schools, they demonstrate higher outcomes, as measured by graduation and dropout rates, than large high schools. Other studies have focused on process indicators which, in a standard input-process-output model, are widely believed to impact student outcomes. For example, Jones et al. (2008) showed that school attendance rates are lower in large high schools (and large school districts) than in smaller schools (and districts) and that this irregular attendance is a precursor to dropping out.

A purely economic-rationalist approach to the organization of schooling holds that the system should adhere to a strict set of economic principles. However, just because it is possible to consolidate schools may not necessarily mean it is always the appropriate thing to do. Opponents of consolidation argue that basing organizational decisions on economics, to the exclusion of other types of evidence, represents an antiquated policy framework. They claim that other factors, such as student safety, discipline problems, and capacity for parent engagement, should be evaluated as part of a broader social policy analysis on how school systems are organized (Cotton, 2001; Meier, 2004; Shakrani, 2008). There may be social costs associated with school closure and consolidation, such as lower student achievement or disengagement with the community, which raise troubling questions about large-scale restructuring. In the longer term, will these social costs outweigh the immediate economic benefits of school closure? What are the long-term effects on a community of closing a school and busing students 30 or 40 minutes to another town? To what extent do the new busing arrangements present safety risks to students? What accommodations will be made for extracurricular involvement? Are there any program delivery options (for example, e-learning) that could maintain program quality and forestall the closure of a school?

Thus, governments often find themselves in an untenable position with respect to school consolidation. Although policy-makers face a growing press for fiscal accountability, school consolidation efforts have frequently met with resistance by organizations and community alliances who oppose amalgamation. These representations invariably involve attempts to prevent or reverse policy decisions, followed, in turn, by political action.

One of the most extensive and polarized school consolidation exercises in recent history is the one on which this book is based: the restructuring of Newfoundland and Labrador's system of denominational education. William McKim, in his 1988 book on denominational education in Newfoundland, described the issue as a "vexed question"—the issue was highly sensitive—both socially and historically, bitterly divisive, and politically radioactive.   There were compelling economic reasons, however, for large-scale consolidation and the unfolding of the "business case" for reform was a key plank in the 1992 Report of the Royal Commission of Inquiry (the Williams Commission), entitled, *Our Children, Our Future* (Government of Newfoundland and Labrador, 1992b, 1992c). This section of the opening paragraph from its *Summary Report* set the direction of the Commission's findings:

> The establishment of this inquiry into the school system has come at a crucial time in our history. Profound political, social and economic changes throughout the world are prompting educators everywhere to reassess the effectiveness and efficiency of their education systems. Despite the significant gains made in education over the past two decades since the report of the last Royal Commission on Education, there remains throughout the province a widespread and well-founded concern about the quality and direction of schooling. (Government of Newfoundland and Labrador, 1992c, p. 1)

Accountability and educational reform: The Newfoundland context

When the Williams Commission brought down its recommendation calling on government to restructure the education system in Newfoundland and Labrador, the accountability movement was gaining strength in Canada. Accordingly, the Commission spent a good deal of its report addressing issues of fiscal accountability (*Chapter 7: Contextual Issues in Educational Finance* and *Chapter 8: Presentation, Interpretation and Conclusions*) and accountability for learning (*Chapter 18: Performance and Accountability*). The new government under Premier Clyde Wells was facing possibly the worst five-year economic forecast of any province in the federation. Although some of the contributing factors to school reform—such as enrolment decline and duplication of infrastructure—were already well recognized, the economic currents that pushed the reform of the education system in 1997 are hard to ignore. The 1990s ushered in a period of extreme economic uncertainty in Atlantic Canada. The decline and eventual closure of the $700 million Northern Cod fishery affected some 31,000 fish harvesters and processors, the vast majority of whom lived in Newfoundland and Labrador (Government of Newfoundland and Labrador, 1998b). A resulting wave of unemployment, out-migration, and urbanization dominated the social and political agenda of the provincial government for the remainder of Premier Wells's term in office and beyond. It was a time when the public and political spotlight turned to education.

Changing the architecture of the province's education system was one way the government believed it could generate significant cost efficiencies, respond to demands for curricular reform, and demonstrate fiscal accountability to an electorate that seemed more concerned about the quality of schools than their religious character. The Williams Commission argued that the fundamental economic principles upon which an educational system should be based were taxpayer equity in the provision of resources for education and equality of access for students in the consumption of those resources:

> [T]he education system must exhibit financial responsibility and accountability for all aspects of the educational process. These principles, however, fail to address a basic practical dilemma: how to ensure equal access to these resources while facing a critical scarcity of means. Whatever the available resources, there are always more demand than can be satisfied. (Government of Newfoundland and Labrador, 1992b, p. 117)

The arguments to reform the Church-run system were both ideological and pragmatic, but, given the economic context, the Commission's emphasis on the pragmatic was timely and strategic. While acknowledging the significant investment the churches had made to the development of education, the Commission took the stance that the continued involvement in the administration of public funds was no longer reasonable, nor viable. The Commission charged that the system was over-administered and duplicative, and that these redundancies—presently underwritten by the taxpayer—could no longer be tolerated, especially in light of the fiscal and demographic challenges facing the province. The report admonished the churches for maintaining their direct role in administering the system "through lobbying activities and political pressure" (Government of Newfoundland and Labrador, 1992b, p. 120).

By the time the Commission reported, the kinds of social changes discussed by McCann (Chapter Four) were becoming entrenched into the Newfoundland way of life. Families were getting smaller and this meant a mounting overcapacity in the school system. Fertility rates, which had been among the highest in the world, were now among the lowest. The tri-denominational educational structure had been slow to recognize the implications of such a profound drop in student enrolment and had no comprehensive plan to consolidate and adjust capacity. As noted by the Commission, "it was not uncommon to see three small denominational schools representing each of the recognized denominations in a community with fewer than 100 students in total" (Government of Newfoundland and Labrador, 1992b, p. 121). Even though the churches did voluntarily undertake some consolidation, almost 90 per cent of schools had enrolments fewer than 500 students. The Commission, with access to accurate demographic projections, understood that the downward enrolment trend which had begun in the 1970s would only accelerate through the 1990s. From the standpoint of economic viability, the system in its present form could simply not be justified.

The next point dealt with the adequacy issue. Lack of funding for education, the Commission claimed, had become a recurring theme. School boards, many of which could be consolidated, had accumulated some $41 million of debt and with deferred construction and maintenance estimated at $150 million, it was unlikely that the problem of inadequate and underfunded schools could be remedied under the denominational model. Many of the educational facilities that had been built by the boards were old and did not conform to health and safety standards such as wheelchair accessibility. Nor were schools able to afford new technology and learning resources. The Commission estimated that to upgrade and replace obsolete buildings would have exceeded $150 million, about 30 per cent of educational expenditures.

The Williams Commission proposed four models for reform of the system, each with a projected cost analysis. Model A (the status quo) set the baseline at $519.7 million. Model B (maximum consolidation under a denominational system) would yield a modest $6.8 million in cost savings. Models C and D were variations on a public, non-denominational system. Model C was portrayed as a "theoretical model designed only to measure the cost of the denominational system" (Government of Newfoundland and Labrador, 1992b, p. 167) with no practical value; it placed the cost of church involvement in education at $13.3 million. Model D was entitled "*A Rational, Non-denominational System*" (p. 183). The Commission estimated some $21.3 million in annual savings under a non-denominational structure with maximum consolidation, and the government pledged to re-invest this money in the new system by funding improvements in educational programs and services.

Other contributors to this volume have documented the referendum process that provided government with the mandate to seek a constitutional change and amend provincial legislation—in effect, removing the churches from any substantive involvement in the administration of schools, and I will not revisit these discussions here. The adoption of Model D—maximum consolidation of schools—meant that the number of school boards would be cut from 27 to 10 non-denominational Anglophone boards and that students would be rezoned to their designated "neighbourhood" school.

In the aftermath of reform

During and after the debates, referenda, senate hearings, constitutional amendment, and passing of the new provincial legislation in 1997, and over the 10-year period between 1989–1990 and 1999–2000, the province of New-foundland and Labrador closed 200 of its 543 schools. Perhaps the direction set by Williams Commission resulted in too much efficiency for the system to absorb. As Table 3 illustrates, although per-student expenditures increased (the result of enrolment decline), by the end of the decade, total public school educational expenditures were, in fact, lower than they were 10 years earlier in 1989–1990, the year on which the Commission based its financial analysis. Over this period of "rationalization" more than 1650 teachers were dropped from the system, and by the end of the period there were urgent calls from school boards and other stakeholders to re-examine the way the system was resourced—in particular, the provincial model used to allocate teachers to school boards. In 1999, government announced the establishment of the Ministerial Panel on Educational Delivery in the Classroom with a mandate to "review how teachers are allocated by the Department of Education and how they are deployed by the boards" (Government of Newfoundland and Labrador, 1999, ¶ 6).

From an economic perspective, one of the troublesome realities of managing a system in continuous enrolment decline is that there are limits to how far efficiency measures can be taken. One thing we can learn from the Newfoundland experience is that when education systems are contracting the political ground is also continually shifting. Whereas, in the past, education policy may have been accepted by a "trusting and quiescent public," this has changed. These are uncertain and risky times. More than ever, we now have to negotiate educational policy with a diverse and impatient public. Policy-makers at all levels find themselves confronted with the fact that what they plan to function as a benefit to all may, in the fullness of time, be felt instead to be a curse by some and be challenged. Such was the case in the aftermath of the newly-restructured education system. The recommendations of the Williams Commission in 1992 were considered to be groundbreaking and forward-thinking. But by 1999, the same government that had implemented many of these recommendations appointed another group of experts to take on the task of resolving a mounting list of system-level grievances. When the Ministerial Panel brought in its report a year later the pattern was repeated. Stakeholder groups praised the work of the panel—in particular, how it handled the difficult task of developing a model of teacher resourcing that was sensitive to the needs of small, rural schools during a period of enrolment decline. But, in 2006, the government of the day appointed another commission to "address the limitations of the current Teacher Allocation Formula" (Government of Newfoundland and Labrador, 2007, ¶ 6).

Table 3: Public school expenditures and teachers, 1989–1990 to 1999–2000

Year	Total Public School Expenditure (millions)	Per cent change from previous year	Per-student Expenditure	Full-Time Equivalent Teachers
1989–90	$519.7	-	$3994	8035
1990–91	$544.1	4.7	$4430	8015
1991–92	$546.8	0.5	$4514	7951
1992–93	$579.8	6.0	$4915	7885
1993–94	$602.1	3.9	$5256	7769
1994–95	$562.1	-6.6	$5099	7521
1995–96	$535.9	-4.7	$5021	7259
1996–97	$569.0	6.2	$5535	7101
1997–98	$528.1	-7.2	$5197	6705
1998–99	$513.3	-2.9	$5271	6453
1999–2000	$517.2	0.8	$5309	6372

Sources: Government of Newfoundland and Labrador (1989-2000, 1998b).

Commissions and educational panels seem to run in cycles—in Newfoundland and Labrador, about every 8-10 years. As both governments and the educational landscape change, policy-makers struggle to respond to the shifting demands of their constituents. The governance of education systems takes place in a political arena; therefore, policy-makers are faced with achieving that tenuous balance between public accountability and political expediency, and they must do so normally within a short window—between election cycles. Commissions are a useful way of gaining external, expert advice, but they also serve a more pragmatic purpose—that of buying time for policy shifts to be planned and funded while deflecting difficult educational problems away from government.

A perfect example of this occurred in 2004, when Newfoundland and Labrador's newly-elected conservative government again went to the education well to help balance the books. Faced with a large current account deficit, the province announced plans to further consolidate school districts in an effort to achieve $6 million in administrative savings. The plan called for a reduction in the number of school districts on the island portion of the province from nine to four—covering significantly larger geographic regions. In its justification for the change the government made the following argument:

> As part of Education Reform in 1996-97, 27 school boards were consolidated into 10 and a French-language School Board was established. Since that time, enrolments have declined by 23%, the number of teachers has been reduced by 17%, the number of schools have been reduced from 432 to 305 (29%), but the number of school districts, district administrators, and district program staff have remained constant or have, in fact, increased. At present there are five school boards with approximately 5000 students or fewer.... Given that enrolment is projected to decline further; possibly reaching 60,000 students by 2011, further consolidation of school boards is warranted. Just four years after the 1996–97 reorganization, the...Report of the Ministerial Panel on Educational Delivery in the Classroom (2000) considered recommending further school board consolidation. It stated: "...some *$13.8 million is dedicated to the operation of school board offices, and efforts to achieve efficiencies through future board consolidation would seem achievable and necessary within the next several years.*" (Government of Newfoundland and Labrador, 2004)

In Chapters Ten, Eleven, and Twelve my colleagues, David Dibbon, Bruce Sheppard, Jean Brown, and Mary Green explore some of the implications of the 2004 district restructuring and raise questions around issues of centralization of governance, authority of school boards, and humanism. I leave this discussion to them. Their analysis of the fallout from the system restructuring of 1997 and, more particularly, the school district restructuring of 2004, provides an important set of perspectives that recast these reforms, not in terms of their economic antecedents, but in a rather more critical light.

Conclusions

Fiscal pressures, the rationalization of educational delivery during demographic downturns, and the need to demonstrate public accountability are all reasons why ministries of education have been turning to educational restructuring as a policy lever. The reforms that took place in Newfoundland and Labrador represent an archetypical case-study in how economic factors were mobilized as a primary factor in shaping public support for the dismantling of an (inefficient) denominational school system and its replacement with a system based on the most cost-effective deployment of resources. We must also recognize that during this period pan-Canadian and transnational factors—a competitive economy, the internationalization of the labour-market, and the shift towards corporate managerial principles—were permeating education in this once isolated and insular province, and these influences also played a key role in changing the architecture of the system. As the Williams Commission wrote in its 1992 summary report:

> [T]here is also a widely held and documented belief that educational standards are too low, and that too many graduates lack the basic and relevant skills required to function in our present society, let alone the modern, global marketplace that is quickly establishing itself as the economic arena of the future. (Government of Newfoundland and Labrador, 1992c, p. 1)

In addition to its demand for fiscal accountability, the Williams Commission was right to highlight the need to modernize the education and was prophetic in its call for students to develop new skills, which are even now—20 years later—still emerging. These days, the experiences of learners are very heavily mediated through digital devices of one form or another. Nowadays, students acquire most of their new information through a complex nexus of e-portals, blogs, social networking tools, video, and electronic text. Information is expanding at exponential rates. According to Jukes (2006), the amount of technical information is doubling about every two years and this is predicted to continue to increase. As educators in the twenty-first century, we need to be somewhat like soothsayers; we are preparing students for the workforce, but no one is sure what jobs and technologies will exist in five years. One thing seems clear: the problems and challenges of the future will almost certainly be mediated through technology. An important point to recognize, therefore, is that schools have a responsibility to educate students to work in these emerging environments. We need to be thinking hard about our pedagogy and about how technology-mediated learning can fit into our education systems.

The way we deliver school programs is changing and will continue to change. The economics of future educational reforms may well be less geared towards gaining efficiencies in traditional delivery modes, such as physical infrastructure, and directed more towards how we can apply technology to deliver high-quality learning experiences, especially in low-enrolment rural schools—something all provinces are bound to have more of in the future. Despite our best efforts to convince education departments otherwise, some teachers will be lost from the system. There comes a point where even the most robust educational resourcing models will not be sufficient to offer a full suite of programs through traditional, classroom-based teaching, particularly in high schools. The notion of one teacher/one class may no longer be a viable and effective model. We already have some good models of e-learning in web-based classroom environments, and these are constantly being refined and improved.

In 2000, the Government of Newfoundland and Labrador established a Centre for Distance Learning and Innovation to allow students to complete programs using virtual classrooms and real time (synchronous) teaching. A student's e-teacher provides instruction via audio and videoconferencing, e-mail, fax, and conference forums. It was a major undertaking and required a significant and sustained financial commitment from governments past and present. Today, a range of programs (e.g., high school and Advanced Placement courses, e-tutoring, and counselling) are being offered by master teachers to students in schools that, individually, would be incapable of offering such programs.

In some cases, particularly in communities where there is more than one school or where communities are in reasonably close proximity, school closures and consolidation are an important and necessary option. Sometimes, when busing distances are reasonable and provision can be made for students to participate in after-school extra-curricular activities, the only realistic and appropriate option may be the rezoning of students to other schools. School boards do need to demonstrate that they are fiscally accountable for public expenditures and to show they are willing to operate within a context of finite financial resources. But, as my colleague Mary Green (Chapter Twelve) suggests, consolidation cannot be forced and must be accomplished in a reasonable and humanistic way.

Michael Apple, in *Ideology and Curriculum* (2004), says that schooling is inherently a "political and moral process" (p. 12) and the factors influencing how we organize schooling are not only economic, but also political and, more importantly, ethical. Schools have always been foundational to community and regional cohesion. I think it is appropriate to continue to ask questions about the economic benefits *and costs* of educational restructuring. How do we see communities of the future? Can a school help to grow a community? What happens when the school is gone? What have we gained and what have we lost?

The challenges posed by declining enrolments are clearly daunting. When the post-war baby boomers left the K-12 system starting in the 1970s, and into the 1980s and 1990s, they did so during recessionary times. The standard policy responses led to large numbers of school closures, teacher layoffs, hiring freezes, and service reductions. Should we expect the same during the current economic slowdown, as enrolments continue to plummet? Or can we be more strategic in our policy responses?

Many of the arguments for educational consolidation are difficult to refute, but with school closure and consolidation may come unintended consequences, such as those so well articulated in the chapters that follow. Given that enrolments in Canada are likely to continue on their present downward course, it seems inevitable that ministries and school boards must be prepared to embrace the opportunities for innovation that declining enrolments present. To continue on a path of wholesale restructuring so evident in the recent reform literature means that we run the risk of repeating a pattern of educational upheaval that, without thoughtful reflection about its consequences, may well result in harm to students and school communities.

Part Two

*Denominational Governance
of Education: Contested Terrain*

Chapter Six

The Abolition of Denominational Governance in Newfoundland– Unnecessary, Unwarranted

Bonaventure Fagan

On December 9, 2001, the Supreme Court of Canada gave notice that it would not hear the appeal of the Roman Catholic appellants of Newfoundland and Labrador against the 1998 constitutional change to Term 17 of the 1949 Terms of Union between Newfoundland and Canada. With that notice, there came to an end the significant story that publicly funded Roman Catholic education had played in Newfoundland for some 150 years. This chapter will consider the process by which those constitutional rights, together with those of others, were removed and argue that the removal was both unnecessary and unwarranted. The impact of these actions has broad implications not only for the specific situation that pertains to denominational rights in the governance of education, but also from the broader perspective of the removal of rights of any minority in this country. The chapter will conclude with a consideration of the appropriate form that public education should take in a democratic country such as Canada in the twenty-first century.

Constitutional framework

The origin of the constitutional rights in education held by Roman Catholics goes back to the 1840s (Rowe, 1964). As others have noted, Term 17 of the 1949 Terms of Union between Newfoundland and Canada (see Appendix A) spelled out the constitutional principle under which Roman Catholics, together with the members of certain other churches, would have their schools. Later, in 1982, Term 17 became part of the Constitution of Canada, and was further protected within Section 29 of the Charter of Rights and Freedoms of 1982. The same rights were extended to people of the Pentecostal faith in 1987.

What Term 17 did, in effect, was to articulate the principle of the operational relationship between government and church in education matters. Thus, the minister of education was "not bound to adopt any recommendation, proposal or advice" of the denominational educational authorities responsible for the exercise of rights (Education Act, 1968). At the same time, the legislature was bound not to enact any legislation or regulation that contravened the rights of the denominations. The relationship was, in other words, symbiotic, one that required good will and respect on both sides, and, for over 150 years, despite disagreements from time to time, that good will and respect won out.

The removal of constitutional rights: 1989–1996

In the revision of Term 17 (see Appendix C), the rights of the Anglican, United Church, Salvation Army, and Presbyterian denominations were removed with the approval of their church leaders—these four churches, along with the Moravian Church, had come together in 1968 to form the Integrated education system. In contrast, the rights of the Pentecostal, Roman Catholic, and Seventh-Day Adventist denominations were removed against their will. Although there was much common ground among the three throughout the process, this chapter confines itself generally to the perspective of the supporters of Catholic education.

What accounted for the process of removing the constitutional rights in education expressed within Term 17? Elsewhere, I have described the socio-political context in Newfoundland and Labrador during the 1980s, noting such factors as the heightened awareness of the theme of change in education circles globally, various challenging "task force" publications commissioned by the government, the negative disposition of the teachers' union (Newfoundland and Labrador Teachers' Association) towards the education system, conflicting polls on the views of the public, post-Vatican II changes within the Catholic church, and the sexual abuse scandal within the local Catholic church of the 1980s (Fagan, 2004, xxvii–xxxv). Galway and Dibbon, in Chapter One, reason that certain global factors, combined with provincial factors, were the "policy drivers" for change when education reform came under consideration. Nevertheless, such policy drivers needed human impetus to trigger the change process. That impetus came with the election of the Liberals under Premier Clyde Wells in May 1989.

I suggest the real issue for the government led by Mr. Wells, as for the Roman Catholic church—albeit from a quite different perspective (Sacred Congregation for Catholic Education, 1965, 1997)—was governance. Naturally, more pragmatic reasons were provided by government for seeking change, principally that, given the economic challenges of the early 1990s, the denominational system cost too much.[1] Poor student performance was also used periodically to suggest an inherent weakness in the system. Yet, at the heart of the matter was governance. To Catholic authorities, it seemed that Premier Wells perceived governance solely in terms of political power—a power wherein the government would have full control over every aspect of education. The premier seemed to think that a single school system was a prerequisite to achieving reform. Implicit in this reasoning was the suggestion that the government had little or no say in the governance of denominational schools. In fact, the government, quite properly, exercised substantial governance over such matters as the curriculum and all the factors that went into student performance and accountability; it alone determined the level of staffing for the various board offices and schools; it alone determined the budget for education. In addition, governance by the denominational authorities in matters such as the certification of teachers was a shared role rather than a responsibility in which the government had no say. Long before any of the policy drivers of the 1980s came into play, the record shows that Mr. Wells, in 1969, identified the Roman Catholic church and the Pentecostal assemblies, in particular, as opponents to the fulfillment of his notion of reform (Government of Newfoundland and Labrador, 1969), a position he still held after he had left politics nearly 30 years later (Wells, 1996).

In August, 1990, the government established the Williams Commission. From the beginning, it seemed clear to the Roman Catholic education authorities that the government intended to suggest that reform of education was impossible within the confines of the rights enshrined in Term 17 (Fagan, 2004). By contrast, the Catholic Education Council, in its 1991 presentation to the Royal Commission, pointed out that the goals of reform that had been identified by the government in the Commission's terms of reference could be achieved within Term 17 (Catholic Education Council, 1991). The record shows, of course, that the Commission, in its 1992 report *Our Children, Our Future* (Government of Newfoundland and Labrador, 1992b), brought back certain recommendations that, if adopted, would see the end of Catholic education in the province.

From the time of the release of the Royal Commission report in 1992 until 1997, Roman Catholic education authorities—embodied legislatively in the Catholic Education Council/Committee or CEC (the bishops as co-chairs, the representatives from various Catholic school boards, legal counsel, and various sub-committees struck to review and provide advice and to ensure a wide base in the Catholic community)—cooperated as fully as possible with the government's declared intent to reform the education system. Far from being anti-reform, the Catholic authorities provided leadership on how that reform might be expressed to the satisfaction of all parties. In meetings with government officials, with other church authorities, with the various Catholic advisory committees, and with the public, Catholic authorities took the position that reform was important and that Catholics should take an active part in all such discussions. Where the Catholic authorities differed fundamentally with the government was over the role that constitutional rights in education might play in that reform. To those authorities, the focus of reform ought not to be the denominational model of governance but what the model was asked to deliver. The decision of the Catholic authorities in 1992 was to cooperate with the government to the greatest degree while clearly enunciating the critical bottom line of ensuring the appropriate elements of governance for Catholic schools so that these schools might maintain their Catholic identity.

And what was the bottom line? To be identified as a Roman Catholic school, the school authorities (most typically, a school board) must have governance over those aspects that ensure the "catholicity" of a school, aspects such as student admission policies, hiring and termination of staff, religious education, and family life programs. Without these, a school cannot be ensured to carry out the Catholic church's mission of serving society through the values and world-view emanating from the teachings of Jesus Christ. In essence, it was this integrity that Term 17 guaranteed and enabled. This constitutional guarantee Roman Catholics did not take lightly. To supporters of Catholic education, a covenant was made, and, once made, a covenant was not to be broken. In discussions with the government, this guarantee did not seem to matter.

The government was quick to adopt the recommendations of the Royal Commission, and there ensued from 1992 onwards a series of on-again, off-again talks between the various church authorities and the government led by Clyde Wells. In those talks there was a desire by all sides (not just the government) to develop a governance model of maximized efficiency (Fagan, 1993). That is what the government said was at the root of its reform drive, even though, on the issue of cost, it was never able to demonstrate the validity of the numbers it was casting about. Indeed, the authoritative source for the supposed extra cost of the denominational system, the Royal Commission's report, *Our Children, Our Future,* had so many disclaimers attached to its findings (see, for example, Government of Newfoundland and Labrador, 1992b, pp. 107–108, 114, 197) they were considered by Roman Catholic authorities to be unreliable. Unreliable or not, the government never hesitated to use them for its own purposes.

Efficiency formed the premise for the 1993 summer talks among church and government representatives. Officially, the government officials were positioned as "resource persons" only (C. Decker, personal communication, July 15, 1993), yet they were very actively engaged in the discussion to find an acceptable and efficient governance structure. Out of that process, the denominational representatives proposed a joint governing board with a committee structure to ensure that the interests of Catholic, Pentecostal, and Seventh-Day Adventist schools were fully met (Denominational Education Councils, 1993). Under the plan, the school board would meet for common issues as a whole, while on those issues that affected only aspects of Catholic governance, for example, the Catholic committee members would meet independently. For Catholic trustees, the proposal was a radical one because it would see an end to the model of autonomous Catholic school boards. Nevertheless, the model was an efficient and constitutionally sound expression of the rights held under Term 17. Similarly, at the provincial level, shared and separate responsibilities were identified.

The government failed to appreciate the significance of the offer and rejected the position of all the churches (because the joint model had been developed collectively). However, because the church leaders representing the Integrated school system had already espoused a common denominational system, in essence, they had little or nothing to lose; the really significant movement had been made by the Catholic, Pentecostal, and Seventh-Day Adventist representatives. What the authorities representing the Integrated education system were pledging in the model was to continue to recognize governance by Catholics over those aspects that would ensure that a Catholic school was indeed Catholic; similarly for Pentecostal and Seventh-Day Adventist governance. In any event, the government rejected the proposal and responded with a position paper entitled *Adjusting the Course* (Government of Newfoundland and Labrador, 1993) that outlined how the new reformed educational system would operate. Other than in religious education, the Catholic people would have no say in the governance of their schools. For the government to equate Catholic education with religious education as a scheduled program and not to recognize that an operational Catholic philosophy as a holistic educational ethos was to either fail to understand the basis of that education or to reject it. Clearly then, the notion of limited governance put forward in *Adjusting the Course* was unacceptable to Catholic authorities.

Throughout these discussions there were several occurrences which suggested to Catholic authorities that the government was not really committed to finding a solution to reform within the parameters of the 1949 Term 17. One of these was its position on joint service schools. Term 17 acknowledged the right of the different churches to establish and operate their own schools, but also provided for the possibility that churches could on free accord come together to operate schools jointly. This provision allowed the Anglican, United, and other churches, in 1968, to form the Integrated system. It also allowed for the creation of a joint service school, a school formed by differing denominational school boards where low population deemed it appropriate to come together under one roof, while retaining governance rights over such aspects as religious education, family life education, and the appointment of teachers. Joint service schools were staffed by each operating school board on a basis proportionate to the student population; similarly, the administration was allocated usually through a shared and/or succession system.

Joint service, then, was a natural and constitutionally available solution to a shrinking student population. As the 1990s progressed, there was a growing number of such schools throughout the province and plummeting student populations clearly indicated that more joint service schools were in the offing. And yet, when the government issued *Adjusting the Course*, the concept of joint service school was replaced by that of interdenominational school wherein governance was restricted to religious education. This limited interpretation of governance was simply not acceptable to Catholic authorities, who, for their part, were prepared to exercise rights with some modification in certain compelling situations, but were not prepared to give up those governance rights on a wholesale basis, nor jeopardize their exercise in such schools. The discussions with the government over *Adjusting the Course* confirmed for Roman Catholic authorities that it was control, not economics nor cost nor performance nor anything else, that was the real goal of the government. Whether the schools were to be interdenominational or uni-denominational (the government's tag for a school of a single denomination), governance, other than in religious education, was perceived by Catholic authorities to be either non-existent or so restricted in its exercise that in fact it was not governance at all. In other words, the adoption of *Adjusting the Course* would see the very character of Term 17 fundamentally changed. That, Catholic authorities could never accept.

In the months that followed, various revisions to *Adjusting the Course* were made, all of which failed to modify the government's stance on the basic issue of governance. The position of the Catholic authorities was simple, straightforward, and consistent: Catholic schools required Catholic governance, after which any number of modifications could be made to the expression of that governance. And the government, while giving the appearance that it understood the Catholic position in face-to-face discussions, would produce yet another statement that was clearly not in keeping with the Constitution of the country.

In the winter of 1994, however, an opportunity arose for a resolution to the impasse that would satisfy the stated goals of the various churches and the government. In an oft-repeated line in various discussions, the church leaders in Integration stated that they were not interested in governance over schools. What they wanted was the continued guarantee that in all their schools they could offer their religious education program. They were in favour of a single denominational system, they said, but they would respect the minority rights held by others, and asked the government to do likewise.

With that understanding a fresh proposal was put on the table in February 1994 (Fagan, 2004). That proposal would see the Integrated schools become open schools with the continued guarantee of the provision of the Integrated religious education program. Governance over the admission of students would be forfeited but not at the expense of religious education. It seemed an acceptable solution. Not so. The church leaders in Integration rejected the proposal on the fear, they said, that their schools would become the common schools. They would only let go the right to govern the admission of students if the Catholics, Pentecostals, and Seventh-Day Adventists did the same thing. This fixation on contingency was a baffling and self-contradictory rejection of a possible solution to the governance issue.

At this point, the government led by Mr. Wells could have exerted a considerable degree of influence to get the church leaders in Integration to accept the proposal. Instead, it renewed pressure on the Catholic, Pentecostal, and Seventh-Day Adventist authorities to give up the one thing that they had said from the beginning could not be given up, namely governance over those aspects that gave their schools their religious identity. To supporters of Catholic education, there certainly seemed to be a disproportionate treatment of the Catholic (and Pentecostal and Seventh-Day Adventist) position in the discussions with the government as compared to that taken towards the Integrated position.

In late November, 1994, the Catholic authorities, under the signature of Archbishop James MacDonald, put forward to Premier Wells a clearly delineated position showing the Catholic commitment to reform (J. MacDonald, personal communication, November 22, 1994). Among the points made in the archbishop's letter were the following:

- ❖ a denominationally based school system (to which the government had already agreed) does not preclude the establishment of separate secular schools;
- ❖ it was agreeable that there be 10 or fewer school boards, comprised of those elected to represent the various denominations in the district;
- ❖ uni-denominational and interdenominational schools should be treated equally in every respect;
- ❖ schools in communities which have only Roman Catholic schools would become interdenominational if that was decided by a majority of the population served by the school;
- ❖ in areas which could support more than one viable school system, Roman Catholic parents would be free to decide whether they wished to send their children to a Roman Catholic school or to an interdenominational school;
- ❖ elected Roman Catholic representatives would have authority in matters which affect their denominational integrity:

  - ◆ general ambience, religious education, family life education and pastoral care, including staff development in these matters
  - ◆ the selection and placement of teachers for Roman Catholic schools, including the termination of placement with those schools;

◈ agreed-to province-wide viability criteria, once established, should be non-discriminatory and based on education criteria, and applied equally to all schools;

◈ a single provincial school construction board was acceptable with provincially established school-construction priorities;

◈ all schools should be treated equally in all respects, including transportation policies, and;

◈ at the provincial level, there needed to be a clear recognition of the existence of statutory denominational rights.

The response of the government was negative, charging that what Catholic authorities wanted was the status quo (C. Wells, personal communication, November 3, 1994). To Catholic authorities, the government's rejection seemed to be imputing to them motives and intentions that were completely unfounded.

During the winter and spring months of 1995, a series of meetings and communiqués between the church authorities and the government centred on questions and revisions of *Adjusting the Course*. At the heart of the questions was the concern that the proposals put forward by the government to that point in time remained contrary to the provisions of the Constitution, a point that Mr. Wells acknowledged (C. Wells, personal communications, November 3, 1994, and May 31, 1995). It had been the Catholic position from the beginning that any reform had to provide for the continuation of constitutional protection for Catholic education. On June 1, 1995, talks were suddenly terminated by the premier and he announced a general referendum would be held in September of that year (Education plebiscite, 1995).

Premier Wells used the results of that referendum to table a resolution in the House of Assembly in the fall of 1995 that allowed Catholic schools to exist "subject to provincial legislation that is uniformly applicable to all schools" (Government of Newfoundland and Labrador, 1995b). Although there was some solace in the fact that, at the last minute, it seemed the government was willing to recognize partially the desire of Catholics to retain their constitutional rights in education, Catholic authorities opposed the resolution and the resulting amendment by the Parliament of Canada in 1996 on the grounds that a constitutional right should never be subject to a provincial legislature and that the model of governance purported to be in the amended Term 17 would collapse at the implementation stage (J. MacDonald, personal communication, October 18, 1995). The Senate, after hearings in the province, recommended that the House of Commons amend the resolution (Government of Canada, 1996). The government led by Mr. Chrétien refused, and the amendment to Term 17 passed in the House of Commons on December 4, 1996. Over the next 12 months, the fears of Catholic education authorities concerning the government's intent regarding the implementation of the revised Term 17 were confirmed.

The removal of constitutional rights: 1996–2001

Prior to passage of the amendment to Term 17, Mr. Wells retired and Brian Tobin had become premier in the winter of 1996. In March of that year, after some urging by Archbishop MacDonald, the government invited church representatives to meet, and over a three-day period a framework of agreement was reached to the satisfaction of church leaders and the government (Government of Newfoundland and Labrador, 1996). The minister of education, Roger Grimes, made much of the agreement because it apparently satisfied the reform goals of the government (Government of Newfoundland and Labrador, 1996). The Catholic (and Pentecostal and Seventh-Day Adventist) authorities also made much of the agreement because it demonstrated quite clearly that the reform stated by the government was achievable within the 1949 Term 17 and therefore the impending amendment (the Wells resolution, as it were) to that term was unnecessary. Most importantly, the framework agreement was only possible because the church leaders in Integration had also fully agreed to its articles. Despite that, representatives of the Integrated authorities backed away from support of the "Framework Agreement," as it was commonly called. The government seems to have perceived this as a sign of discord among church leaders and decided to move ahead with amending Term 17 (F. Mifflin, personal communication, May 27, 1996).

This was a key event in the story of denominational education reform. The disposition of the Integrated representatives toward the "Framework Agreement" had significant implications for the course of events that followed. It is not clear why the government under Mr. Tobin did not exert its considerable influence on the representatives of the Integrated system to accept the principles of the agreement in which they had just fully participated. Instead, over the next several months—from the perspective of Catholic authorities—considerable pressure was placed on Catholic, Pentecostal, and Seventh-Day Adventist representatives until they could give no more, and when no more could be given, the government took all.

I argue that once again, as in 1994 with the Wells Government, when a reasonable solution to the impasse between the government and churches had been proposed, the Tobin Government failed to seize the opportunity to provide a fair and balanced resolution that would meet the stated goals of all parties. When the Tobin Government went about the implementation of the 1997 amended Term 17, there was no coherence among the constitutional statement, provincial legislation, and the directives of the minister of education; as such, the Catholic and Pentecostal authorities concluded that they had no choice but to seek an injunction against the implementation of the model that was to take effect in September 1997. In short, the injunction was granted, in large part on the grounds that the minister of education's actions had rendered the constitutional rights "meaningless" and "illusory" *(Hogan v. Newfoundland (School Boards for Ten Districts)*, 1997a). Catholic and the Pentecostal authorities were directed to make decisions on the appropriateness of school closures as recommended by the province's new interdenominational school boards. The Catholic authorities exercised the Court's directive agreeing to close some 35 Catholic schools. Another 31 were approved for joint service arrangements; and, based on the free determination of a simple majority of Catholic parents in certain communities, six Catholic schools were released to become interdenominational (Catholics OK, 1997). At this point, however, it appeared to Catholic authorities that nothing they could do would satisfy the government. Mr. Tobin proceeded with another referendum and armed with the results once again amended Term 17, this time to remove completely the minority rights in education of Catholics and others, a deed accomplished by Parliament in the fall of 1997 (Government of Canada, 1997e; House of Commons).

Minority rights before the courts

Much has been made of the results of the referendum held in 1995 and of the second one held in 1997. Perhaps too much authority is accredited to those two events in regard to the subsequent actions of the provincial legislature and the Parliament of Canada. What is known for certain is that resolutions were brought forward twice in the province's legislature, the first to remove some of the constitutional rights of Catholics and others, the second to remove the rights altogether. Those actions resulted in the 1997 and 1998 amendments to Term 17 by the Parliament of Canada. How various segments of society, including Roman Catholics, actually voted may be interesting but is of no binding consequence—the votes held no authority legislatively or legally. Nor did the results hold any authority for the supporters of Catholic education.

One critical aspect about both referenda that Catholic authorities disputed was that, because the rights held in education and exercised by Roman Catholics were minority rights, *Catholics were the sole determiners of what should become of those rights*. The rights had been planted in the 1840s and recognized ever since, including by the 1949 Term 17, the Constitution of Canada, and the Charter of Rights and Freedoms. One of the perceived principles of a minority right in Canada is that it must not be put to the test by a vote of the general population. In its presentation to the 1997 Special Joint House Committee in Ottawa, the Catholic representatives noted that there was a constitutional convention in Canada to the effect that "minority rights in Canada will not be eliminated without the consent of the holders of those rights" (Catholic Education Council, 1997). Yet, both the governments led by Mr. Wells and Mr. Tobin ignored that convention by putting the continued existence of Catholic and other minority rights in education to a general referendum. The outcomes appeared to give the governments of Newfoundland and Labrador and of Canada the needed rationalization to do what they intended to do.

Catholic plaintiffs took their case against the 1998 change in Term 17 to the Supreme Court of Newfoundland, first to the Trial Division and, on failure there, to the Appeal Court. The case centred on four arguments, each affecting minority rights:

(1) the process of the September 2, 1997, referendum was invalid and unfairly conducted;
(2) the consent of Roman Catholics is required for any amendment to the educational rights of Roman Catholics contained in Term 17 of the 1949 Terms of Union between Newfoundland and Canada;
(3) in Canada the consent of the minority affected is required before any abrogation of those rights;
(4) if an amendment to the Constitution was permitted, the general amending formula applied, not the bilateral formula. (*Hogan v. Newfoundland (Attorney General)*, 1999)

These arguments touched on certain cornerstones that had been identified by the Supreme Court of Canada in the *Reference re Secession of Quebec* (1998). In that case, the Supreme Court, having identified "respect for minorities" among the "four fundamental and organizing principles" of the Constitution, went on to observe that minority rights, "religion and education rights" among them, may well have been the result of political compromises but "that does not render them unprincipled. Rather, such a concern reflects a broader principle related to the protection of minority rights," which the Court then identified as an "independent principle underlying our constitutional order." The Court pointed out that "the protection of minority rights was clearly an essential consideration in the design of our constitutional structure" and "continues to exercise influence in the operation and interpretation of our Constitution" (*Reference re Secession of Quebec*, 1998).

As in the judgment of the Trial Division (*Hogan v. Newfoundland (Attorney General)*, 1998), that of the Appeal Division also went against the Roman Catholic plaintiffs (*Hogan v. Newfoundland (Attorney General)*, 2000). In both rulings, the Justices seemed determined to avoid making reference to key events that had negatively affected the plaintiffs over the previous three years. In the Appeal Court's judgment, the Terms of Union provided no legal basis to challenge the 1998 proclaimed revision of Term 17. Secondly, the Court rejected the argument that any amendment to the Constitution would require the general amending formula. Thirdly, the Court found that the plaintiff's use of the *Reference re Quebec Secession* went too far in interpreting its findings. Of critical importance, however, the Court went on to conclude that "the constitution entrusts minority rights to the majority."

Because in November of 2001 the Supreme Court of Canada declined to hear the appeal of the Catholic plaintiffs, the ruling of the Supreme Court of Newfoundland on this matter of constitutional protection of minority rights in Canada still stands. From that perspective, it would seem that minority rights may not be, as previously supposed by the Canadian public and certainly by the various minorities affected, protected from the will of the majority. Furthermore, the ruling that the use by the plaintiffs of the *Quebec Secession Reference* findings was erroneous begs to be clarified. If the Supreme Court of Canada were to agree with the Newfoundland Court on that issue, it would appear to contradict the Supreme Court's identification of minority rights as one of the four cornerstones of this country, with explicit reference included to "religion and education rights." If, on the contrary, the Supreme Court were to rule that indeed all minority rights are protected from arbitrary legislation by governments at the provincial and national levels, then the appeal of the Catholic plaintiffs would be shown to be both just and proper.

Conclusions

The removal of the minority rights in education held by Roman Catholics and enshrined in the Terms of Union with Canada and subsequently in the Constitution of Canada and the Charter of Rights and Freedoms (as with the rights of Pentecostals and Seventh-Day Adventists) was without precedent. Catholic authorities had supported the principle of reform, despite the perceived lack of substance to the repeated refrain of the government (based on the disavowed figures of the 1992 Royal Commission) that the denominational system was costing too much. On the issue of student performance, the government's public statements seemed less about academics and more about politics. On the issues of excessive cost and poor student performance, then, the amendment to the 1949 Term 17 was, to supporters of Catholic education, absolutely unnecessary.

Throughout the early 1990s, on behalf of the Catholic people with rights in education, the Catholic education authorities had negotiated in good faith with both the government and with the other church leaders; they had made substantial proposals on how reform might be carried out; they had demonstrated forcefully that the stated goals of the government— efficiency chief among them—could be achieved within the parameters of the 1949 Term 17. Over those years of negotiation, Roman Catholic authorities remained at the table determined not to let escape this chance to find unity in an acceptable model of reform. In the end, unity could not be found. For supporters of Catholic education, the unwarranted removal of their minority rights left them in September, 1998, with no publicly funded schools for the first time since the 1840s.

In short, supporters of Catholic education believe that the removal of the minority rights of Roman Catholics in education in this province was an injustice: a covenant was made; a covenant was broken. The fact that some Roman Catholics willingly participated in this removal of rights does not diminish the injustice of what has transpired. Indeed, that sense of injustice was only more deeply ingrained when Government seized for use without compensation all Roman Catholic school property (land and buildings) (Schools Act, 1997).

The government of this province, Newfoundland and Labrador, bears the major responsibility for this injustice. Solutions were achievable within the parameters of the 1949 Term 17 and the government failed to achieve them. Solutions may even have been achievable within the revised 1997 Term 17; yet the government of the day, through inadequate legislation and directives contradictory to the new constitutional term, likewise failed to find those solutions. The federal government also bears responsibility for this injustice. As the national government, Parliament is charged with protecting the Constitution and its provisions, with particular vigilance for minority rights. In not meeting this responsibility twice within a 12-month period, the federal government failed the people of this province and the people of Canada as a whole. Finally, by deciding not to hear the appeal of the Roman Catholic plaintiffs, the Supreme Court of Canada failed to use the opportunity to bring clarity to apparently contradictory constitutional matters. By their actions and inactions, both levels of government and of the courts may well have exposed all minority rights in this country to the expressed will of the majority. Although it is true that our governing structures can learn from mistakes, it is equally true that precedent lends legitimacy to repetition.

Despite, however, their conviction that a covenant was broken when their schools were taken from them, and while resignation can never erase injustice, supporters of Catholic education wish the public system currently in place in the province every success. The education of all our children in intellectual and cultural matters is of critical importance to the service of the people of our province, our country, and indeed of the world. For their part, Roman Catholics whose children must attend the public system must not be reticent about what is required to ensure the education system lives up to their expectations.

Afterword: Can denominational rights co-exist with educational secularism?

The change in the education system in Newfoundland and Labrador gives us pause to examine the question of what model of publicly funded education ought to obtain in a country like Canada (see Stapleton, Chapter Seven, for a description of the current educational context throughout the nation). In essence, there are two such models of organization for public education. One would see a single form of public secular schools under the direction of public secular boards. In this model, the best interests of the state are seen to be exercised in a school system that on matters of religion and moral values would remain neutral. That would be the case even if the school system had a program in religious education, as it does at the moment in Newfoundland and Labrador (see Hodder, Chapter Nine). The theory is that such a single stream of education is, among other things, easier to administer, treats everyone the same, causes fewer difficulties with the individual rights of teachers, and is economically more efficient. In Chapter Thirteen, for example, and despite the promising results of an aggressive inter-religious linking of students through computer technology, Austin and Hunter seem to suggest that the secularization of religious schools in Northern Ireland would provide the ideal means of developing good social relations among Catholics and Protestants.

The other model of organization of public education runs counter to the first. This perspective calls for a school system that recognizes in its organization and governance the right of parents to see their children educated in the values of those parents. That includes secular values as well as religious values, for in one way or another all schools are value-laden (Sacred Congregation for Catholic Education, 1965). The reality, however, is that for many parents, secular values are often perceived as a contradiction to their religiously-held convictions, as, in turn, their religious values are often unacceptable to those parents who espouse a secular outlook. Those deepest of convictions require an equally deep "respect" for the position of the other; alone, the politically correct "tolerance" is a hollow gesture.

Yet, in postmodern society, the single model of education seems to result in the muting of religious convictions. If, as one of the underlying premises of this book posits, our society is becoming more secularized, it is equally true that a large portion of the Canadian social fabric has retained its religious heritage (Bibby, 2006). Simply put, the increase in secularization does not mean that people of faith must be forced to park their convictions when it comes to the public education of their children. There is room for both kinds of schools. That is healthy for Canada, as it is currently for Australia, England, Germany, and other countries. And the "public" aspect of education would ensure that the differing systems do not become unbridgeable solitudes.

A parental values model of education would see a partnership in governance between the government and the structures which represent the parents, both the religious-minded and the secular-minded. All schools would be treated to an equal share of the education budget. The government would set the standard of viability, applicable equally to all schools. The government would be responsible, for example, for the general curriculum, the certification of teachers, monitoring performance, ensuring building and safety codes. Collaterally, the philosophical "integrity" of the school would be the sole responsibility of the parental structures. It is this latter model of education that the Government of Newfoundland and Labrador had an opportunity to see in place in the reform talks of the 1990s. Instead, in its desire to remove the rights of certain religious groups, in particular Roman Catholics, Pentecostals, and Seventh-Day Adventists, it missed the chance to reorganize the system in such a way that all groups, including the secular-minded, would have schools that meet a common standard of viability and where children would be educated in the values, religious or secular, of their parents. This would be a model of education worthy of any democratic country, including Northern Ireland, and most certainly a natural fit for Canada, where the recognition of minorities is said to be a cornerstone of our society.

Chapter Seven

Denominationally (Religiously) Segregated Education in Canada

John J. Stapleton

The design of education in Canada has changed considerably since 1962 when I began my teaching career in a Catholic high school in St. John's, Newfoundland. As a boy growing up in the central Newfoundland town of Grand Falls-Windsor, I attended Catholic schools; all my classroom teachers and principals were religious sisters and brothers. There were still many sisters and brothers teaching in the schools of Newfoundland in 1962, but this era was about to end. Similarly, I had no inkling that the whole denominational school system would be abolished 36 years later, ending not only the schools themselves but also such institutions as the annual Jones Shield hockey series between St. Michael's Regional High School and Grand Falls Academy, which was a significant athletic, social, and cultural event of my childhood. Across the rest of the country in 1962, I saw a wealth of differences in educational systems: a provincially supported confessional system in Quebec, a partially funded separate school system in Ontario, no public support for private schools in most of the country including Manitoba and British Columbia, and publically funded separate school systems in Alberta and Saskatchewan.

Who knew that half a century later Canada would have such a drastically altered educational landscape? Today, constitutionally protected public school systems based on religious rights enjoyed by Protestants and Roman Catholics exist only in Ontario, Saskatchewan, and Alberta, although they existed in Manitoba until 1890, and until 1998 in Quebec and in Newfoundland and Labrador. Public denominational school boards and schools may be operated by statute in Nunavut, the Northwest Territories, and the Yukon, but these are not constitutionally protected. No public denominational schools exist in the remaining provinces. All provinces permit the establishment and operation of private faith-based schools in accordance with their acts and regulations, but financial aid in the form of operating grants is allocated only in Quebec, Manitoba, Saskatchewan, Alberta, and British Columbia. No such grants are available in Ontario or in the Atlantic provinces, although it might be noted that Ontario, which has many private schools, briefly provided in the early years of the first decade of the twenty-first century a measure of tax relief to parents that was related to tuition charged by these schools. Quite a change indeed from 1962!

Canada's 10 provinces and three territories contain 13 different educational designs which are the products of their different histories. Some jurisdictions have ended the public denominational school system as part of their educational reform initiatives, but it still exists in Ontario, Saskatchewan, and Alberta despite arguments that it should be eliminated in these provinces as well (Smith & Foster, 2001c). Throughout my career I have been a proponent of publicly funded denominational school boards and recognize this as a contentious issue—one worth further examination. The purposes of this chapter, then, are (1) to describe the current status of constitutionally protected public denominational education in Canada, and (2) to outline the arguments that have been advanced both for eliminating and for preserving the current arrangements in Ontario, Saskatchewan, and Alberta.

Constitutionally protected public denominational schooling in Canada

It is generally considered that Canada's constitutional arrangements consist of the Constitution Act, 1867 (formerly known as the British North America Act), the Constitution Act, 1982 including the Canadian Charter of Rights and Freedoms, the amendments to these Acts that have been made over the years (there have been nine since 1982 including four regarding education—three for Newfoundland and Labrador, one for Quebec), the Acts creating the provinces that came into the Dominion after 1867, the Royal Proclamation of 1863, and the various treaties signed between the Government of Canada and First Nations (Bezeau, 2007).

It is helpful to recall a little Canadian history at this point but it should be noted that a thorough discussion of our constitutional history in education is beyond the scope of this chapter.[1] The Constitution Act, 1867 was passed by the British Parliament approximately 250 years after the founding of Quebec in 1608 and just over 100 years after the formal transfer of control of the country from France to England in 1763 as part of the Treaty of Paris. Between 1608 and 1867, education was a significant part of colonial life; the first schools can be dated to the 1630s in New France, and significant legislation was passed in the period to govern education in Canada East and Canada West after 1841, including the famous Scott Act of 1863 which is generally perceived to be the legislative basis of Catholic school rights in modern-day Ontario. In fact, given his influence in establishing educational rights for Catholics, Richard Scott of Ottawa is considered a hero in Catholic school circles. Flynn (2003) retells a story by Carl Matthews, S.J., of Scott, a backbencher from Ottawa, introducing separate school legislation as a private member's bill in 1861, 1862, and 1863. In the last of these years, it passed in the Parliament of Canada with the support of John A. Macdonald. The day of its passage, May 6, the Archbishop of the Archdiocese of Toronto, John J. Lynch, sent Scott a telegram saying "PLEASE ACCEPT ASSURANCE OF PERPETUAL GRATITUDE OF CATHOLICS OF CANADA" (pp. 29–30).

With Roman Catholics and Protestants possessing rights to education prior to 1867, how then were these to be treated when Canada East and West, Nova Scotia, and New Brunswick entered into Confederation? As is well known, Section 93 of the Constitution Act, 1867, sometimes referred to as the "Confederation compromise," states that "In and for each province, the Legislature may exclusively make laws in relation to education subject to the following provisions," and these latter include the significant first one that says, "(1) Nothing in any such Law shall prejudicially affect any right or privilege with respect to denominational schools which any class of persons have by law in the province at Union." Clearly then, if a denominational group had a legally enshrined right regarding education prior to Union, it retained that right after Union, which in a sense rendered the Constitution Act, 1867 a transmittal document. If this first provision was very important for the retention of denominational rights, the second provision is widely considered to have been the agreement that made Confederation possible: "(2) All of the powers, privileges, and duties conferred and imposed in Upper Canada on the separate schools and school trustees of the Queen's Roman Catholic subjects shall be and the same are hereby extended to the dissentient schools of the Queen's Protestant and Roman Catholic subjects in Quebec." Subsections (3) and (4) of Section 93 allow for appeals to the federal government in those cases in which Ontario and Quebec approve new legislation prejudicial to denominational educational rights, and for the enactment of remedial laws by the federal government that would overturn such provincial legislation. As to the other provinces, Manitoba entered Confederation in 1870 with a denominational school system, British Columbia in 1871 and Prince Edward Island in 1873 without such provisions, Alberta and Saskatchewan in 1905 with denominational rights that had been confirmed by the Ordinances of the Northwest Territories in 1901, and Newfoundland in 1949 with a denominational school system. As to the three territories, the Constitution Act, 1871 assigned to Parliament responsibility for their governance, and subsequently this body created territorial governments in the Northwest Territories, Yukon, and Nunavut through legislation that allows for the creation of separate schools for Protestant or Roman Catholic minorities.

What exactly is meant by denominational rights? Generally, this means that Roman Catholics and Protestants have the right to organize a school district; to elect a school board to establish and manage schools in that district for its resident pupils, including the right and responsibility to set policies that protect the denominational nature of the schools; to receive public funding to build and operate the schools; and to be exempt from taxation which supports the public schools of that district. This last right was more significant when school boards in much of the country had the right to levy local taxes on property. Supporters of the public denominational school board would have to pay the tax levied by their board, but they would be exempt from local taxes levied by the public school board. Because most provinces have eliminated local property taxes as a means of financing education, preferring instead to levy a provincial property tax to support education, this right is not as important as once it was. It should also be noted that denominational school boards must comply with provincial acts and regulations regarding education, as Section 93 makes the province responsible for this function.

Canada's educational history, then, contains efforts to secure in legislation the rights of certain religious communities regarding education. However, it is also replete with cases wherein provincial legislation and constitutional amendments to federal legislation have been used to abolish those rights. The provisions of Section 93 have been tested many times. Soon after Confederation, the province of New Brunswick eliminated funding to Catholic schools. Catholics challenged this decision, but the provincial initiative was upheld by the courts on the grounds that the rights of Catholics to publicly funded education had never been enshrined in law. Later, perhaps the best known legal case in educational history of this country—the Manitoba School Question of 1890–1896—occurred when the Province of Manitoba passed the Public Schools Act of 1890 which effectively ended the Quebec-like confessional school system that had been constructed in 1871 following the Parliament of Canada's passage of The Manitoba Act. Section 22 (2) and (3) of this Act were identical to Section 93 (3) and (4) of the Constitutional Act, 1867, and these became the basis of the ultimately unsuccessful challenge of the Roman Catholic community to retain public support of its school system.

These challenges to denominational education rights have continued into our own age. In 1997, with the consent of the Government of Quebec, the Parliament of Canada amended the Constitution Act of 1867 by approving Section 93A which reads, "Paragraphs (1) to (4) of Section 93 do not apply to Quebec." This provision paved the way for the province to replace denominational school boards with ones organized linguistically (Boudreau, 1999). Furthermore, following contested referenda in Newfoundland and Labrador, the province petitioned the Government of Canada to change the provisions of Term 17 which governed the entry of that province into the Union in 1949. Consequently, Canada's Parliament approved a constitutional amendment in 1997 to create a secular system to replace the denominational system then in place, and another in 1998 to abolish the denominational school system (Fagan, 2004). Currently, the only constitutionally protected rights to religious education are in Newfoundland and Labrador where access to courses in religious education is provided on the grounds that they are not specific to a particular religious denomination and to religious observances when requested by parents.

Another constitutional document that bears upon the question of religion and education is the Charter of Rights and Freedoms, 1982. Section 2(a) grants everyone the fundamental freedom of conscience and religion, and Section 7 grants the right to life, liberty, and security of the person; however, these are not unlimited rights as Section 1 guarantees such rights and freedoms subject only to such "reasonable limits prescribed by law as can be demonstrably justified in a free society." Moreover, concerning equality rights, Section 15(1) states that "every individual is equal before and under the law and has the right to equal protection and equal benefit of the law without discrimination based on race, national or ethnic origin, colour, religion, sex, age, or mental or physical ability." Two observations arise from an initial consideration of these rights. First, it would appear that parents could make an argument for the existence and support of schools that foster their religious convictions on the two-fold justification that such would accommodate their rights to religious freedom and to the pursuit of liberty. Secondly, those opposed to government support for only one group, e.g., Roman Catholics, on the basis that such a benefit is discriminating on the basis of religion, would seem to have a solid point. However, the Charter also contains Section 29 which states that "Nothing in this Charter abrogates or derogates from any rights or privileges guaranteed by or under the Constitution of Canada in respect of denominational, separate or dissentient schools." This would seem to be strong protection for the legal defense of denominational schools, but as we have seen, it did not provide protection for such schools in Newfoundland and Labrador and Quebec in the 1990s. At the end of the first decade of the twenty-first century, the situation is as follows: (1) all provinces and territories have public school systems; (2) some provinces have public denominational school systems to accommodate the constitutionally enshrined rights of Roman Catholics and Protestants; (3) the territories whose existence depends on the Parliament of Canada have legislation that permits the existence of public denominational school boards and these exist in the Yukon and Northwest Territories, and (4) while most denominational school boards are Catholic (the English Catholic and French Catholic school boards of Ontario, the Catholic school boards of Alberta and Saskatchewan, and the public denominational boards in the Yukon and Northwest Territories), there are at least three denominational Protestant school boards in Canada—one each in Ontario (Penetanguishene), Saskatchewan (Englefeld), and Alberta (St. Albert).

Statistics Canada (Blouin, 2008) reports that the public and public denominational school boards of the country educated approximately 93 per cent of the approximately 5.2 million students who attended Canadian schools in 2005–2006. Data provided by the Canadian Catholic School Trustees Association (G. McNally, personal communication, December 4, 2008) indicate that approximately 15–16 per cent of that population is enrolled in public denominational Catholic schools. The percentages in Ontario, Alberta, and Saskatchewan are higher because of the formal systems that exist there, and the Catholic school boards of these provinces enrol approximately a third, a quarter, and a fifth of the total school populations respectively. The numbers are substantial—the English and French Catholic school systems of Ontario numbered 622,447 full time equivalent (fte) students in 2007–2008, Alberta had 129, 032 fte students, and Saskatchewan 35,554 fte students.[2]

It is clear, then, that there are sizable public denominational school systems in Canada based on constitutional rights of Roman Catholics and Protestants. It is also clear that our history is replete with challenges to those systems based on arguments for and against their abolition. The following section outlines what those arguments are.

The case for constitutional amendments to abolish public denominational school systems

At the outset, it should be noted that periodic waves of effort to improve or reform education are common in Canada. We are currently in a period that is strongly focused on the improvement of student learning, particularly for students facing disadvantages, and to that end, initiatives have been launched by provincial governments to increase retention and graduation rates, to improve literacy and numeracy scores in provincial, national, and international tests, and to close the achievement gaps between defined groups of students. Such policies have addressed curriculum, special education, technology, accountability, parent and community involvement, safe schools, nutrition, teacher and administrator development, school choice, school finance, and school board consolidation. Consequently, it is not surprising that another target of reform is public denominational school systems.

The educational rights of Roman Catholics garnered attention in the Ontario provincial election of 2007 as a by-product of the promise of John Tory, the leader of the Progressive Conservative party, to provide public support to private faith-based schools which receive no financial support from government. (Note the distinction between the public denominational system and private faith-based schools.) This quickly became the major issue of the election. Poll data showed that 70 per cent of Ontarians opposed the proposal, and its consideration by the public brought the issue of the existence of the English Catholic and French Catholic public denominational school systems into the limelight. The One School System Network (OSSN), a coalition of a dozen or so organizations including Education Equality in Ontario and the Canadian Civil Liberties Association (CCLA), weighed in on the issue with CCLA proposing that not only should provincial funding not be extended to faith-based schools, but also that Ontario should seek a constitutional amendment to abolish the existence of separate school systems (CCLA, 2007). In the aftermath of the election which was won by the Liberals, columnist Michael Valpy (2007), in assessing the election's winners and losers, claimed that one loser was the Roman Catholic Church, whose leaders he claimed would have preferred that the subject of denominational rights in education remain below the radar. Furthermore, given the recent history of constitutional challenges to denominational schooling, he predicted that the Catholic school system would be gone in 10 years.

It has not been only in Ontario that issues pertaining to the operation and existence of Catholic school systems have been raised. In Saskatchewan, a public challenge to the ability of Catholic school boards to receive public operating grants for non-Catholic students has been awaiting resolution for several years (Donlevy, 2005). In Alberta, issues have arisen when Roman Catholic residents have used their rights to create a new separate school division or to enlarge an existing one which then opens a school in a jurisdiction that has witnessed the close of a school by the public school division because of insufficient enrolment, and that new separate school then enrols both Catholic and non-Catholic students. Unsurprisingly, this has raised the ire of the public school board. In the Northwest Territories, the legislation permits people who are non-Catholics to run for office on the public denominational Catholic school board, a fact that has to this point been unsuccessfully challenged by the Catholic community in the courts (Borst, 2008).

Given that Ontario has the largest public denominational school system and because the issue was raised in the last provincial election, this chapter will focus on the case that might be made for abolishing the educational rights held by Roman Catholics and Protestants in that province based on the following nine reasons. First, Ontario is a secular and increasingly diverse society. Although religion is important to many people and although the academic study of religious beliefs and practices ought to be part of the curriculum of schools, it is an inappropriate use of public moneys to foster the beliefs and practices of a particular religion. The proper places for encouraging faith formation are the home and the place of worship, not the school.

Second, it is demonstrably unfair and a violation of Section (15) of the Charter of Rights and Freedoms to bestow a public benefit on the adherents of one religion, Roman Catholics, that is unavailable to those from other religions. The United Nations Human Rights Committee ruled on November 5, 1999, that Canada is in violation of the International Covenant on Civil and Political Rights because of Ontario's funding of Roman Catholic schools and not those of other faiths (Zur, 2003). Smith and Foster (2001c) put the case more forcefully:

[T]he lingering discrimination in several jurisdictions in favor of Catholic and Protestant religions over all others...is permissible by virtue of the shield afforded by Section 93 of the Constitution Act, 1867 and Section 29 of the *Canadian Charter*. The shield is necessary because the privileges are incompatible with *Charter* rights and standards. As a matter of public policy, it is both unacceptable that such discrimination be allowed to continue and repugnant that this is sanctioned by a constitutional provision. (p. 259)

Third, while it is acknowledged that Roman Catholics and Protestants in three provinces have well-defined historic and constitutional rights, it is equally true that those protections, rights, and privileges reflect a situation that existed in the nineteenth century when it was clearer that Catholics attending public schools had legitimate concerns that public schools were really educational institutions infused with Protestant values. Such Catholic-Protestant divisions no longer exist, and there is no need for Catholics to dissent from existing public schools by establishing their own school districts, school boards, and schools. Although this generation has inherited the tradition of public and public denominational school boards, this does not mean the current structure has to be kept in perpetuity, and indeed recent changes in Newfoundland and Labrador and in Quebec provide roadmaps for abolishing the archaic denominational rights of Roman Catholics and Protestants.

The fourth reason is that the public school is one of the most important integrative mechanisms of our society, and as such it should be kept strong. There is wide consensus on this point, as has been revealed by past reports that have examined the case for and against public support for private schools (Government of Manitoba, 1959; Shapiro, 1985). The fact that a large number of Catholic students are removed from public schools means that those who attend public schools are denied the benefits that come with interacting with them. Put bluntly, public schools need the attendance of Catholic students because without them, the equality of educational opportunity of the children and adolescents who attend public schools is lessened. Equally, Catholic students are deprived of the benefits that come when they attend the same school as their fellow students from diverse and no religious backgrounds.

Closely aligned with the argument concerning educational equality is number five—the argument for social cohesion. Canada is a diverse, multicultural society that recognizes and values differences. It is important that citizens be able to communicate effectively with each other. Having children and adolescents from different creeds learn from each other in the same school is the most effective way of creating a new generation of citizens respectful of difference but with an ability to work together.

Sixth, schools established by a particular denomination, unwittingly, can adopt a proselytizing, even indoctrinating, role which may undermine the capacity of the individual student to become a morally autonomous agent. This is not an appropriate role for any school.

The seventh argument is based on economics. The current system is complex and costly, especially because many administrative costs used to operate the system are duplicated. It is inefficient to create multiple school board divisions in the same geographic region with all the attendant costs that arise from having to service them. This is a particularly cogent argument as we go deeper into a period of declining enrolments. Ontario, for example, will experience a decline of as many as 500,000 students in the next decade (People for Education, 2008).

Eighth, Ontario can profit from the experiences of other provinces that have had the courage to battle the "vexed question" (McKim, 1988) of denominational rights. In the absence of research that shows that negative effects resulted from the major changes that were legislated in Manitoba, Newfoundland and Labrador, and Quebec in the past or even in New Brunswick or Nova Scotia when those jurisdictions ended support for church-sponsored schooling, one can assume that the changes fostered educational improvements.

Finally, there no longer are any real differences between Catholic and public schools in this secular age, particularly now that Catholic schools have been enrolling increasing numbers of non-Catholic students. All of the above arguments have been forwarded as rationales for the abolition of denominational schooling. However, as in all debates, there also exist philosophical, historic, legal, educational, and political reasons for retaining public denominational school systems. The following section will consider these arguments in light of the Ontario experience.

The case for the continuation of public denominational school systems

There are seven primary arguments for supporting the continuation of Roman Catholic and Protestant denominational rights in education and for the public denominational school systems that flow from those rights. First, although Canadians are used to referring to education as a provincial responsibility, we sometimes forget that this is in the context of whether or not it is the federal or provincial governments who have duties in this field. Such talk tends to obscure the long-held position of the Catholic church that parents have the primary responsibility for the education of their children and that part of this responsibility concerns the religious and moral education of their children, always keeping in mind that the child is to grow to become an autonomous adult. A corollary to this teaching concerns the role of the state, namely, that the role of the state is to support parents in the fulfillment of their educational obligations. Consequently, if Catholics want to establish Catholic schools, they have the right to do so, and it is the responsibility of the state to support those schools (Miller, 2007).

Second, the rationale for public denominational schools is every bit as persuasive today as it was at the time the schools were first established. The traditional argument accepted by governments in the nineteenth century regarding Ontario and the Northwest Territories (the forerunner of Alberta and Saskatchewan) was that the adherents of the religious minority should not be subjected to beliefs and practices at variance with their own. In districts that were primarily Catholic, Protestants did not want to be taught by nuns and priests. Although Catholics might agree that today's public schools are not Protestant, and furthermore that they would concede that there is much in public schools that they would support, for example, the goals of preparing students for citizenship, for lifelong education, and for the world of work, they would likely argue that the full development of the student—the moral and spiritual as well as the academic, the physical, and the emotional—is simply not possible in a public school. The underlying ethos of the public school is based on relativism or even secular humanism and as such promotes a world-view that is at variance with the Catholic world-view. From time to time, this conviction of Catholics can be expressed more publicly as we have seen in recent incidents in Quebec. Following the abolition of the confessional school system in 1998, the province mandated that the new regime permit students to enrol in one of three options—moral education, Protestant religious and moral education, or Catholic religious and moral education. In 2005, it announced that beginning in 2008, all schools including private schools would have to include the mandatory program titled Ethics and Religious Culture (ERC). Clearly, this is a serious attempt to introduce important topics into the curriculum. However, Loyola, a Jesuit Catholic high school in Montreal, examined the curriculum of ERC, decided that it was inappropriate for its school, and applied to the minister of education for an exemption, arguing that its own religious education program was equivalent. The minister denied the request with the result that the school applied to the Superior Court in Quebec for redress. In its statement, Loyola noted that the world-view promulgated by ERC was based on an ideology known as normative pluralism (Loyola High School & Zucchi, 2008). In a ruling issued September 1, 2009, Justice Jean-Guy Dubois rejected the request and concluded their right to freedom of religion was not being violated. In his 42-page ruling, Dubois reasoned that the course teaches about all religions and is not coercive; hence, there was no threat to freedom of religion. The Association of Catholic Parents in Quebec quickly rejected the judgment, stating that it deprives citizens of all faiths the fundamental right of parents to guide their children in religious and moral development according to their own convictions (Catholic Civil Rights League, 2009).

The third argument, involving the legal basis of public denominational school boards and schools in Ontario, Saskatchewan, and Alberta, is a strong one that has been confirmed in judicial rulings over the years. Opponents of the system agree that this is the case; their argument is that the system itself is wrongheaded in this era and that constitutional amendments ought to be introduced by the affected provinces and Government of Canada to remove these legislative protections. The effect of such constitutional amendments would be to remove the rights of minorities that have been enshrined in legislation. It can be anticipated that adherents of continuation would argue that abolition of their rights without their consent is inappropriate.

The fourth, and one of the strongest arguments put forward by those wishing to abolish public denominational school systems, is that they violate the principle of equality found in Section 15 of the Charter. Thus, why should Roman Catholics and Protestants but not other religious groups have access to public benefits? A first response to this is rooted in history. Just as the "Confederation compromise" made Canada possible in 1867, the inclusion of Article 29 was essential to the approval of the Charter. Without this Article, the probability that the Constitution Act, 1982 would become law was low. Consequently, it is inappropriate less than 30 years later to eliminate a section that was critical to the passage of the entire Act. A second response arises from the observation that Canada promotes group as well as individual rights. Take the case of linguistic rights for example. Section 23 of the Charter endows specific minority language (English and French) education rights to Canadian citizens, thereby excluding speakers of other languages and all landed immigrants. Or consider aboriginal rights.

Section 25 of the Charter protects the group rights of certain Aboriginal peoples that are recognized by the Royal Proclamation of 1763, by treaties, or by land claims settlements. At this moment in history, group rights for recognized linguistic and Aboriginal groups are not challenged but the educational rights of certain religious groups are. It is simply unfair to single out one group of the several who have Charter rights with a view to abolishing those rights.

The fifth argument is actually a counter-argument to those who support reforms on fiscal grounds. The claim that cost savings would be associated with the abolition of separate school systems in Ontario and indeed in all three provinces is likely to be illusory. Experiences with school board amalgamations normally show that while some administrative costs might be shaved as a result of eliminating staff positions in school board offices, there are likely to be as many or more costs that accrue as a result of such matters as the harmonization of collective agreements.

The sixth argument is that proposals to secure constitutional amendments, to abolish public denominational schools, and to create amalgamated school systems will consume time and effort and are likely to sap energies that would be better spent in solving more pressing issues of educational reform. Certainly, adherents of public denominational schools are not opposed to educational reform, and there are plenty of examples that demonstrate the willingness of leaders of these systems to change, including the voluntary amalgamation of school districts of their own denomination. On the other hand, they are likely to resist strenuously initiatives to abolish the existing systems, and they will have considerable resources to assist them in their struggle. Take the two Catholic systems in Ontario, for example. First, they are sizable, numbering as noted earlier about a third of the 2 million students of the province. This approximates the total public school enrolment of British Columbia and is larger than all provinces other than Quebec. Secondly, Ontario contains an extensive Catholic leadership infrastructure far in excess of the capacity that Newfoundland and Labrador had during the debates of the 1990s. This infrastructure includes the Ontario Conference of Catholic Bishops, the Ontario Catholic School Trustees' Association, the Ontario Association of Parents in Catholic Education, the Ontario English Catholic Teachers' Association, the Catholic Principals' Council of Ontario, the Ontario Catholic Supervisory Officers' Association, the Ontario Catholic School Business Officials' Association, the Institute of Catholic Education, and the Association Franco-Ontarienne des Conseils Scolaires Catholiques. Third, the Catholic population of On-

tario itself is large. One can anticipate that the resources of these organizations would be mobilized to resist strenuously proposals to change the status
quo. Those with a sense of history that dates back further than the Newfoundland and Labrador and Quebec decisions may recall that the Manitoba struggle of the 1890s lasted seven years, involved considerable
political and judicial effort, affected the 1896 federal election, and even
stimulated the intervention of Pope Leo XIII who wrote an encyclical titled
Advari Vos on the issue in 1897. In short, the political costs of ending the
current arrangements are likely to be very high, and the Ontario political
party which would have to bear them would have to consider seriously their
worth.

    The final argument is that the large Catholic English and French sys-
tems of Ontario provide a public service, especially when seen against the
policies at the secondary school level that allow students to decide which
school they will attend. Together with the public schools, they constitute
something akin to a free market which supports initiatives to provide quality education. These arguments, and variations and extensions of them,
will be used by those who have denominational rights in education to counter those who propose that such rights be removed and subsequently that
public denominational school boards and systems be abolished. What then
are we likely to see in the near future?

Conclusions: Looking ahead

Even a cursory examination of the arguments for retention or abolition of
public denominational schools leads to the conclusion that both are based
on values, and as such, it is likely that good people on both sides will continue to disagree. That said, I suspect that while the issue is likely to heat up
in the next decade, there will be no major changes in the short run; as to the
distant future, it's anybody's guess. The trend towards greater secularization in Canadian society is powered by many forces, and it might ultimately
prove to be unstoppable. Those favouring constitutional amendments
which will pave the way towards abolition can be expected to articulate
various methods by which this can be done.

    On the other hand, I expect that there will be significant efforts by
leaders of public denominational school systems, especially Catholics, to resist efforts toward abolition. It is likely that these leaders will work to show
that Catholic schools graduate students who become exemplary citizens
and that they add to the social cohesion of the provinces in which they are

located and of Canada more generally. Second, I would expect them to develop strategies that build commitment among those already in the system—teachers, administrators, parents, and students—to the continuation of the system.

Whatever happens on the general question of continuation or abolition, episodes will occur periodically that cause difficulties for the adherents of both public and public denominational school systems. As the effects of declining enrolments are ever more keenly felt, several questions will warrant the attention of school system leaders. What should be done when the spirit of the Constitution is used for more pragmatic reasons, such as when a public school division closes a school in a rural area because of declining enrolment and the adherents of the religious minority use their right to establish a separate school district to enrol not only adherents of their own religion but all the other students of that community who might even constitute a majority of the student population? What rules will govern joint-service agreements between public and public denominational school boards as they attempt to keep schools open in rural communities? What should be done when the original intent of Catholic schools to foster the Catholic faith is affected by secularization, when sizable numbers of students in, for example, a Catholic school are non-Catholics? There will be arguments from public school supporters that the Catholic school should not receive provincial grants for such students. Catholics, on the other hand, will contend that not only does provincial legislation on school choice require them to accept these students if there is sufficient room and if the students and their parents willingly accept the rules under which the Catholic school operates, but also that acceptance of such students is consistent with the evangelization mission of Catholicism. Clearly, the times will call for mutual respect and willingness to cooperate among the adherents of both systems.

As noted in the introduction, I have witnessed a considerable amount of change concerning denominational education in Canada during my professional teaching career, and the greatest changes have occurred in the past decade. If the past is indeed prologue, I imagine that the future will bring changes of comparable magnitude. What will happen to public denominational school boards is unclear, but I do believe that they have served the public interest in the past and that they continue to do so.

Chapter Eight

Legal and Constitutional Considerations in Denominational Education Reform

Glenn Loveless

In much of the world, including Canada, religious organizations have played a major role in the development of education, as "the church was often the only institution with the organization, the knowledge, and the teachers needed to establish schools" (Warren, 1988, p. 102). Historically, throughout the territories that would eventually become Canadian provinces and territories, Christian churches and organizations were frequently instrumental in establishing schools. While Christian groups continue to construct and manage schools in Canada, as Canada's mosaic has become more multicultural, organizations from other religious backgrounds have also established schools in various provinces. Even though faith-based schools continue to exist in Canada, sometimes with support from the public purse, many citizens question the role of religion and religious groups in the education systems of a modern, multicultural society. These views, along with economic considerations, changing values, and competing interests, have contributed to governments taking steps to restructure and reform their education systems, sometimes in ways that impact on the roles of classes or groups of people in a province's education system.

When governments consider making changes in their education system, the reforms are often the subject of intense debate, particularly if the potential implications are far-reaching. If the changes are fundamental in nature, particular groups of people may lose rights, power, and influence; for example, in 1998 when the education system in Quebec changed from being denominationally-based to language-based, the Christian churches lost their role in governance. At other times, groups stand to gain rights, power, or influence; for example, Francophone parents gained in most provinces when official minority-language school boards were established in the 1980s and 1990s. Similarly, Aboriginal groups achieved gains when they were granted the right to manage and control the education of their children. Although most education-related changes tend to generate public discussion, those which impact the governance of education tend to be particularly intense.

Since Confederation in 1867, provinces have, from time to time, introduced significant, sometimes quite fundamental, changes to their systems of education, some which may be truly categorized as reforms. Young and Levin (1999) define reform, in this context, as referring to "programs of educational change that are government-directed and initiated based on an overtly political analysis (that is, one driven by the political apparatus of government rather than by educators or bureaucrats), and justified on the basis of the need for a very substantial break from current practice" (p. 1). From the mid-1980s to the first few years of the twenty-first century every province in Canada has restructured or reformed its education system. As these were the first major education reforms since the proclamation of the Constitution Act, 1982 (which includes the Canadian Charter of Rights and Freedoms), the jurisdictions frequently found themselves considering legal and constitutional issues within the context of Canada's new constitution, sometimes with limited legal precedents.

The number and types of restructuring and reform initiatives since the mid-1980s have been varied and extensive. All provinces have reduced significantly the number of school boards. As part of the education reform initiatives, one province (New Brunswick) eliminated school boards altogether for a period of time (Fleming, 1997; Lessard & Verdy, 2007); all English-speaking provinces introduced French minority-language school boards (Loveless, 2008; Martel, 1991); one (Alberta) broadened parental choice and included charter schools in its publicly funded education system (Young & Levin, 1999); one (Ontario) extended full public funding to separate, i.e., Roman Catholic, schools (Zinga, 2008); one (Quebec) replaced denominational school boards by linguistic school boards; and one (Newfoundland and Labrador) replaced denominational school boards by a "unified non-denominational system" (Zinga, 2008, p. 7) and reduced "religion in education" to non-denominational religious education courses and the right to hold religious observances (see Hodder, Chapter Nine).

While provinces have a constitutional right to restructure and reform their education systems, the Constitution Act, 1982 has impacted education policy across Canada. Among the earliest post-Charter issues to be tackled was that of official minority-language rights in education, with every jurisdiction establishing at least one official minority-language school board (Loveless, 2008; Martel, 1991). One of the thorniest issues, however, and one which required serious consideration of the relationship between the current constitution, the British North America Act, 1867 and the Terms of Union for each province, was the question of rights of religious denominations in education.

The genesis of education rights in Canada

Among other matters, the British North America Act, 1867 divided legislative powers between the federal and provincial governments, with education being identified as the exclusive responsibility of the provinces. As Fleming and Hutton (1997) state:

> The defining moment in Canadian history—and, indeed, the defining moment in the history of Canadian school governance—was Confederation. Passage of the British North America Act in 1867 (renamed in 1982 the Constitution Act, 1867) established Canada as a nation, and set out the legal framework under which public institutions were to develop. Under the terms of this legislation, provincial legislatures "assumed full legal responsibility for education" within their jurisdictions.... The British North America Act, in essence, furnished the legal basis for the centralization of school governance. (pp. 1–2)

The British North America Act, 1867, then, made provision for each province to put in place structures to support the provision of education services within its own boundaries. Consequently, Canada, instead of having a federal Department of Education, has ten provincial and three territorial education systems, with each having its own distinct characteristics and the ability to make its own educational decisions, so as to respond to its particular circumstances, subject only to the limitations of the Charter.

Denominational rights

While the initial Confederation compact gave provinces constitutional authority over education, it "limits the exercise of provincial authority in education. A fundamental part of the Confederation compact was a recognition of reciprocity of educational rights and privileges between the Catholic and Protestant minorities in Ontario and Quebec respectively" (Dickinson & MacKay, 1989, p. 49). Historically, this Confederation compromise has been the object of much public debate and litigation, both in provincial courts and the Supreme Court of Canada. It has also been the key issue in arguably the two most fundamental education reform initiatives in Canada—Quebec and Newfoundland and Labrador—where the governance rights of Christian denominations were eliminated.

Although the British North America Act, 1867 gave provinces exclusive right to legislate education in Canada, the right was not unfettered. Section 93 of the British North America Act, 1867 provided particular constitutional rights to Christian denominations, notably:

❖ protection against legislation which prejudicially affects any right or privilege with respect to denominational schools which any class of persons had at the time of union with Canada;

❖ provision of identical powers, privileges, and duties to separate Roman Catholic schools and school trustees in Upper Canada and dissentient Protestant and Roman Catholic schools in Quebec; and

❖ the right to appeal provincial education legislation, which a denomination perceived to have a prejudicial effect on its rights or privileges, to the Governor General in Council, with the Parliament of Canada having the power to make laws to remedy the situation.

The main purposes of Section 93 were to establish exclusive provincial control over education and "to temper this legislative authority by prohibiting legislative action with respect to *certain* provisions respecting *certain* persons" (Smith & Foster, 2001a, p. 400). Sections (3) and (4) also provided an appeal mechanism for groups if provinces implemented legislation and policies which "prejudicially affect" groups holding denominational rights. Therefore, as Dickinson and MacKay (1989, p. 50) have observed, "the Legislature may regulate [denominational education rights] as long as the regulation does not 'prejudicially affect' their denominational character."

While Section 93 initially applied only to the four founding provinces of Canada, namely Ontario, Quebec, New Brunswick, and Nova Scotia, every province included a similar provision, which provided education rights for Protestant and Roman Catholics, in its terms of union with Canada. As Warren (1988) notes:

Originally applicable to Ontario, Quebec, New Brunswick, and Nova Scotia, Section 93 was applied to British Columbia in 1871 and to Prince Edward Island in 1873. Slightly modified versions of the Section became part of the statutes which were adopted when Manitoba joined the federation in 1870, Alberta and Saskatchewan in 1905, and Newfoundland in 1949. (p. 103)

Section 93 and similar provisions in each province's terms of union with Canada provided the constitutional basis for denominational schooling in various Canadian provinces, for example, separate (i.e., Catholic) schools to Grade 10 in Ontario, Protestant schools in Quebec, and separate schools (i.e., Roman Catholic or Protestant, if they were a minority in a school district) in Alberta.

As discussed in earlier chapters, when Newfoundland joined Confederation in 1949, included in its terms of union was a provision (Term 17) that provided protection for particular denominations with respect to any rights or privileges these denominations held at the time of union with Canada (Appendix A). This provision also ensured that each denomination would receive public funds for education on a non-discriminatory basis for its denominationally-run schools and colleges. Term 17 had the effect of enshrining constitutional rights with respect to the governance of education on several Christian denominations, namely Roman Catholic, Anglican, United Church of Canada, Salvation Army, Congregational, Presbyterian, and Seventh-Day Adventist. In 1987, the Pentecostal Assemblies was added to this list (Government of Canada, 1987; *Hogan v Newfoundland. (School Boards for Ten Districts)*, 1997a, 1997b); Penney, 1988).

Although a more secular value system has become the norm in each province and territory of Canada, the Constitution Act, 1982 includes a section which provides, and to some extent reinforces, guarantees related to denominational and separate education. Section 29 states:

Nothing in this Charter abrogates or derogates from any rights or privileges guaranteed by or under the Constitution of Canada in respect of denominational, separate or dissentient schools.

As Warren noted in Chapter Two, when the churches sensed that the Charter could threaten the system of denominational schools, they, along with then Premier Brian Peckford successfully lobbied for the inclusion of Term 29 in the Charter. Yet, two sections of the Constitution Act, 1982, in particular Sections 15 and 2 which make it unconstitutional to discriminate against individuals on several bases including religion, seem to be at odds with Section 29, which discriminates in favour of particular Christian denominations. While Sections 15 and 2(a) clearly conflict with Section 29, the courts have ruled that Section 29 rights are not to be abrogated by Sections 15 or 2(a). To do so would require a constitutional amendment (Dickinson & MacKay, 1989).

In post-Charter years, provinces have adjusted their education systems in various ways, for example, establishing official minority-language school boards, changing the role of religion in education, and providing aboriginal Canadians with the right to control their children's education. Because each province has exclusive jurisdiction in education, each one has established a distinct education system with some having roles for religious groups in the publicly-funded system. As Foster and Smith (2002) note, many variations exist across Canada with respect to the application of Section 93:

> In three provinces—Alberta, Ontario and Saskatchewan—constitutionally entrenched rights and privileges granted by law at the time of union continue to exist for minority denominational schools, Catholic or Protestant. In one province, Newfoundland, constitutionally protected denominational rights have been reduced to: (1) courses in religion provided they are not specific to a particular denomination; and, (2) religious observances where requested by parents. In six provinces—British Columbia, Manitoba, New Brunswick, Nova Scotia, Prince Edward Island, and Quebec—and the three territories—the Yukon, the Northwest Territories and Nunavut—there are no constitutionally guaranteed rights or privileges with respect to religion in schools. (p. 4)

It should be noted that some of the provinces which do not provide constitutional guarantees for faith-based schools (e.g., British Columbia, Manitoba, and Quebec) do, nevertheless, provide a level of public funding for such schools subject to certain conditions (e.g., alignment of school curriculum with provincial curriculum, suitably qualified teachers). Others have provisions in their legislation which permit the operation of faith-based, as well as other types of schools (e.g., private schools), albeit without public funding.

Official minority-language education rights

Because the British North America Act, 1867 gave provinces the exclusive right to make laws respecting education, each province passed legislation governing education. In some cases, the legislation had the effect of impacting negatively a particular segment of the religious minority in a province (e.g., the Francophone linguistic minority which was largely Roman Catholic). For example, according to Mahé (2002), "before the 1890s, French-speaking Catholics in the Prairies had the power to govern their schools and the right to instruct their children in French.... In 1916, legislation was passed [in Manitoba] to prohibit the teaching of all languages other than English in public schools" (p. 1). Furthermore, Denis and Li (1988) state: "The historical evidence indicates that the Francophones were unable to maintain their language largely as a result of Anglophones successfully passing laws restricting French in schools since 1892" (p. 351). Constitutionally, provinces had the right to pass such legislation which negatively affected the ability of the Francophone minority to maintain their language and culture, but which did not "prejudicially affect" their denominational rights.

The proclamation of the Constitution Act, 1982 established another limit on provinces' legislative authority in education in that it also included a section whose objective "was to encourage the linguistic and cultural vitality of the official language minorities" (Martel, 1991, p. 17). Section 23 provides French and English citizens of Canada, who reside in a province in which their mother tongue is that of the linguistic minority, with the right to have their children receive, from public funds, primary and secondary instruction in the minority language if they meet one of the following tests:

- ◈ the parents' first language learned and still understood is that of the English or French minority of the province in which they reside;
- ◈ the parents received their primary school instruction in Canada in English or French, or;
- ◈ the parents have children who have received, or are receiving, primary or secondary school instruction in English or French.

The right to education in English or French applies wherever the number of children of Section 23 right-holders is sufficient for the provision of education from public funds. Furthermore, if there is a sufficient number of children, Section 23 provides the right to have instruction delivered in separate minority-language educational facilities.

The introduction of Section 23 of the Charter into the Canadian legal and educational landscape led to a decade of litigation and court references which clarified the educational rights of English and French linguistic minorities in Canada, including the right to govern their children's education where numbers warrant (Loveless, 2008).

Legal and constitutional lessons in education reform

Provincial governments and the Canadian courts have considered the roles of religion and religious organizations in education from many perspectives, including governance, taxation, hiring and firing practices, religious observances, and curriculum. A concrete example of the important considerations is illustrated in Newfoundland and Labrador's educational reforms which changed the entire character of the provincial education system from one with only denominational school boards to a public system with provision for non-denominational religious education courses and religious observances. Warren (Chapter Two) provides us with a full discussion of these events.

Section 93 of the British North America Act, 1867 and similar provisions in subsequent Terms of Union for other Canadian provinces, including Term 17 in Newfoundland's Terms of Union with Canada in 1949, had the effect of "grandparenting" the educational rights of particular Christian groups in the Constitution (Smith & Foster, 2001a). These sections have been the source of considerable litigation across Canada. Some of these provisions, which imposed restrictions on provincial legislatures, were also central to the reform debates in Newfoundland and Labrador.

Provinces contemplating major reform initiatives must consider the legal and constitutional implications of the changes being considered. Some reforms, which impact on constitutionally guaranteed rights such as the removal of Christian denominations' governance rights in education by Newfoundland and Labrador and Quebec, can only be accomplished by a constitutional amendment, while others can be accommodated within each province's terms of union with Canada. The Newfoundland and Labrador reform process involved two constitutional amendments—the first, in 1996, which significantly reduced the role of Christian denominations in the governance of education, and the second, in 1997, which removed the governance rights completely.

Reforms requiring a constitutional amendment

One of the most interesting observations with respect to the Constitution Act, 1982 is that it does make provision for faith-based discrimination in education. Section 29 clearly protects the education rights that particular

Christian denominations had "by law" (not simply by practice) when that province joined Canada. This "denominational rights" section provided protection for certain classes of religious groups (Roman Catholics or Protestants) when educational reforms were implemented within the particular province's terms of union with Canada. On the other hand, education reforms that require a constitutional amendment, such as those undertaken in Newfoundland and Labrador, must consider the legal and constitutional rights of individuals and classes of people who have rights under the existing Constitution as well as the potential implications of the reforms for other jurisdictions.

Denominational rights of classes of people

Section 29 of the Constitution Act, 1982, which provides protection for denominational rights in education, enshrines in the Canadian constitution the rights that particular Christian denominations had "in law" when they signed their terms of union with Canada. Smith and Foster (2001a) state with respect to Section 29:

> Section 29 can be regarded as an essential safeguard of section 93 rights.... The major impact of section 29, depending on how it is interpreted, is on its limitation of the *Canadian Charter*; thus,...rights granted by section 93 are not affected by the provisions of the *Canadian Charter*. (p. 405)

In accordance with Section 1 of the Constitution Act, 1982, denominational rights, like others, are "subject only to such reasonable limits prescribed by law as can be demonstrably justified in a free and democratic society." With that caveat, denominational rights in education are protected as long as the constitution is not amended in such a way as to impact those rights.

The nature of denominational rights in education contained in Section 93 and the terms of union of different provinces with Canada are an important consideration for provinces. According to Smith and Foster (2001a):

> Sub-section (1) of section 93 defines the restriction of provincial legislative autonomy in relation to two sets of elements. First, the only provisions which the provincial government cannot infringe upon are "rights and privileges" which were provided for "at the Union" (i.e. upon Confederation in 1867) "by law". Thus, any advantage or authority enjoyed in practice (*de*

facto) but not provided for by law (*de jure*) at Confederation is not protected and any legal rights provided *after* 1867 can be withdrawn by the government at will. Second, protected rights are limited to those which existed for a "Class of Persons" "with respect to Denominational Schools" and which would be "prejudicially affect[ed]" by provincial legislative action. The class of persons envisaged, Catholics and Protestants, like the rights themselves, is defined by religious belief. Only provincial legislation which is prejudicial to these denominational rights is prohibited. (p. 411)

When the Government of Newfoundland and Labrador initiated discussions with Christian churches with respect to their role in education, the constitutional rights of the classes of people, described in Newfoundland's terms of union with Canada in 1949, with governance rights in education, were clearly of paramount importance both to the classes and the government. The churches and their legal advisors were of the opinion that their existing constitutional rights in education were well protected by Section 29 unless the constitution itself was amended. When the churches and the government were unable to agree on the role religious groups should play in Newfoundland and Labrador's education system, the provincial government examined the constitutional amendment option.

The Charter provides various amending processes that may be employed, under certain conditions, to change particular rights in a single province. Among these processes is Section 43 which makes provision for the Governor General to proclaim constitutional amendments if authorized by resolutions of the Senate, the House of Commons, and the legislature of the province to which the amendment applies. Furthermore, Section 46 describes how the procedures for amendment under sections 38, 41, 42, and 43 may be initiated either by the Senate or the House of Commons or by the legislative assembly of a province. This was the process used by the Government of Newfoundland and Labrador in 1996 and again in 1997 to amend its terms of union with Canada, which initially changed and subsequently removed the governance role of Christian denominations in education.

Ensuring equality rights

Equality rights often revolve around discrimination, a term whose legal definition has been expressed as follows in *Andrews v. Law Society of British Columbia* (1989):

[D]iscrimination may be described as a distinction, whether intentional or not based on grounds related to personal characteristics of the individual or group, which has the effect of imposing burdens, obligations or disadvantages on such individual or group not imposed upon others, or which withholds or limits access to opportunities, benefits, and advantages available to other members of society. Distinctions based on personal characteristics attributed to an individual solely on the basis of association with a group will rarely escape the charge of discrimination, while those based on an individual's merits and capacities will rarely be so classed. (Foster & Smith, 2002, p. 27)

Following the 1995 referendum, which changed but did not remove entirely the churches' role in education, the provincial government enacted legislation to give effect to the amended Term 17 (Appendix C). This constitutional amendment still made provision for uni-denominational schools (e.g., Roman Catholic, Pentecostal, or Seventh-Day Adventist) and for the election of denominational representatives to interdenominational school boards. However, the Legislature was given the right to establish the conditions under which uni-denominational and interdenominational schools would be established. Government legislation and ministerial directives intended to give effect to the amended Term 17, in the opinion of particular churches, contravened Section (b) of the revised Term 17 in that they appeared to favour the designation of schools as interdenominational, thereby making it more difficult for school boards to designate schools as uni-denominational. At the request of the Roman Catholic and Pentecostal churches, the Newfoundland Supreme Court, Trial Division issued an injunction requiring that the consent of the Roman Catholic and Pentecostal churches be obtained before closing uni-denominational schools which met the province's school viability criteria. In other words, the courts required the Government of Newfoundland and Labrador to abide by its constitutional amendment with respect to denominational rights in education contained in the amended Term 17 by passing non-discriminatory legislation.

The implementation of legislation, regulations, and ministerial policy directives following the first amendment of Term 17 in 1996 brought into play, then, the issue of discrimination. As the trial judge acknowledges, "Terms 17(b)(i), 17(c), 17(d), and 17(e), ...recognize a right in classes of persons to have uni-denominational schools publicly funded on a non-discriminatory basis." Yet, Section 82 of the Schools Act, 1996 states "a school shall be an interdenominational school unless the requirements set out in the regulations for designation as a uni-denominational school are satisfied" (*Hogan v. Newfoundland (School Boards for Ten Districts)*, 1997, ¶ 52). Judge Barry thought that a court would find sections of the Schools Act, 1996 unconstitutional and, consequently, in *Hogan v. Newfoundland (School Boards for Ten Districts)* (1997a), he stated:

> In these circumstances I conclude the appropriate approach of this Court is to restrain school boards from closing, without the consent of the Roman Catholic or Pentecostal Education Committee, as the case may be, any schools which operated as Roman Catholic or Pentecostal for the school year 1996–97, where the expressed parental preference for a uni-denominational school has indicated a number in favour sufficient to make it a viable uni-denominational school under the minimum standards or requirements for adequate schooling employed by the Department of Education and the school boards for 1996–97, after allowing, in a non-discriminatory fashion, for the changes necessary to recognize the declining student population and reduction in teacher allocations. (¶ 82)

The government, both in its legislation and ministerial directives, had expressed a clear preference for interdenominational schools. In this case, the trial judge ruled that the discriminatory legislation and ministerial directives would have imposed a disadvantage on the classes of people wishing to establish uni-denominational schools in accordance with the 1996 Term 17. In Judge Barry's opinion, a trial judge would find sections of the provincial legislation and ministerial directives unconstitutional, likely discriminatory, in the sense that they established conditions which made it difficult, if not impossible, for school boards to establish uni-denominational schools in accordance with parents' wishes, as provided for in Term 17.

Minority rights considerations

In Newfoundland and Labrador, the Roman Catholic, Pentecostal, and Seventh-Day Adventists relied heavily on the "minority rights" provisions of the Charter in their constitutional and legal deliberations (Fagan, personal interview, November 25, 2008). At the time, Roman Catholics comprised approximately 38 per cent of the population of the province, Pentecostals just over 7 per cent, and Seventh-Day Adventists about 0.1 per cent (Fagan, personal interview, November 25, 2008). The Newfoundland Supreme Court, both Trial Division and Appeals Division, rejected this argument when presented by the Roman Catholic church (*Hogan v. Newfoundland (Attorney General)*, 2000; *Hogan v. Newfoundland (School Boards for Ten Districts)*, 1997a), it being the largest single Christian denomination in the province, and the Supreme Court of Canada refused to hear the case (Fagan, 2004). Although Section 43 of the Constitution Act, 1867 and similar provisions in each province's Terms of Union with Canada was intended, among other things, to provide a level of constitutional protection for education rights of particular Christian denominations who were in a minority in a given province, the courts, in the last decade of the twentieth century, ruled that a Christian denomination (Roman Catholic), in a province in which the dominant religion is Christianity, does not have a constitutionally guaranteed right to governance in education where the provincial government, with the consent of the Parliament of Canada, wishes to amend the constitution to remove such a right.

Potential impacts on other provinces

The Christian denominations in Newfoundland and Labrador were of the view that the removal of denominational education rights would set a precedent for other provinces, but the courts rejected this argument. Because provincial legislatures have exclusive authority to enact education legislation, and because each provincial education system in Canada is unique, changes made in one province do not have implications in another jurisdiction. Provinces that wish to make such changes may do so, but there is no precedent. Section 46 makes provision for provincial legislatures to petition the Senate and House of Commons to amend particular sections of their terms of union with Canada. This is what the Government of Newfoundland and Labrador did in 1996 and again in 1997, and what Quebec did in 1997, to remove the educational governance rights of Christian denominations.

The Newfoundland and Labrador and Quebec cases illustrate the fact that provinces may amend the Constitution with respect to matters that do not impact other jurisdictions, such as changing the status of denominational rights in education. In both cases, the Parliament of Canada established committees to receive input from interested parties; however, permission of the affected classes of persons was not required for the Senate and House of Commons to grant the constitutional amendment. Although, in Newfoundland and Labrador, it may be possible to conclude that the people, including the affected classes of persons, had expressed their support for the amendment through referenda, this was not the case in Quebec where no such process was followed.

The constitutional amendments affecting Newfoundland and Labrador and Quebec represent profound educational governance changes involving the removal of the governance rights of Christian denominations in education. But other provinces, notably Ontario, have made significant changes to their education systems within the framework of the Constitution Act, 1867. As one of the original signatories to the Act, "Ontario had a system of Roman Catholic separate schools established both within law and in practice at the time of Confederation" (Bezeau, 2007, p.9). The Ontario legislation in effect in 1867, and which is protected by Section 93 of the Constitution Act, 1867, gave Roman Catholics broad rights in education. As Bezeau (2007) states:

> Roman Catholics were authorized to establish separate schools for Roman Catholics and to elect trustees to manage them. The trustees could levy taxes on persons declaring themselves to be separate school supporters and such persons were exempted from taxation for the public schools, then called the common schools. Separate school trustees were given the same powers and responsibilities as common-school trustees, including the right to a share in provincial or municipal grants for the common schools in proportion to pupil attendance. (p. 9)

Since, as Zinga (2008) notes, "Ontario has...been the site of controversial challenges to denominational rights over the years" (p. 7), the courts have clarified the nature of the Section 93 rights that are constitutionally protected. The ruling in *Ontario English Catholic Teachers' Assn. v. Ontario (Attorney General)* (2001) specified that:

> Section 93(1) of the Constitution Act, 1867 guarantees denominational school boards the right to fair and equitable funding, and to control over the denominational aspects of their education program, as well as those non-denominational aspects necessary to deliver the denominational elements. (p. 16)

Within this legal and constitutional context, the Government of Ontario introduced major education reforms which, when subjected to constitutional challenges, satisfied the constitutional test. In the mid-1980s, the Government of Ontario introduced regulations and legislation which extended secondary school funding for separate school boards to the end of high school. According to Zinga (2008):

> The extension of full funding to the separate school was accomplished through Bill 30, an amendment to the Education Act. The constitutionality of Bill 30 was challenged in the Court of Appeal of Ontario and the Supreme Court of Canada (Bill 30, 1987) and was declared constitutional by both courts. (p. 8)

Bezeau (2007) adds:

> Seven justices of the Supreme Court decided, in one of the most important court decisions in the history of Canadian education, that the province had not only the right, but also an obligation, to pass Bill 30 or similar legislation. (p. 13)

Although Bill 30 extended funding for separate schools, it did not make provision for public funding for other faith-based schools. Not surprisingly, then, other religious groups challenged the constitutionality of the legislation in the courts, claiming that it was discriminatory in that funding one particular religious group, namely Roman Catholics, contravenes Section 15 (the freedom of religion and equality provisions) of the Constitution Act, 1982. However, the Supreme Court of Canada (*Adler v. Ontario*, 1996) declared the Act to be constitutional. The legal and constitutional decision has not, however, quieted the debate, with some groups calling for a constitutional amendment to eliminate all denominational rights in education and others urging the Government of Ontario to extend funding to other faith-based schools on a non-discriminatory basis. During the 1997 provincial election campaign, the progressive conservative leader, John Tory, launched a controversial plan to extend public funding for education to other religious denominations. Tory was defeated and his plan to expand denominational education never materialized. While campaigning against Tory, Premier Dalton McGinty was quoted as saying the plan would "take us backward to an era of conflict and cuts" and would cost the public school system in Ontario a half a billion dollars (Alphonso, 2007). Supporters of Tory's plan for their part argued that the McGinty approach, which advocated the status quo—funding for separate Catholic schools only— amounted to discrimination (Alphonso, 2007).

To further reform its education system, in 1997 Ontario passed the controversial Education Quality Improvement Act which "effectively eliminated the ability of school boards to levy the property tax and which centralized all education finance at the provincial level" (Bezeau, 2007, p. 13). While the Act removed local autonomy, it "provided that public and separate school boards…were to have equal access to revenues on a per pupil basis. The Act also placed limits on the ability of school boards to make spending decisions" (Goudge, 2000, p. 1), but prevented the Minister from interfering with the denominational aspects of school board operations. The Supreme Court of Canada (*Adler v. Ontario*, 1996) concluded "that the right of a school board to receive revenue in a certain way was not a denominational right and so was not protected" (Bezeau, 2007, p. 13). The court's ruling confirmed that the legislation was consistent with the constitution.

As the Ontario cases demonstrate, there is flexibility within the current legal and constitutional framework of Canada to enable provinces with religious groups whose rights were protected in law at the time that province joined Confederation to reform their education systems as long as the reforms do not infringe denominational rights of protected groups or those non-denominational aspects required to give effect to protected denominational rights. Although Ontario has a legal and constitutional right to extend funding to other faith-based schools on a non-discriminatory basis, these rights are not seen to be protected by the constitution. On the other hand, the Quebec and Newfoundland and Labrador cases suggest that Ontario does have a mechanism within the Constitution Act, 1982 to eliminate funding and governance rights for all faith-based groups.

Religious curriculum and observances

As outlined in Chapter Nine, the revised Term 17 (1997) and Schools Act, 1997 make provision for religious education curriculum that is non-denominational and for the provision of religious observances when requested by parents. With respect to curriculum, the provincial Department of Education has developed a religious education program that teaches about various religions and states categorically that it is to have no proselytizing intent. Foster and Smith (2002) cite a 1990 Ontario Court of Appeal decision (*Corp. Of the Canadian Civil Liberties Assn v. Ontario (Minister of Education)*, often cited as the Elgin County case), as follows:

> The crucial issue…is whether the purpose and the effects of the regulation and the curriculum are to *indoctrinate* school children in Ontario in the Christian faith. If so, the rights to free-

dom of conscience and religion under s. 2(a) of the *Canadian Charter of Rights and Freedoms* and the equality rights guaranteed under s. 15 of the Charter may be infringed. On the other hand, it is conceded that education designed to teach about religion and to foster moral values without indoctrination in a particular religious faith would not be a breach of the Charter. It is indoctrination in a particular religious faith that is alleged to be offensive. (pp. 45–46)

While Newfoundland and Labrador's legislation and policies giving effect to the 1997 Term 17 have not yet been contested in the courts, the province's religious education curriculum would appear to satisfy the equality provisions of the Charter in that it teaches about different religions and is intended to foster moral values.

The legislation does not, however, describe a process to enable parents, who do not wish their children to participate in religious instruction, to give effect to their wishes. This may be an important issue in the future when a parent or guardian, who does not wish to have his or her child participate in the religious education courses, challenges existing school board processes. The courts have generally been more favourable to an "opting in" versus an "opting out" approach. Case law, at least in Ontario, suggests that "merely allowing persons to opt out [of religious education and exercises] is insufficient accommodation" (Foster & Smith, 2002, p. 63).

The current Term 17 (Appendix D) indicates that religious observances shall be permitted in a school where requested by parents (Government of Newfoundland and Labrador, 1997b). This would appear to apply to "religious observances" from any particular faith, on a non-discriminatory basis. Otherwise, it may be a breach of the equality provisions of the Charter.

Reforms within existing terms of union with Canada

Most education reforms in Canada have been undertaken within the particular province's existing terms of union with Canada. Section 93 of the British North America Act, 1867, supported by Section 29 of the Constitution Act, 1982, has been used by governments to enact reform measures, some of which have been challenged by individuals and groups. Aside from denominational rights in education, which are being clarified through court decisions and references, provinces must consider issues such as minority rights, equality rights, and the right to religious freedom when contemplating reform initiatives. In other words, while Christian denominations have protected constitutional rights in education, they are not absolute. That being said, provincial legislatures may not pass laws which "prejudicially affect" the denominational rights that particular classes of persons held "in law" at the time the province joined Canada.

Section 93 of the British North America Act, 1867 does not seem to prevent a province or territory from extending public support to faith-based schooling. Where a province decides to take such action, however, Section 15 of the Constitution Act, 1982 would seem to require that it be done on a non-discriminatory basis, that is, not be limited to a particular faith. Furthermore, such faith-based schools do not appear to enjoy constitutional protection.

On the basis of Section 93, the Supreme Court of Canada indicated that separate schools (i.e., Roman Catholic schools) in Ontario were entitled to public funding to the end of Grade 12. Jurisprudence to date suggests that provinces have the authority to regulate "with the proviso that such government authority does not extend to *abrogating* such rights" (Smith & Foster, 2001a, p. 418). Furthermore, Supreme Court of Canada decisions suggest that, as long as funding for separate schools is fair and equitable, in comparison to public schools, legislation will not violate Section 93. The government of Ontario also used Section 93 provisions, which provide constitutional protection for the Roman Catholic minority only in that province, to deny public funding to other faith-based schools. As Smith and Foster (2001a) note, "The only denominational groups envisaged by Section 93 are Roman Catholics and Protestants" (p. 409). Provincial structures, for example, school boards, are not, however, protected by Section 93. This enables provinces to consolidate and even abolish school boards. Furthermore, as Smith and Foster (2001a) point out, and as affirmed by the Supreme Court of Canada, "school boards do not enjoy any constitutionally protected right to *reasonable autonomy*" (p. 446) (for a more complete understanding of the issues surrounding autonomy of school boards during the reform process, see Chapter Ten).

Provinces such as Ontario, Alberta, and Saskatchewan which provide funding to faith-based schools also need to consider legal and constitutional issues related to human resources (e.g., hiring and firing of teachers). Various courts suggest that occupational qualifications of a denominational nature (e.g., a teacher in a Roman Catholic school), while discriminatory, can be imposed on an employee who occupies a position with denominational elements. However, such occupational qualifications may not be imposed on employees whose positions do not include denominational components, even in a faith-based institution. "It would appear that hiring and other employment practices are protected by Section 93 provided they are necessary to maintain the denominational aspect of the school" (Smith & Foster, 2001a, p. 447).

Most provinces choose to make adjustments to their education system within the existing terms of union with Canada; however, when fundamental or foundational changes are required, they may chose to seek a constitutional amendment. The process for amending the constitution to accommodate a provincial government's desire to undertake fundamental education reforms has been established in both Quebec's and Newfoundland and Labrador's education reform initiatives. Whichever process is followed by provincial governments, which have the exclusive right to pass education legislation, constitutional and legal issues must be carefully considered.

Conclusions

Throughout the Confederation period, Section 93 of the British North America Act, 1867 and sister provisions in the various terms of union have been the object of many court cases and references. Furthermore, since the proclamation of the Constitution Act, 1982, the new Canadian constitution has been used as a yardstick to evaluate provincial education legislation and policies and to enable provinces to make changes—sometimes fundamental changes—to their education systems.

Several provinces, after signing their original terms of union with Canada, have enacted legislation and policies that grant religious bodies the right to have faith-based schools, with or without public funding. In some cases, provinces have expanded the number of organizations, religious or otherwise, with the right to have and govern schools. Examples include British Columbia's decision to permit and partially fund faith-based schools and Alberta's decision to grant different organizations the right to operate charter schools with funding from the provincial purse. The various court decisions would suggest, however, that only those religious organizations, that is, Protestants and Roman Catholics, which had the right to operate schools at the time the province joined Canada would have a constitutional right to such schooling in that province. The fact that the courts have rejected constitution-based petitions by faith-based groups in Ontario, other than Roman Catholics who operate the separate schools in that province, would support this conclusion.

Given Ontario's multicultural, multi-ethnic mosaic, and considering mounting external pressures, either to continue to fund separate Catholic schools as presently exist, or to extend funding to other faith communities, the issue of educational governance has yet to be settled. Those interested in educational change will, no doubt, be watching closely to see how the present and future governments in Ontario address these matters. Will Ontario use its constitutional lever to quell the voices of those groups advocating for a single public education system? Will the province stay the course and continue to fund the demographically dominant Catholic school system to the exclusion of other faith-based groups? Or will it act within the current legal framework to extend funding to other denominations?

While the British North America Act, 1867 provided what appeared to be permanent constitutional protection for particular Christian denominations in education, and the Constitution Act, 1982 further entrenched these rights, the Quebec and Newfoundland and Labrador experiences indicate clearly that the current Canadian Constitution provides mechanisms for changing these rights. Because the existing constitution of Canada has provisions for making constitutional amendments on matters that affect only one jurisdiction, as is the case with education in Canada, the legislatures of Quebec and Newfoundland and Labrador were able to petition the House of Commons and Senate of Canada to amend the Constitution of Canada as a means of changing denominational rights in education (Government of Canada, 1997a, 1997b, 1997c, 1997d, 1998; Government of Newfoundland and Labrador, 1997b; Smith & Foster, 2001a; Young & Bezeau, 2003).

In both cases, the permission of those groups, whose governance rights in education were negatively impacted, was not needed. The only requirement was for the provincial legislature to obtain the consent of the House of Commons and Senate in order to bring about the constitutional amendment. In each case, denominationally-based school boards were replaced by other types of school boards, further supporting Smith and Foster's (2001a) contention that school boards do not enjoy constitutional protection.

The Newfoundland and Labrador reform process would suggest that provincial governments must be careful to ensure that their education reforms, including the legislation, regulations, policies, and programs required to enact the reforms, are non-discriminatory. Following the province's first constitutional amendment in 1996, the provincial government introduced legislation, regulations, and ministerial policy to give effect to the constitutional change which a provincial court ruled to be discriminatory in that they favoured interdenominational over uni-denominational schools and ordered the province not to enact the offensive conditions. Furthermore, as part of the education reform process, the province developed religious education programs that were non-denominational in nature in that they teach about and celebrate different religions and make provision for religious observances of any faith when requested by parents. The Newfoundland and Labrador education reform process, then, supports Foster and Smith's (2002) claim that "[p]ublic school authorities must provide educational services in an environment that is not polluted by intolerance, in which students may participate, without discrimination based on religion" (p. 64).

Over time, provinces, for whatever reasons, may wish to reform their education systems, including those aspects related to the roles of various groups and organizations in the governance of education. Because education is exclusively a provincial responsibility with education reforms generally not impacting other jurisdictions, the Constitution Act, 1982 provides a mechanism for provinces to make constitutional amendments that affect how their education systems are governed. Given each province's multicultural and multi-ethnic mosaic, and a general decline in religiosity among adherents to traditional Christian faiths, Canadians have probably not seen the last major change to educational governance.

Chapter Nine

The Impact of Educational Reform on Religious Education and Religious Observances

Bryce Hodder

Since the restructuring of the Newfoundland and Labrador education system in 1997, there has been much discussion and some misinterpretation regarding what these reforms have meant, both for religious education and for religious observances in schools. Taking a series of denominationally-based religious education programs and designing a single program to replace them are not without challenges. The development and implementation process, while largely complete, has taken considerable time and discussion. And even as the development of new resources continues, there is still debate over the appropriateness of religious observances in public schools, especially those observances that involve the entire student population. Although there are many jurisdictions in which religious education is part of the school curricula, one of the key differences between the Newfoundland and Labrador school system and other secular systems is that in the former, by constitutional amendment, provision is made for religious observances.

The restructuring of the education system has resulted in fundamental questions about schooling and the role and design of a religious education program. Do schools have a role in helping shape a student's spiritual development? If so, how much emphasis should be placed on our Christian heritage within the broader spectrum of faith systems? Should Christianity be given more significant emphasis in a program of religious education? Is there a danger of Christianity being marginalized?

In what follows I give consideration both to religious education and to religious observances in the context of the resolution to amend Term 17 of the Constitution Act and the substance of the "new" Term 17. The events leading up to the 1997 consolidation were considered in Chapter Two. In this chapter these events are recast in terms of their impact on (1) the philosophy of and rationale for continued religious instruction in schools, and (2) the new rights of various faith communities.[1]

Religious observances in schools

Until 1997, selected Christian denominations, together with the Department of Education, had governance over the education system in Newfoundland and Labrador. The road to reform was lengthy and contested, as is evident from the accounts of previous authors. As part of the new system, the citizens were assured that all schools, other than those that were privately operated, would be required to offer religious education courses that would be developed as part of the provincial curriculum. Assurance was also given that provision would be made for religious observances in the schools.

Article Three of the present version of Term 17 states: "Religious observances shall be permitted in a school where requested by parents." This article is perhaps the one most misunderstood in the amended Term 17. Some school administrators, teachers, and parents have interpreted this article to mean that celebrations and religious observances can no longer be carried out in schools, such as is the case in some other provinces in Canada and in some other countries. For example, in the USA, prayer and Bible reading for devotional purposes are forbidden in public schools. However, students have the right to pray "in a non-disruptive manner when they are not engaged in school activities or instruction and subject to the rules that normally pertain in the applicable setting" (US Department of Education, 1988). By way of contrast, in France, no religious activities are permitted in state schools.

In Canada, the legislation regarding religious observances varies among the provinces, but for Newfoundland and Labrador, Article Three of Term 17, rather than curtailing religious observances in schools, provides a broader perspective than had been the case before reform. Before 1997, only students and parents belonging to the Christian denominations governing the denominational system could be assured that provision would be made in the schools for their religious observances. With the new Term 17, provision for religious observances, if requested by a parent, is mandated to accommodate students of all living belief systems. This does not necessarily mean that the entire school population has to take part in the observance or celebration, but provision has to be made, if a parent requests it, for a student to observe or participate in religious observances within the school during school time. In keeping with the new Term 17, the Schools Act, 1997, under "Religious Instruction and Observances", states:

10. (2) A parent of a student in a school may request of the school principal, giving the principal reasonable notice, that a religious observance be held in the school.
(3) A principal of a school shall, in accordance with the by-laws of the board, comply with a request of a parent with respect to a religious observance. (Government of Newfoundland and Labrador, 1997c)

Making provision for and permitting religious observances to take place may entail providing a "private" space and time where the student(s) can carry out a religious observance that is a requirement of their belief system. How has this played out so far in Newfoundland and Labrador? Because there are areas of the province where every student in the school is of Christian background, in reality Christian observances and celebrations such as Christmas and Easter assemblies are often organized by school personnel and usually include the entire school body. However, some school personnel have taken the position that there are so many legalities and other factors to consider when organizing an assembly for a religious observance, it is best not to have any religious observances held within in the school. Therefore, depending on one's faith perspective, the new Term 17 can be viewed as having negative or positive consequences with regard to student involvement in religious observances and celebrations.

To date, in schools where religious observances have been carried out, there has not been a court challenge. One reason for this may be the fact that in schools in which there are students of living belief systems other than Christianity, provision is made as stated in the Schools Act for any student to be excused from a religious observance. The Schools Act states: "Where a student's parent requests in writing, the principal of a school shall excuse that student from participation in a course in religion or a religious observance conducted in the school" (Government of Newfoundland and

Labrador, 1997c, Sec. 10 (1)). This, however, is not always done in the most desirable manner, because often the only provision made is that the excused student is given permission to stay home during those observances or to wait in some other area of the school while the other students partici-pate in the religious observance. With limited personnel, many schools find it difficult to make other arrangements for students who do not partici-pate in any school function that includes the majority of the students.

As the population of Newfoundland and Labrador becomes more multicultural and multi-faith in nature, the issue of the total school popula-tion being involved in the religious observances of specific faith communi-ties will likely have to be examined. From my experience, this has caused concerns in some urban areas where there are significant numbers of stu-dents who are adherents of various living belief systems.

That being considered, however, the most significant change resulted from Article Three in Term 17, in that, since 1997 provision must be made for each student to participate in religious observances at school, regardless of their living belief system.

The development of a new religious education program

The process leading up to the implementation of the new religious education curriculum began with the development of a new religious education frame-work in October, 1997. Its development would be protracted, but it would be within this framework that the new religious education curriculum would evolve. To begin the process of developing a new curriculum for religious ed-ucation, a vision statement was written. The wording of this statement would be foundational to much of what followed in the development of the new religious education curriculum. The vision statement reads as follows:

> The Newfoundland and Labrador religious education curricu-lum is shaped by a vision of enabling and encouraging students to grow religiously, spiritually and morally into informed, caring and contributing members of society, who appreciate their own belief and values, and the beliefs and values of others, and who understand the contribution that Christianity and other reli-gions make to human life. (Government of Newfoundland and Labrador, 2002a, p. 5)

In recognition of the Christian heritage and culture of Newfoundland and Labrador, Christianity is singled out in the vision statement. It should be made clear, however, that there was no implied intent to use Christianity as a benchmark to "measure" the validity of other living belief systems or to infer that a comparative religious education curriculum was being developed.

Concurrently, while the framework was being developed, an examination of existing resources from the former denominational systems was carried out to determine which ones could be used in the "new" system during the interim period, until new resources were produced. To achieve this task, curriculum working-groups were struck consisting of teachers from the former Pentecostal, Roman Catholic, and Integrated systems to help determine which of those existing resources were the "best fit" with the outcomes stated in the new religious education framework document. These working-groups also began work on the new religious education program and the development of resources for that program.

In early 1998, focus groups were conducted around the province to discuss the draft of the religious education framework document and to receive suggestions and reactions to the proposed new religious education program. These sessions were by invitation, with representatives from the various Christian denominations found in the province, other living belief systems, educational institutions, and others with an interest in religious education. As the process continued, the provincial Department of Justice became involved, examining the framework document as well as the recommended resources presented by the curriculum working-groups. In its review, the Department of Justice focused on the balance of representation of various living belief systems, gender balance, multicultural representation, statements of faith not being delivered as statements of fact, and other criteria. As part of the process, new curriculum guides were developed that provided direction regarding which sections of the interim resources would be included in the interim program and which would be excluded because they were deemed inappropriate for the reformed education system. New general curriculum outcomes were also developed, making provision for an inclusive religious education program with statements of methodology and appropriate activities. Upon completion of the curriculum guides, work began on developing new student and teacher resources for the program, many of which would be custom designed. "Faith readers," recommended by their communities, also became involved in the process with the purpose of reviewing all resources to ensure, as much as possible, that the information was accurate and acceptable. Because of the sheer number and diversity of stakeholders, this process took considerable time, but significant emphasis was placed on ensuring that all living belief systems included were given fair and accurate representation, that sound pedagogy was used, and that from a legal perspective the prescribed criteria were met.

Rationale for religious education in schools

Why is it important to study religious education? When the aforementioned religious education framework document was developed, the contributors took great pains to articulate a series of statements that provide a rationale for religious instruction. In this section, I consider some of these statements.

First, the presence of religious education as part of the school curriculum is critically important to those who believe in the value of religious instruction. Part of the rationale mirrors questions that students commonly ask about how they can make sense of the world, such as: Where do we fit into the scheme of things?; What makes us different from other living things?; What is the source of suffering?; How can happiness be found?; and, What happens after death? These questions are examined by all major living belief systems, and the philosophy of the religious education program since the 1997 reform is that students should receive the opportunity to reflect on these questions from the perspectives of various living belief systems. This requires sensitivity; the age/grade of the students must be considered in deciding when to introduce certain topics, materials, and activities. A religious education program cannot provide conclusive answers to the profound questions given above, but religious education provides a forum where such questions can be examined—indeed, perhaps it is the only such forum in the school curricula. Although the religious education program in Newfoundland and Labrador examines how various living belief systems explore these questions, it in no way negates the importance of students understanding the position of their own belief systems on questions of such importance. In a world that is truly multicultural and multi-faith, the vision statement for religious education recognizes that "each person should value and celebrate his/her own faith (religious heritage or commitment)" (Government of Newfoundland and Labrador, 2002a, p. 5). However, the program also recognizes the value of the practices and beliefs of other faith communities. Regarding the importance of religion and belief and the profound questions of life, Andrew C. Clarke, General Secretary for the International Association for Religious Freedom in a pamphlet prepared for his organization, says the following:

> Religion and belief are motivating forces that guide our existence and make it meaningful. We should listen carefully to the form(s) that the faith and beliefs of others take while accepting

our own human limitations to know truth absolutely. What we can rightly demand is religious freedom and what we correspondingly must supply are the highest ethical standards of responsible conduct. (Clarke, 2004, p. 1)

The religious education program ensures that in addition to the vital role of parents and society at large in exploring these profound questions of life, students are provided the opportunity to examine how various living belief systems have responded to some of these questions.

Second, the world's population is continually shifting and as people move, cultures and beliefs move with them. There are many cultures in which religion is such an integral part that it is difficult to separate the religion from the culture, and in fact, it is not uncommon to hear such phrases as Muslim culture or Christian culture. Many practices in many cultures, even when not recognized as such, had their origin in religious beliefs. Students need to be informed about this phenomenon in order for them to have a better understanding of the world. Religious education endeavours to help students understand that just as their practices and belief systems are important to them and to their families, the same is true for all people who are adherents of other living belief systems. The program discussed here is designed on the premise that "religious and denominational intolerance will be eliminated only when people are more understanding of the intrinsic worth of religious views and traditions that are not their own" (Government of Newfoundland and Labrador, 2002a, p. 7).

Third, students need to appreciate that most living belief systems have sacred writings and all teach values, ethics, and morals. The *Atlantic Canada Framework for Essential Graduation Learnings in Schools* states that the mission of public education is "to enable and encourage every individual to acquire, through lifelong learning, the knowledge, skills and values necessary for personal growth and the development of society" (Atlantic Provinces Education Foundation, 1996). In addition to the six Essential Graduation Learnings outlined for all Atlantic Provinces, there is a seventh for Newfoundland and Labrador: *graduates will demonstrate an understanding and appreciation for the place of belief systems in shaping the development of moral values and ethical conduct.* Religion has been a determining factor in the history and cultural heritage of Newfoundland and Labrador. It is recognized that although living belief systems have sometimes been responsible for conflicts, these same belief systems have also helped to bring about resolution, peace, and social justice. It is believed that an effective religious education program will enable students to appreciate the relationship between religion and history and to appreciate that belief systems are a major contributing factor in current and international events. In order for students to comprehend this feature, the relationship between living belief systems and their historical and societal contributions should be approached from a multi-faith perspective. As part of the rationale, as well, consideration is given to the impact and contributions of belief systems in the areas of literature, architecture, art, music, film, and theatre. Again, the new program enables students to gain an appreciation for this impact through the study of various living belief systems, and not just one.

Fourth, since "young people develop intellectually, physically, emotionally, socially, and spiritually" (Government of Newfoundland and Labrador, 2002a, p. 8), it is important to have a religious education component in the school because the school should consider the development of the whole child. If the purpose of the school is to educate, and not to proselytize or indoctrinate, then each of the above components of development can best be examined using an inclusive approach for religious education. Students live in a pluralistic society and a religious education program must recognize this pluralism as it attempts to help them develop intellectually, physically, emotionally, socially and spiritually. It is recognized that this can be seen as threatening for those of the opinion that only one "truth" should be presented to students. In *The Courage to Teach*, Parker J. Palmer makes the following statement:

> As long as we inhabit a universe made homogeneous by our refusal to admit otherness, we can maintain the illusion that we possess the truth about ourselves and the world—after all, there is no "other" to challenge us! But as soon as we admit pluralism, we are forced to admit that ours is not the only standpoint, the only experience, the only way, and truths we have built our lives on begin to feel fragile. (Palmer, 1998, p. 38)

In their personal search for meaning, it is important that students acquire the knowledge, understanding, and skills needed to reflect on and critically interpret the teachings and practices of many, not just one, living belief systems. John Bowker (2002) acknowledges that religious education can mean different things and include different approaches, but supports the notion that religious education falls under the domain of academia and therefore belongs in the school curricula:

> We have to appreciate all that religions have meant to people in constructing through their lives virtually all the memorable

achievements of what we now call civilization. Because religions matter so much, those who belong to them become "edgy" (to say the least) when they perceive the necessary boundaries of the system coming under threat. The study of all this, and in particular of the dynamics of religious systems, is manifestly an academic subject. (Bowker, 2002, p. 216)

Approached as an academic subject that is of importance in the holistic education of a student, religious education deserves to be viewed as having the same value as other academic subjects.

Defining religious education

Defining religious education is a challenging task and there are many interpretations of what it means and what it should entail. Religious education methods and programs vary, depending inevitably on the prevalence of religious beliefs and practices, or lack thereof, within a given country or area of a country and on the governing powers of the state and school. However, where religious education is included in the curriculum, a specific approach is usually taken. Michael Grimmitt (as cited in Jackson & Steele, 2004) describes three major types or concepts of religious education in schools around the world: learning religion or educating into religion, learning about religion, and learning from religion (Hull, 2001). A synopsis for each follows:

(1) *Learning religion or educating into religion:* A single religious tradition is taught as the religious education curriculum, and is taught from the insider perspective. Teachers engaged to teach the curriculum are expected to be believers in the religion. The purpose and expected outcome of instruction is to have students become adherents of the faith being taught or to strengthen their commitment to it. This type of religious education is often described as confessional religious education. The religion being taught is the one that is believed to be the true one and students are expected to accept this. As a result, students are expected to live their lives according to the teachings of that religion or of a particular denomination or sect of that religion.

(2) *Learning about religion:* This is the "religious studies" approach. Religion is taught from the outsider perspective and not from the insider perspective. Texts that are sacred for specific liv-

ing belief systems (e.g., the Bible for Christians and the Qur'an for Muslims, are not taught as being sacred but often taught as being literature only). Learning about religion is more of a historical or critical approach. This kind of religious education is sometimes referred to as "education in comparative religion." Students will learn about the beliefs, practices, and traditions of living belief systems but there will be no attempt to have students believe in or practice any of the faith traditions. The student's search for moral and spiritual values is not usually considered in this approach.

(3) *Educating or learning from religion:* Here an opportunity is provided for students to reflect on the different teachings and practices of various living belief systems. Students are encouraged to develop their own views on major religious and moral issues. Students are put at the centre of the teaching and their experiences are brought into consideration. The assumption is that students of all ages can gain educational benefit through the study of religion and through reflecting on the teachings of various religions.

Two points should be noted here. First, a society that is secular and/or pluralistic is not likely to embrace the first approach, "Learning Religion," as a method or philosophy for religious education. Second, the third approach, "Learning from Religion," is not used in most parts of the world, although it is the one that many educators agree will lead to a better understanding of others and a greater appreciation for freedom of religion. It is this third approach that seems to best serve students in a multicultural and multi-faith society.

In the province of Newfoundland and Labrador, there is an attempt to have students *learn from* living belief systems. This attempt is not limited to a single living belief system—in the framework document under "Principles Underlying the Program", it is stated:

This religious education curriculum is non-confessional. In such a program it is essential that faith, beliefs, doctrines, practices and history of Christianity and other religions be covered with respect. No attempt to indoctrinate, proselytize or present a biased view would be appropriate. (Government of Newfoundland and Labrador, 2002a, p. 9)

The document also states:

> [T]he learning environment will foster inquiry, reflection, decision making and the experiential within the classroom and school. (Government of Newfoundland and Labrador, 2002a, p. 3)

Including the experiential component is one significant way that this program differs from religious studies or "learning about religion." This is often the area that teachers find most difficult because there is always the question of what is appropriate regarding the experiential in religious education. This question is considered in the religious education teacher guides and the Department of Education curriculum guides. Activities included in the curriculum that are of an experiential nature have been reviewed by adherents of living belief systems and suggestions have been made by the Department of Justice, especially around areas of sensitivity. Also, teachers have had input regarding the appropriateness and practicality of activities that would be considered experiential. It is never the intent that practices or traditions of any faith community be presented in such a way that students are experiencing them in inappropriate ways or in an attempt to proselytize or indoctrinate. In support of the inclusion of an experiential component in religious education programs, consider the following quotation from Nord and Haynes's book, titled *Taking Religion Seriously Across the Curriculum* (1998):

> In educating students about music we are not content to have them read about the beliefs of composers and musicians, nor is it sufficient for them to scan sheets of musical notation or study acoustics. It is in *listening* to music—or better yet, in *performing* it—that students can grasp *from the inside* what music is all about. They make sense of music by experiencing it.... Similarly, scientists often claim that it is only in *doing science* that students can learn what science is.... For any number of reasons we can't require students to practice religion, but they can acquire some imaginative and vicarious sense of what it means to experience the world religiously from autobiographies and even better, from literature, drama, film, and art. (Nord & Haynes, 1998, p. 51)

The "experiential" can be interpreted in different ways and can be experienced at different levels. It is the degree to which the experiential will be part of the program and the selection of what will be experienced that is of utmost importance in the classroom. For example, it may be acceptable for students to participate in eating food that is considered part of a religious festival, but it may not be acceptable for students to take part in prayers from a living belief system; similarly, it may be appropriate for students to listen to music from a particular living belief system to better understand that system, but it may not be appropriate for them to learn to sing or perform religious music as part of their religious education program. The purpose of the experiential should be to help students better appreciate and understand the living belief systems they are studying.

Recognizing and celebrating diversity

The new religious education curriculum recognizes and celebrates the diversity of beliefs and practices within our classrooms and society at large. Attempts have been made to conceptualize diversity as positive and to help students appreciate the richness that diversity can bring. Students, as referenced in the religious education framework, are taught to appreciate their own belief system, if they are adherents of one, and to appreciate and respect the belief systems of others in the knowledge that for each person who is an adherent of a living belief system, it is of importance to them (Government of Newfoundland and Labrador, 2002a). As society becomes more multicultural, it becomes imperative that our education systems have a broad world-view. In today's education systems, an exclusive approach to religious education cannot be supported if holistic education is to be taken seriously. Education systems must be inclusive, and that is nowhere more applicable than in religious education. In Newfoundland and Labrador, every attempt has been made to have an inclusive approach to religious education.

Key principles of the new religious education curriculum

The provincial religious education curriculum gives emphasis to Christianity in recognition of the heritage and contemporary society of Newfoundland and Labrador. The 2001 census (Statistics Canada, 2001), which provides the most recent Canadian statistics regarding religious affiliation, reports that the population of this province was 512,930, with 303,200 persons stating they were Protestant and 187,405 persons stating they were Roman Catholic. The remainder of the population, 22,325, stated they were adherents to other Christian denominations or to other belief systems, or that they were not adherents of any belief system. These statistics would be somewhat different today as a result of the increase, since 2001, in the number of adherents to non-Christian living belief systems in the province, particularly in the St. John's area. However, because religious statistics are only collected in every second census, it is impossible to know how significantly the demographics have changed. Nevertheless, it is imperative that the provincial religious education curriculum recognizes the province's heritage and recognizes that students live in a global society and in a country that is multicultural and multi-faith.

If this line of thought is followed, students should be informed about the influence of religion locally and globally. They should be given information on the founders, beliefs, main practices, symbols, and festivals of various living belief systems. Although the new religious education program is not a comparative study, students will learn some of the similarities and differences among the living belief systems being studied (Government of Newfoundland and Labrador, 2002a, p. 9).

One of the principles underlying the program is that religious education should be taught with sensitivity and respect for all living belief systems and their adherents. Religious education must occur in a classroom environment in which respect and sensitivity are shown and prejudiced attitudes are discouraged. Only in this environment will students be able to appreciate how a person's world-view can be shaped by their religious beliefs:

> Understanding a religion is not a matter of knowing a few *facts* about it or being able to recite its core *beliefs*; it is more a matter of being able to make sense of the world in a particular religious way. It requires a different gestalt or consciousness, an appreciation of how the different dimensions of that religion shape a world-view. (Nord & Haynes, 1998, pp. 50–51)

Another of the key principles states, "This religious education curriculum acknowledges that the essence of all interfaith dialogue is the awareness that human beings share essential truths and experiences (Government of Newfoundland and Labrador, 2002a, p. 9). The new program, while recognizing there are differences of beliefs and practices, endeavours to help students understand and appreciate the essential truths and experiences common to most of humanity and emerging from the teachings of living belief systems. It is not a matter that "all should be the same" but that all should be able to value the diversity of beliefs and practices among humanity.

Conclusions

Canada has become internationally recognized as a multicultural and multifaith country. Across the country, the cultural and religious landscape continues to change, reflecting a growing diversity of cultures and religious beliefs and practices. If there is one commonality among much of the world's population, it is a profession of belief in that which might be called the spiritual or an ultimate reality. However, most education systems do not examine this spiritual or religious side of humanity. In fact, Newfoundland and Labrador and Quebec are the only provinces in Canada that have a religious education program for all grades. I suggest that the religious education program described in this chapter is unique, in that it recognizes a religious heritage that can never (and should never) be denied, while challenging students to reflect on and gain knowledge about the multiplicity of practices and beliefs inherent in the various living belief systems. Because it is non-confessional in approach, this program also enables students to reflect on and make personal decisions regarding their own spirituality and religious traditions.

But, more than 10 years after the 1997 reform, there are still some unanswered questions. The first area of concern relates to the question of how much program emphasis should be placed on Christianity. Canada's (and Newfoundland and Labrador's) religious and cultural history is predominately Christian. Should Christianity, therefore, be taught as one belief system among several or should it be given more significant emphasis? If taught as one among many, is there a danger of Christianity being marginalized? A second area of contention, for some, is whether the education system should be responsible in any way for passing on the traditions of a particular faith or attempting to ensure that students become committed to or remain committed to a particular faith community. What is, or should be, the role of the education system regarding a student's spiritual development and/or religious beliefs and what is the role of the home and faith communities to which students belong? A third area of concern is what is appropriate by way of experiential learning in a religious education program?

These are questions which will continue to be debated for some time and may hinge on an individual's understanding of what is meant by religious education and his or her perception of the role of living belief systems in a student's education. Undoubtedly, they will need to be considered in future iterations of the religious education curriculum and as other provinces continue to grapple with questions of religious and cultural diversity in schools.

There have been dramatic changes in the way religious education is delivered in Newfoundland and Labrador schools since 1997 and in the way religious observances are carried out in some schools. There is a greater recognition that a person should be able to express one's faith or lack of faith in a "safe" environment where one's beliefs and right to hold those beliefs is respected. There is also a greater emphasis on helping students appreciate the intrinsic worth of each living belief system for its adherents. The focus is much more on understanding and acceptance in the hope that the differences that have been divisive in the past will not be a part of future generations. Recognizing that not everything about diversity is positive, the religious education program developed since reform in 1997 endeavours to help students see the positive and value the richness of diversity while supporting what is taught in the home and in the belief systems to which students may belong.

Part Three

Impacts and Challenges

Chapter Ten

Systems Challenges to the Sustainability of Meaningful School Reform

Bruce Sheppard

Canadians are, for the most part, supportive of public education and hold high expectations for schools and school boards. The business plan of the Nova Scotia Department of Education (2009), for example, reveals that public education is viewed as an essential component of each citizen's and the province's future health and prosperity. Similarly, the Ontario Ministry of Education (2008) notes that:

> a strong publicly funded education system is the foundation of the competitive economy and cohesive society...(p. 15) and...is vital to the prosperity of Ontario...(p. 2). The schools' role is... to help students develop into highly skilled, knowledgeable, caring citizens who contribute to [a] strong economy and a cohesive society. (p. 1)

In addition, in Newfoundland and Labrador, the strategic plan of the Department of Education (Government of Newfoundland and Labrador, 2008c) states that "education levels are a key indicator of individual economic success which fuel the province's achievements in both national and international environments" (p. 10).

Beyond the lofty expectations set out in provincial government statements such as those articulated above, the majority of Canadians expect schools to promote citizenship education and political engagement; develop social skills and technological competence; promote healthy living; develop students' abilities in, and foster an appreciation of, the arts, music, and our cultural heritage; strengthen common moral values; prepare students for post-secondary studies; and develop employability skills and prepare them for the new knowledge-economy (Canadian Council on Learning, 2007; Ungerleider, 2003). At the same time, it appears that citizens in all provinces expect their public school system to ensure that their children perform above the national average on national tests such as the Pan-Canadian Assessment Program (PCAP), and at least on par with the best in the world on international tests; for example, the Program for International Student Assessment (PISA). Additionally, there is an overarching universal recognition in the articulated goals of all schools, school districts, provincial governments, and the Canadian School Boards' Association, that schools must be safe, caring environments that exist as meaningful social spaces for children and adolescents, rather than just places to be endured as they prepare for adult life.

From purpose to practice

There is little doubt that the expectations Canadians hold for their public schools are exceptionally high. As a matter of fact, given the varied and somewhat competing expectations, it may be nigh impossible for provincial governments or the public school system to meet these expectations. Goodlad (2001) has noted that the level of priority placed on educational purposes tends to shift according to two competing social-political realities, the *hard-and-tough* and *soft-and-tender*. During the *soft-and-tender* times the purpose of education is focused on the development of a caring, wise, thinking, responsible, sane citizen who has the resources to contribute to the social and economic welfare of self and others and the enjoyment of life. Advocates of those times contend that the only meaningful purpose of education can be to develop individuals' desire and ability to be lifelong learners, and that what is learned in schools must be authentic and must enable students to learn who they are, and how to respond to challenges they will face in order to live a fulfilling life (Goodlad, 2001; Littky, 2004; Starratt, 2004). Starratt (2004), for example, argues that "high-stakes testing of the *hard-and-tough* times shrinks the vision of teachers [and leads to] inauthentic...superficial learning" (pp. 1–2). In the *hard-and-tough* times, the advocates of accountability dominate. These advocates contend that the most important criterion of success is meeting defined performance standards on achievement tests. They adhere to a *back-to-the-basics* agenda that focuses primarily on mathematics, science, reading, and writing, and believe that the curriculum can be aligned to focus on these priority areas. They believe that standards for success must be established in each of those priority areas, assessment instruments must be developed to measure whether all students meet those standards, and schools and educators must be rewarded or punished accordingly (Brooks & Brooks, 1999).

Given the emphasis placed upon provincial, national, and international tests by the provincial governments and the growing emphasis of accountability models, it appears that Canadians have entered a period that can be likened to Goodlad's *hard-and-tough* times. Provincial curriculum documents describe the more inclusive purposes of education, but in reality educators are held accountable for student performance on only a narrow portion of those purposes as assessed through provincial testing regimes that place priority on English language, mathematics, and science. Such schizophrenic expectations place considerable stress upon public school professionals. It should not be surprising, therefore, that some teachers have moved away from the *softer* educational purposes in order to focus primarily on the provincially tested topics in designated subject areas. Such a narrowing of focus comes at the expense of other curriculum areas (Laitsch, 2006), and thereby supports claims that what gets assessed gets valued (Stoll & Fink, 1996).

Education and globalization

Throughout the last decade or so, public schools, school boards, and provinces in Canada have been subjected to increasing critique with respect to their performance on goals most valued by the *back-to-the basics* critics such as the Atlantic Institute for Market Studies (2008) and the Fraser Institute (2008). While governments and school boards have sought to defend themselves against such attacks, they have become increasingly dependent upon the same narrow accountability measures that these groups have advocated from the beginning (Hargreaves & Fink, 2006; Sheppard, Brown, & Dibbon, 2009). It appears that this shift has occurred largely as a consequence of globalization (Taylor, Rizvi, Lingard, & Henry, 1997) and the resulting increase in the influence of the Council of Ministers of Education, Canada and the Organization for Economic Cooperation and Development (OECD) on provincial policies, structures, and governance. Canada, like other member countries of the OECD over the course of the last three decades, has turned from Keynesianism in favour of OECD's globalization agenda and the concomitant management practice of *corporate managerialism* (Taylor et al., 1997). As a consequence, it is not surprising that education in Canada mirrors that of other OECD countries, or even that there has been a blurring of provincial boundaries in respect to public education.

Although it is likely that public school educators have thought little about the influence of corporate managerialism on their work, there is little doubt that they readily recognize many of the structures, processes, and agendas that are consistent with this management practice and how these have impacted their daily work. In Chapter Five, Galway describes some of these structures and practices: a focus on efficiency and effectiveness; reduced spending on education; the creation of larger school districts with fewer staff; and an increased emphasis on strategic planning and school development at the local level with a concomitant loss of local autonomy over the format of these processes or the determination of accountability measures. In addition, while there is a continued rhetoric of increased local governance, and local school councils have become prominent throughout many OECD countries, in reality governments and their officials who may or may not have educational expertise make all (or at least most) of the key decisions regarding education. "Instead of [educational] organizations having the autonomy to consider, plan, and launch their own change initiatives...,external forces such as [governments] and...policy-makers, the courts, and various experts have set the change agenda" (Hall & Hord, 2006, p. 1). Of even more concern is that "education is increasingly regarded as a commodity, [rather than] a public good" (Shaker & Grimmett, 2004, p. 29) as the public education agenda is frequently determined by "what interest groups...can persuade governments to do" (Taylor et al., 1997, p. 3), rather than on the basis of more ideal public purposes.

Consequently, professionally initiated innovation has been displaced, and the autonomy of educational leaders and teachers has been eroded to the point that they have become little more than mere functionaries who are expected to implement centrally determined curricula while at the same time being subjected to increased accountability for their students' performance on standardized or provincially designed tests (Mulford, Silins, & Leithwood, 2004). There appears to be little consideration of the fact that professional educators are knowledge workers and leaders who have the professional expertise to lead and make key decisions regarding the organization of schools and student learning. Similarly, school boards have had little input into the government-driven agendas related to public education, and have had little control over the consequences of them. In spite of that, school boards have had frontline responsibility for implementing these government agendas, and as a result have become the primary target of the public's loss of confidence in the public education system. As expected, this has increased public support for even more centralized control by the government.

Within the context of the corporate managerialist agenda, most provinces in Canada have implemented their own testing program and the ministers of education issue regular press releases touting the success of their education accountability initiatives using test scores as evidence (Shaker & Grimmett, 2004). For instance, in Newfoundland and Labrador these measures include public examinations at the high school level and criterion-reference tests in mathematics and English Language Arts in Grades 3, 6, and 9 and science in Grade 9. Additionally, the Council of Ministers of Education, Canada (2007) place considerable weight on PISA and PCAP results that are focused on student achievement in mathematics, reading and writing, and science. Although the focus on testing in Canada has not become high stakes in comparison to the *No Child Left Behind* program in the USA (Brennan, 2004; Laitsch, 2006; Nichols & Berliner, 2005; Raudenbush, 2004), it has created significant pressure on parents, educators, and students to focus on improving test scores in the assessed subject areas. As a consequence of this focus on testing and outcomes, there has been an overemphasis on traditional direct instruction at the expense of other valuable student-centred teaching and learning approaches such as collaborative learning (Kagan, 1994) or guided inquiry (Kuhlthau, Maniotes, & Caspari, 2007) that have been shown to better facilitate the learning of other "important lessons our children should learn" (Littky, 2004, p. 5). As a result, gains in test scores often come "at the expense of other goals...including equity; curricular relevance; and student interest" (Grubb & Oakes, 2007, p. 29). Those of us who have been monitoring this phenomenon in Canada are beginning to observe the truth in Kohn's (2002) warning:

> If the sole goal is to raise achievement (in the narrowest sense of that word), then we may end up ignoring other kinds of learning. It's difficult to teach the whole child when you are held accountable only for raising reading and math scores. (p. 20)

By international standards, students in public schools in Canada perform very well. Even though PISA results of the performance of 15-year-old students in science, mathematics, and reading vary by province, Canadian students perform among the best in the world in each of those subjects (Bussière, Knighton, & Pennock, 2007). In those provinces where students scored slightly below the Canadian average on those tests, when socio-economic status and parent education levels are considered, those students are shown to have generally performed on par or above the Canadian average. This is not an argument that schools in Canada do not need to improve. If the public education system had been truly successful in the past, it is likely that the education levels and perhaps the socio-economic status of current parents might be at the Canadian average. For instance, Newfoundland and Labrador has the highest percentage of parents of any Canadian province who have no post-secondary education (44 per cent compared to 32 per cent in Alberta where students scored the highest) and the lowest SES index in the country (an index of .11 as compared to an index of .43 in Alberta) (Bussière et al., 2007). The connection between education and socio-economic status is a vicious cycle that is somewhat of a "chicken and egg" question, as low levels of education are a major determining factor of low socio-economic status while the converse, low socio-economic status, is a major variable in determining success in school. This challenging self-sustaining cycle was clearly evident in findings of a recent study of intermediate students in Newfoundland and Labrador (Atlantic Evaluation and Research Consultants, 2008). The researchers found that 31 per cent fewer students with mothers who had less than high school education and 40 per cent fewer students who reported having very few books in the home[1] aspired to getting a post-secondary education in comparison to the those who reported being most advantaged in these respects.

Also, while the graduation rate from high schools in Newfoundland and Labrador is on par with the Canadian average (Statistics Canada, 2005), a graduation rate of 75.3 per cent for male students and 81 per cent for female students (Government of Newfoundland and Labrador, 2007b) is not at a preferred level. And what about developing a desire to learn? In the study by Atlantic Evaluation and Research Consultants (2008) reported above, researchers surveyed intermediate students' attitudes toward their school experiences in Newfoundland and Labrador. Survey results revealed that 83 per cent of the students stated that they enjoyed learning new things; however, only 55 per cent admitted to liking school and even fewer (47 per cent) of those students indicated that they found school interesting. As for students' perception of relevance of their course work to their future, the courses that students perceived to be most useful were as follows: mathematics (96 per cent), English language (88 per cent), and science (85 per cent). These are the courses that have been the focus of provincial, national, and international assessments. The courses perceived to be the least relevant were music (39 per cent), art (38 per cent), and religious education (38 per cent). In addition, only 70 per cent and 64 per cent respectively viewed physical education and healthy living as relevant courses—a finding that may be somewhat surprising in light of a nationwide campaign over the last few years to promote healthy and active living. Similarly, those who believe that an essential purpose of public education is to foster a Canadian identity, to provide students with a sense of pride in their heritage, and to encourage them to assume their democratic and moral responsibilities within Canada and around the world, will likely consider our education system to be underachieving as only 66 per cent considered French (second language) and 61 per cent social studies to be useful or somewhat useful. While these results of students' attitudes toward school are from one province only, given the commonalities of the educational experiences and the similarities in graduation rates in public schools across Canada, it is likely that similar student attitudes exist across the country. If one accepts the assumption that an essential component of breaking the cycle of poverty and low education is through the provision of improved educational opportunities and increased curriculum relevance, then reform of the public education system is essential.

Toward an understanding of meaningful school change

Unfortunately, most observers of the school systems in the Western world have concluded that educational reform is challenging. In spite of constant talk of educational reform and volumes of literature about it, the most significant elements of today's schools remain the same as they were over the last 100 years (Schlechty, 2001; Starratt, 2004). For instance, Schlechty (2001) opines that schools have not kept pace with our changing social context. Even though we have shifted "from a society in which only the culturally elite and intellectually gifted were expected to achieve high levels of academic competence to a society in which nearly all students are expected to perform at levels once assumed to be the purview of a few" (Schlechty, 2001, p. 10), "schools are not much different...than they were fifty years ago" (p. xi). Starratt (2004) holds a similar dim view of the performance of public schools, stating that "despite sincere efforts of many [school personnel], the schooling process remains a huge waste of students' time and taxpayers' money" (p. 2).

In reality, student learning is impacted by multiple factors, many of which appear to be outside the direct control of educators (Kohn, 2002; Leithwood, Louis, Anderson, & Wahlstrom, 2004; Wang and Walberg, 1991), and therefore, little meaningful sustained change in education is likely to be achieved without the recognition that "education is a system, not a collection of parts" (Emery, 2006, p. 2). For instance, Leithwood et al. (2004), in an extensive review of the research relating to the factors that influence students' learning, identified the following general categories: student and family background factors; various sources of leadership (parents, community leaders, the province, school districts, school personnel, etc.); policies and practices; school and classroom conditions; and teachers' professional community. It is readily apparent that each of the aforementioned categories is composed of multiple variables. For instance, school and classroom conditions include variables such as class size, teacher workload, student exceptionalities, and student behaviour issues, each of which has been found to have considerable impact on student learning. Obviously, in light of such complex, systemic challenges, the belief that the imposition of simplistic accountability models is an effective approach to bringing about meaningful school reform is unrealistic and naive. As a matter of fact, while educational professionals recognize the need for change, they become frustrated by such simplistic approaches to educational reform and by the constant barrage of competing demands and oftentimes ill-conceived initiatives that appear to be thrust upon them from all parts of the educational system and the larger community as more and more groups and individuals with differing political and ideological perspectives begin to view themselves as having ownership of the educational system (Jenlink, Reigeluth, Carr, & Nelson, 1998; Young, Levin, & Wallin, 2007). As a result, rather than embrace educational reform, schools and school districts continue to operate largely as isolated bureaucratic organizations that attempt to fend off what they perceive to be attacks from the outside, rather than to embrace change. In response to this circumstance, there has been a growing body of empirical evidence that has fuelled support for the importance of organizational learning as a promising approach for bringing about meaningful, sustained improvement in schools and school systems (Fullan, 2005a; Giles & Hargreaves, 2006; Hall & Hord, 2006; Leithwood et al., 2004). As it applies to schools and school systems, the term "organizational learning" (more typically referred to as "professional learning community" in schools) refers to the professional, organizational, and leadership capacity and processes within a school or school district to maintain and improve organizational performance based on experience and collaborative learning with the intent of improving students' learning (Sheppard et al., 2009).

Although I share the optimism related to the potential of organizational learning and the development of schools as professional learning communities, I am concerned that the term, professional learning community, has been co-opted by many schools, school districts, departments of education, and consulting firms as the current label of choice (the buzzword of the day) without any consideration of its theoretical underpinnings or the growing evidence base. Simplistic recipes that offer immediate transformation of a school into a professional learning community continue to proliferate as many schools announce that they are professional learning communities without having any of the attributes or characteristics that have been identified as most valued in those communities (Hall & Hord, 2006). In reality, a school that is a professional learning community displays a number of specific key attributes or conditions that are both facilitative and symptomatic of organizational learning (Sheppard et al., 2009).

Employing an organizational learning framework requires recognition that schools are just one component of a complex adaptive organizational system composed of multiple dynamic interrelated subsystems that determine the organization's directions. As complex adaptive systems, schools recognize their unique relationship with other schools, the local community, the school district, and other levels of the environment that mutually determine one another. Improvement efforts are not solely reliant upon initiatives where cause and effect can be easily identified, as is expected in traditional school development or strategic planning models; rather, emphasis is placed on the broader possibilities where the cause-and-effect linkages are not so apparent and where learning and school development occurs through the successes and failures of experimentation (Emery, 2006; Pascale, 2001). Emphasis is placed on action learning and strategic thinking, rather than on traditional strategic planning. It recognizes the limitations of the traditional approach to strategic planning that is completed by senior administrators and/or a leadership team with an apparent assumption that because it is planned, it will be executed and change will occur (Redding & Catalanello, 1992). It assumes that change is complex and adaptive, and that it occurs as a multiple dynamic interrelated web of learning cycles that simultaneously, consecutively, and intermittently spiral forward in a nonlinear fashion (Sheppard et al., 2009). Recognizing and accepting such a reality allows one to recognize that focusing on isolated school level factors or developing static strategic plans by consulting with selected groups only, will likely result in disappointment, as has been the case with repeated attempts by legislators to impose simplistic solutions.

In sum, there has been considerable convergence of views that the primary barriers to growth and sustainability of meaningful educational reform are the existing bureaucratic hierarchical structures and the accompanying organizational and professional cultural norms (Mulford et al., 2004; Murphy, 2007; Schlechty, 1997; Sparks, 2005) that remain dominant in our schools, school boards, and governments (Kouzes & Posner, 2003). The challenge, then, is how to encourage organizational learning in an environment in which the authoritarian hierarchy and the professional norms related to schooling remain deeply entrenched in the minds of formal leaders and followers as not just the best way, but the only way of organizing. It would be naive to believe that the solution can be found through the elimination of hierarchies (Leavitt, 2003) or through government mandate, and similarly naive to expect this to occur at the school level in any pervasive fashion without school district intervention and support. In fact, my colleagues and I have argued:

> While there are some examples of successful schools and school districts that are professional learning communities, these are isolated cases that appear to have had minimal impact on public education overall. If collaborative leadership and organizational learning are to become the norm for schools, rather than something that occurs randomly in isolated cases as appears to be the current circumstance, the school district has the most potential for fostering that change. (Sheppard et al., 2009, p. 34)

Even though the evidence in support of school districts as an important agency in facilitating and sustaining school and classroom reform has grown over the last decade or so (Fullan, 2005a, 2005b; Hightower, Knapp, Marsh, & McLaughlin, 2002; MacGilchrist, Mortimore, Savage, & Beresford, 1995; McLaughlin & Talbert, 2003), it must be acknowledged that the continued existence of school districts remains a double-edged sword. Those districts that have been found to have particular characteristics have a positive influence on school reform whereas other districts inhibit reform. The characteristics of successful districts that have been identified include: a shared vision of improving education for each student, an emphasis on individual professional learning, a focus on teaching and learning, collaborative leadership, and system-wide organizational learning (Elmore, 2002; Fullan, 2005a; McLaughlin & Talbert, 2003). While the evidence is convincing that large-scale meaningful school reform that is focused on the improvement of student learning is more likely to occur with the support of strong school districts, I concur with Fullan (2005a) that "it is not possible for districts to move forward over time if the larger system [government] is not a partner in fostering the sustainability agenda" (p. 80).

In the remainder of this chapter, I explore the challenges presented to school districts by successive governments in Newfoundland and Labrador that have inhibited their ability to lead a sustained meaningful reform agenda. My data sources include semi-structured interviews with 36 senior educational administrators (including current and past school board superintendents and assistant superintendents, school board trustees, and senior level department of education officials) and relevant district and provincial documents within Newfoundland and Labrador. The interview design and process were informed by Kvale (1996) and the analysis of all the data including document analysis generally followed the procedures outlined by Miles and Huberman (1994) and Glaser (1978).

Challenges to organizational learning in Newfoundland and Labrador

Strategic planning

The planning model imposed upon public bodies such as schools and school boards in Newfoundland and Labrador (Government of Newfoundland and Labrador, 2005) appears to act as an inhibitor of meaningful change as it relies on the traditional approach to planning that has been recognized as passé (Hamel, 2001; Mintzberg, 1994; Mintzberg & Lampel, 2001; Redding and Catalanello, 1992). Indeed, Hamel (2001) contends that strategic planning "doesn't produce strategy, it produces plans" (p. 187). Mintzberg (1994) holds a similar dim view of conventional strategic planning models, arguing that they fit best in a classic bureaucracy that is epitomized by formalization, centralized authority, and standardization of work and stability. In such classic bureaucratic organizations the strategic plan allows those at the top to set the direction and determine the processes to achieve it, thereby serving a similar purpose as blinders to a horse—to keep it going in the desired direction. Mintzberg contends that this model does not do well in dynamic professional environments such as school systems that are loosely coupled, intensely political, and operate according to deeply held cultural norms. In fact, he maintains that when it is imposed on these systems, it results in a huge waste of time and resources.

My colleagues and I (Sheppard et al., 2009) observed an example of the conventional strategic planning process in one school district. The school district had developed a strategic plan through a lengthy process of consultations that were led by senior district administrators and a steering committee. It contained 10 laudable goals that were approved by the school board and distributed to all schools; however, no implementation plans had been developed for any one of those goals. It appeared to assume that "someone else" at "some other time" would further develop the plans, and that the planned goals would then be achieved. In reality, it was little more than a document to gather dust on a shelf. The approach to strategic planning in schools (school development planning) mirrored the district approach and therefore was equally unlikely to have had any meaningful impact on teaching practices or student learning. In addition, there was considerable informal evidence that the school development process was weighted heavily toward the data gathering, and that it had little impact on actual school improvement. In fact, we were told by several teachers who were members of their school development team that they had spent three years on planning, but had not developed action plans, let alone commenced action. One teacher suggested that the data they had gathered were now outdated as the majority of students, their parents, the school council members, and many teachers were no longer associated with that school.

Even when plans are well developed with detailed action plans and defined evaluation periods, the usefulness of detailed upfront consultations and planning prior to action, rather than as an ongoing component of action, is questionable. Analysis of data from one school district revealed that following months of consultations and multiple strategy sessions, the school board had completed a written strategic plan. The plan contained multiple action-learning cycles for each of the action plans that they believed would bring progress toward the attainment of their vision which was "to challenge and develop the learning and achievement capabilities of each student in safe and caring learning environments." Unfortunately, within two months of the finalization of their plan, the government dissolved the school board through legislation. Although the vision survived the government restructuring because it was similar to that which was held in each of the other predecessor districts with which they were consolidated, progress was halted, or at least dramatically slowed, because the goals, objectives, and strategies in the former district were unique to only one region of the new district. The budget commitments that had been made by the former board were based on that board's fiscal realities and were no longer applicable to the new board that was dealing with a comparatively smaller budget allocation and reduced staffing levels. As well, while the new school board held a two-day retreat early in their first year to consider strategic directions, it was not in a position to develop or approve a long-term strategic plan as school board elections were to be held in September of the following school year. Even though the school board endorsed an interim strategic plan that was an amalgam of the plans of the preceding school districts, in reality, the adopted plan served little purpose as its agenda was completely filled in dealing with the immediate structural, administrative, and policy components of the newly formed district. In essence, even though the strategic planning process of the previous school board was founded upon the principles of adaptive planning and organizational learning, it was tailored to fulfill obligations related to the government's mandated strategic planning process, and therefore, as a result of a legislated government school restructuring event, it became little more than yet another perfunctory exercise.

Government control of financial and human resources

The K-12 school system in Newfoundland and Labrador is funded entirely by the government. Teachers, district educational personnel, and senior administrators are paid directly by the government, and the remaining budget is allocated to school boards as a grant with specifically designated components (as opposed to block funding) that include instruction, repairs and maintenance, school secretarial, maintenance wages, operations, and most recently, information technology. As a result of the manner in which the government allocates the funding to school boards and because of strong political pressure to budget within the designated components, school boards have had little discretion in their budgeting process. A particular challenging aspect of the government's approach to budgeting for boards has been in the government's total control of capital expenditures and the reduction of the budget allocation for repair and maintenance. During the mid-1990s, as the government became increasingly obsessed with reducing the provincial debt, capital spending in education was drastically reduced. As well, the funding for repair, maintenance, and cleaning was reduced (from a rate per square foot of $0.96 down to $0.55) as a cost-cutting measure and remained at that lower rate until 2007 when it was increased to $0.92. For more than a decade, school boards were restricted in their ability both to purchase cleaning and maintenance supplies and to enter into preventative maintenance contracts. By 2005, the capital needs had reached a crisis point. Many of the province's children and school personnel were working in uncomfortable and unsafe buildings because of leaking roofs and windows and the build-up of dust and mould. Such a challenging context left school boards with little choice other than to focus on the provision of safe and comfortable facilities for students and school personnel, rather than on improving teaching and learning processes. It appears that in spite of a significant effort on the part of the government and school boards over the last two to three years, the problems created by the lack of funding for school maintenance continues to divert attentions away from the improvement of student learning as school and district personnel continue to deal with multiple air-quality problems that have resulted from past underfunding (Auditor General, 2008).

As well, historically, the government's budget allocation to school districts for instruction has been inadequate to meet the cost of purchasing learning resources, assessment tools, technology hardware and software, and instructional equipment for schools. In fact, until 2007, in spite of increasing pleas from school councils and school boards, the costs related to the purchase and maintenance of new and emerging information technologies were largely ignored (Warren, Curtis, Sheppard, Hillier, & Roberts, 2003). Another source of concern for school boards in respect to the new and emerging technologies has been the government's relative inaction in respect to the consolidation of financial, personnel, and student records through the use of a common provincial data warehouse that would reduce duplication and improve efficiencies throughout the system. Several senior school district officials have expressed considerable frustration that in spite of increasing centralized control by the government that has resulted in what they perceive to be interference, in this one area in which school boards have expected leadership from the government, it has not been forthcoming.

Government control of the teacher allocation formula for classroom teachers, program specialists, guidance counsellors, and school administrators has been problematic as well. This formula has created challenges related to program delivery in small schools and has contributed to large class sizes in larger schools. Even more problematic, at least until recently, has been the control by personnel at the department of education of the allocation of categorical special education teachers to schools. The ISSP and Pathways Commission (2007) noted the limitations of such a top-down approach:

The overwhelming message gleaned from the...hearings was that the ISSP and Pathways models resembled a good idea gone awry, a sound concept which has lost its focus.... [And] of equal concern was the approval process for...applications for categorical service. Once developed, applications are forwarded to the Department of Education for approval. All stakeholders noted the irony in a system of decision making where those who know the child the least, have the final decision over their programming. (pp. 6, 54)

The recent changes to both the teacher allocation model (Teacher Allocation Commission, 2007) and to the ISSP and Pathways program delivery (ISSP and Pathways Commission, 2007) appear to be meaningful attempts to improve these processes.

The government also maintains control of contract negotiations for all school and district personnel, including teachers, support staff, and district administrators. In recent years, issues related to senior district administrator contracts have resulted in low morale at that level and have made recruiting of high quality candidates a challenge. As well, during the first half of this decade, two lengthy support-staff labour strikes diverted attention away from the teaching and learning agenda. Although these aforementioned labour problems were not necessarily a function of government control, the reality is that they resulted in a loss of trust and lowered morale. Given the evidence that reduced levels of trust and low morale have been found to inhibit organizational learning, it appears that the government's tight control over budgets, personnel, and labour negotiations may have limited, rather than facilitated, the sustainability of meaningful educational reform.

School district restructuring

Perhaps the greatest negative impact on sustainability of meaningful educational reform in Newfoundland and Labrador has been two major legislated educational restructuring initiatives. The first restructuring, initiated by the Royal Commission of Inquiry into Delivery of Programs and Services in Primary, Elementary, Secondary Education (Government of Newfoundland and Labrador, 1992b), was legislated in 1996. It resulted in the elimination of a Christian denominational educational system and the reduction of school boards from 27 anglophone school boards to 10 and the creation of a French Language School Board. In 2004, a second restructuring of school boards led to the reduction of the 10 anglophone boards to four. While the long-term impact of these restructuring initiatives may be judged as positive (*short-term pain for long-term gain*), the short-term (10-15 year) impact has been the diversion of attention of educational leaders away from a teaching and learning agenda.

While most interviewees were convinced of the need for the elimination of duplication of services that existed under the Christian denominational system, collectively they shared a concern that it diverted attentions away from student learning. In referring to the first restructuring time period beginning in 1992, one senior district administrator observed that his school board "felt under siege," and commented that for an entire decade there was very little focus on instructional leadership or student learning. A director of education from another school district made a similar observation:

> During those years, the politics and the demands of that exercise certainly detracted...the senior decision making energies of all the professional educators in the province as well as the elected school board members.... I think the system probably suffered...from a drift in terms of focusing upon student learning...because of that.

And yet another director of education lamented that, "if there was ever a time that there was no focus on the child that was it!"

Much of the lost focus on student learning during the period leading up to the actual legislated change was related directly to the political debates between the government and the churches. However, following the actual legislated change, the teaching and learning agenda continued to be hijacked because of the requirement to eliminate any duplication of schools that had existed because of the denominational system. Because the process of eliminating duplication required multiple school closures, it was both highly legalistic and mired in political controversy, as revealed in the following comment that is reflective of the common view of all district-level respondents:

> The media was consumed with it, and most school closure decisions were challenged in the courts. As a result, there was nothing else that the school board and district personnel, including program specialists, could focus on. Our agenda relating to teaching and learning that we had started earlier was ignored.

As noted above, this particular restructuring event reduced the number of anglophone school districts by 17. Even though the newly constituted school boards were responsible for more schools and for larger geographical areas, the staffing allocation for district-level personnel in each school district office was similar to that which had existed in any one of the previous 27 districts. As a result, the workload of school district personnel became unmanageable, as indicated by one director of education of that time period:

> For directors and assistants directors, it became a 24-7 job. We had a new Schools Act that redefined authority and a new involvement of the minister of education. It was onerous. A lot of new people had to learn new roles.

An assistant director of programs in another school district, who otherwise expressed considerable support for the legislated reform, was quite distressed over what he perceived to be the unreasonable staffing levels allocated by the government in the context of the major structural reforms that school boards were expected to manage:

> The political masters decreed change, and the people in the system were expected to make it work. Stress levels and work hours increased significantly. Senior administrators worked tremendous hours, nights, and weekends.... Much time was required setting up administrative structures and consolidating schools.

He noted, furthermore, that these additional administrative responsibilities diverted attentions away from student learning: "It probably took three years or more before we got back to the curriculum based issues (e.g., resource based learning)...trying to get away from chalk and talk. Schools were left in many ways to set their own direction." Another senior district administrator, while sharing a similar view in respect to the demands of school system reconfigurations, indicated that the newly created districts were understaffed in respect to available supports to schools and classroom teachers:

> Prior to 1996–1997 we had the optimal system for support to schools and teachers. Up to the end of 27 boards we had program coordinators for each subject area, and there was support from board office for all teachers. Then, following restructuring, the administration levels were decimated and the level of

support from program coordinators for teachers was turned on its head.... The impact on teachers was very traumatic. They were used to knowing who the director, assistant directors, program coordinators, and other support staff were. They were used to seeing us visit their schools and classrooms. That connection with the school board office was gone. They did not feel part of the system anymore. That closeness [and] that familiarity was missing.

To complicate matters further, under the new restructured school system, district officials began to observe increased government control. The new Schools Act gave increased power to the minister of education and his or her officials, and district administrators began to observe more direct engagement of provincial politicians in educational issues. For instance, one director of education stated that he and his colleagues found it challenging "to work within this new political influence. In public meetings around school closure and construction, Cabinet Ministers and MHAs were [many times] in attendance, and sometimes they would pull the rug right out from under me."

All of our interviewees from districts throughout the province were unequivocal that the first restructuring that commenced in the early 1990s refocused, for at least a decade, the attention of school boards, school personnel, and parents toward structural and governance issues and away from issues that directly related to teaching and learning in schools. Paradoxically, during the same time period, the government became more focused on the measurement of student outcomes. The following comment by a senior department of education official of that era confirms that paradox:

The department of education was focused on efficiency and the measurement of effectiveness—getting the biggest bang for the buck—and they were concerned for outputs in respect to student scores on provincial tests. [However], there was little concern for new programs to improve teaching and learning.

The school boards were just beginning to re-establish a focus on teaching and learning when the 2004 restructuring occurred. As a consequence of this latter restructuring initiative, the school district focus was once again on issues of structure as the existing school boards became little more than caretaker boards for several months while the new boards struggled with their new role. In addition, all district-level educational personnel became focused on personal-professional welfare issues as most were declared redundant. To further complicate matters, within a few weeks of the government's announcement of school board restructuring, all the school boards were engaged in managing a lengthy support-staff strike. Although the basic school board restructuring event occurred within the designated timeframe of five months, the newly formed school boards and their senior administrators reported that the newly designed system was underfunded and understaffed. For instance, one school board reported that they were forced to declare redundant 40 per cent of the district-level support and instructional personnel. This greatly reduced the possibility of the direct engagement of district professionals in the delivery of program support at the school level, leading one director to comment as follows:

> From an administrative perspective, I will say we made it work, but from an instructional leadership view, I don't think anyone was under any illusion that things were happening in schools the way they normally did.... The ranks of district consultants and program coordinators were decimated!

The following comment from one school principal three years after the school district restructuring event supports the accuracy of the previous observation that the school districts' attentions were diverted away from the classroom and student learning:

> Prior to the 2004 restructuring of school districts, 80 per cent of the classrooms in my school were connected to the internet and several classrooms were set up as professional learning centres; however, since then there has been very little emphasis on the integration of technology in the teaching and learning process.

It appears that school districts are now much better funded and staffed. There is an emerging level of optimism among senior administrators at both the department of education and the district level, and there is an emerging collaborative climate and a more unified sense of educational direction than in the past. Notwithstanding this new optimism, those who have continued in senior posts at the school district level recognize the negative impact that the 2004 school district restructuring has had upon district initiatives that had been focused on improving teaching and student learning. The only respondent that spoke positively of the 2004 restructuring process was an individual who had been a senior official with the department of education at the time it occurred. The common view expressed by school district administrators is best illustrated by the response given by one senior district official. When asked to identify a word, phrase, or metaphor that best described his district's culture and any changes that might have impacted that culture in recent years, he responded with "the 2004 restructuring put us off the rails." However, after a brief pause, he offered an alternative metaphor. He referred to it as "a landslide" and offered the following elaboration:

> Prior to the former districts coming together we had three fertile fields (3 districts) and then, with restructuring we had a major landslide. We have spent the last three years scraping off the debris and removing the boulders.... The soil is fertile once again... lots of seeds have been planted that we believe will bear much fruit/crop. People are beginning to buy in and I feel good about where we are. However, had this landslide not happened, and had the same amount of energy and resources been expended as was necessary to do the cleanup, it is hard to imagine where we might be right now. The reform effort served a crippling blow to the education system...[and] the many gains that would have otherwise been reaped have been lost forever.

In spite of the emerging optimism of those district administrators who are currently working at the district level, the general view of most senior district officials is that since the 2004 legislated restructuring of school districts, government and its officials have assumed near total control over school boards. For instance, one school district official suggested that prior to the 2004 restructuring, the department of education officials and their political masters believed that the directors of education held too much local power. In his view, the changes in legislation in 2004 gave control to the government and its senior department of education bureaucrats. Another senior district administrator observed similarly, that since 2004 "this government has become so influential in education that everyone has kowtowed to them." This view was supported by a senior official of the teachers' association, as well:

> In the current structure no single district director, school board chair, or provincial school boards association challenges the government any more. The current climate stifles independent thought. The word controlling comes to mind.... The more the Department of Education and the Minister takes a top-down approach in directing the districts, the more things [programs] become politically driven.

Whether or not it was the government's intent to assume more control over the public education system, from the perspective of the vast majority of our interviewees inside and outside of school districts, this has become a reality.

In addition to the widespread perception that the newly created school boards are controlled by the government, there appears to be a growing view that the geographical region for which each board is responsible is too large. A high profile representative of the Federation of School Councils commented:

> Under the previous system of school boards there was a person (a program specialist) responsible for/assigned to school councils to help train them and to encourage positive parental involvement. There was good team building between boards and school councils. There was little turf protection. This support was eliminated through the latest government restructuring of school boards. Now nothing exists to help school councils. Bigger boards make it much more difficult for parents to get answers. In fact, parents say they get quicker answers from the Department of Education since restructuring. The current system is disjointed and fragmented, and there is a lack of cooperation and trust among organizations. In the current setup, I don't see the value of having school boards at all.

The teachers' association representative shared similar views, noting that he has lost confidence in the new school boards. In his view, trust between agencies such as school boards and teachers' associations is contingent upon the establishing of strong relationships which has not been established since the 2004 restructuring largely because the boards have become too large to manage:

> We find it is more difficult to meet directly with district leaders... we can't get to them, anymore. We used to be able to pick up the phone and talk to the directors. The whole basis for the government's latest round of school board restructuring was dollar savings. Our position is that you can't reduce the number of boards to four and expect there will be the same attention to things as before. The phrase "the tyranny of the immediate" is very much the case today.

Beyond the directly observable effects of restructuring upon school districts and schools and the relationships with major educational stakeholder groups, perhaps little recognized is the extent to which restructuring interrupted the growing school district-community partnerships in support of both improved student learning opportunities and community development, particularly in rural regions of the province. For instance, several school districts took the lead role in working with community partners to champion the development of the information and communications technology infrastructure throughout their geographical region. An assistant director who worked as a partnership coordinator in a school district opined that much leadership has been lost as a result of school board restructuring:

> Government does not see the larger role that a school district can play within a community. The role of the district was similar to the [leadership] role that teachers played during the 1950s and 1960s when we had a school in every community.... In a sense, the school board became that individual teacher in the larger [district] community.... It provided the leadership that I think we've lost...as a result of school board restructuring.

The following observation by a senior district administrator—although more optimistic than most about the future benefits of the government's educational reform agenda over the past two decades—summarizes the most commonly held view of the impacts of restructuring upon student learning:

> While it appears that we may now be poised to offer a better education to our children than in the past, we may have done a disservice to a whole generation of students in the process of getting here as attentions have been diverted away from the core business of K-12 education—student learning.

If this is indeed an accurate perception, it should be of considerable concern to all who hold the power to engage in such restructuring activities. Furthermore, it suggests that if restructuring of school systems is deemed necessary, careful consideration must be given to how potential negative impacts upon current and future students can be mitigated.

Conclusions

There is growing evidence that the key to building sustainability of reforms is to build leadership capacity at the multiple levels of the educational system and that schools, districts, and government must work together (Sackney, 2007). Unfortunately, the common corporate managerialist approach that is typical of many OECD countries is not conducive to meaningful school reform. Within that approach, rather than working in partnership with school boards, some governments have chosen either to control them or to eliminate them altogether. In many jurisdictions similar to Newfoundland and Labrador, the government has chosen to downsize and restructure school boards as a means of achieving efficiencies while at the same time they have reduced their level of autonomy through legislation. Although such an approach may give the appearance of improved efficiencies and heightened levels of accountability, and may even produce short term gains in test scores, evidence from the Newfoundland and Labrador experience suggests that the engagement of such an exercise over a long period of time is likely to stifle meaningful improvements in teaching and learning processes. In fact, there is considerable evidence that the level of central control inherent in such an approach may improve fiscal and bureaucratic accountability and force district and school personnel to follow the rules and regulations of the government; however, it does little to foster the kind of creative thinking and organizational learning required to facilitate meaningful sustained educational reform (Duffy, 2004).

My colleagues and I (Sheppard et al., 2009) have concluded that a more successful approach to sustainable educational reform is as follows:

> For governments...to work with successful school districts and researchers in the field of leadership to ensure that school boards and district leaders are aware of and understand the emerging empirical evidence in support of collaborative leadership and organizational learning and to support them as they engage in the challenging work of transforming themselves from traditional hierarchical bureaucracies to dynamic professional learning communities. (p. 132)

Although this alternative approach is complex and challenging and there is no clear road-map on how to bring it about, it holds more promise than doing nothing or repeating the failures of the past. What is most certain is that constant government-imposed school board restructuring and the imposition of more centralized government control that is accompanied by an intensifying focus upon a narrowly defined student testing regime are not in the long-term best interest of authentic student learning, social justice, or the continued development of an enlightened democratic society.

Chapter Eleven

The Impact of Education Reform on School Board Governance

David Dibbon, Bruce Sheppard, and Jean Brown

The existence of school boards is a reflection of society's deep-rooted belief that educational governance should reflect community and regional values and priorities. Typically, school boards are created through provincial legislation, commonly termed as Schools Acts and/or Education Acts. Among other things, a Schools Act identifies school districts and their boundaries, the composition of boards, powers and duties of the board, powers of the minister, and duties of the board's director of education. What separates school boards from most other government entities is that, usually, their members are publicly elected.[1] In this way they are similar to municipal councils, and like municipal councils, school boards have historically been granted autonomous status, despite the fact they are often funded directly by government.

Historically, school boards have been free to make educational decisions independently from the daily machinations of provincial politics, provided they act within boundaries specified in the legislation that governs them. Legislation usually contains safeguards to permit a government to take disciplinary action against a board; such action may include the suspension or dissolution of a board, or dismissal of some if its members, should it become evident that a board is acting in an irregular, improper, or improvident manner (Schools Act, 1997).

There are numerous examples of government intervention into school board operations in recent years. For example, in 1985, the government of the day in British Columbia exercised its jurisdiction to "dismiss the Vancouver School Board trustees and appoint an official trustee to administer the affairs of the school board" (Ungerleider, 2006, p. 80). In December, 2006, in the province of Nova Scotia, the minister of education dismissed all 13 elected members of the Halifax Regional School Board because of interpersonal conflicts and failure to comply with the code of ethics. The minister stated, "This board has failed to meet the performance standards set out under Section 64 (6) of the Education Act. Sec. 64 states that a school board, in carrying out its responsibilities under this act, shall meet education program services and performance standards established by the minister" (Canadian Broadcasting Corporation, 2006, p. 1). There have been at least five recent cases in Ontario in which governments have intervened in the work of school boards for failing to balance their books. The Progressive Conservative government took over the Toronto District School Board, Hamilton-Wentworth District School Board, and Ottawa-Carlton District School Board in August, 2002, and in 2006 the Liberal government sent in a supervisor to manage a budget deficit in the Dufferin-Peel Catholic District School Board (Rushowy & Brown, 2008, p. 2). In a more recent case, the minister of education in Ontario appointed a supervisor to oversee the "financial management and administration of the Toronto Catholic District School Board" (Queen's Printer for Ontario, 2008-2009a, p. 1). In making her decision the minister stated:

> The board's actions have called into question the trustees' credibility, and as a result, I have no confidence in their ability to continue to manage the board's affairs. My actions today will ensure that this board is put back on track so that it can make responsible decisions that are in the best interests of students. Public confidence in this board must be restored. (Queen's Printer for Ontario, 2008–2009a, p. 1)

Given their autonomous nature, it is natural that school board actions sometimes cause tensions between them and the governments who create and provide for them. Particularly in today's political milieu, with increasing media scrutiny, competing demands for resources, and increased accountability, provincial politicians are more interested in, and sometimes vocal about, school board policy and decisions. For example, in the recent case in Ontario, while the minister of education acknowledged school board trustees as important partners in publicly funded education she clearly stated that "families and taxpayers rely on them to govern their boards and make spending decisions in a transparent and accountable way" (Queen's Printer for Ontario, 2008–2009b, p. 1) and that they would be held accountable to that standard. In some recent instances in Newfoundland and Labrador, provincial politicians have publicly challenged board decisions with respect to school closures, with the effect of delaying or altering decisions that had already been taken by school boards. In one very public case, in the midst of an election campaign, the premier of the province stepped in and stated openly to the people of Bishops Falls that a school in their community, that had been scheduled for closure by the Nova Central School Board, would not close; he stated "We're satisfied...the school is viable" (Jackson, 2005, p. 4). The premier said "this was not a sign that government is prepared to overrule school boards but if boards...make decisions that are wrong decisions, then we have a responsibility to make the right ones" (Jackson, 2005, p. 4). Subsequent to that public statement, in a special school board meeting, held in April 2006, the Nova Central School District (2006, p. 2) moved to revisit their earlier motion to close the school in question and replaced it with another motion that would see the school remain open.

It is against this backdrop that we chose to report on the findings from data collected during the first year of an ongoing four-year leadership study in which the authors are engaged. Although we did not set out to investigate or examine governance, accountability, or autonomy at the school board level, the evidence that emerged from a series of interviews that we completed with 25 former and current senior educational administrators revealed that government mandated educational reform that occurred over the span of 12 years had considerable impact on school board governance, accountability, and autonomy. It is this impact that we examine in this chapter.

The evolution of school board governance in Newfoundland and Labrador

School boards in Newfoundland and Labrador have a history dating back to the early 1800s. Newfoundland's representative colonial government, created in 1832, drafted the colony's first Education Act in 1836 (Rowe, 1964). The Act established a public system of education administered by local school boards. Although it was intended to be non-denominational in nature, it did include a provision for local clergy as board ex officio members. The Act of 1843 marked the beginning of legislative provisions for the denominational system of education and denominational school boards, naming the Roman Catholic and Protestant denominations (Rowe, 1964). Rowe also documents the fact that subsequent Acts (e.g., 1858 and 1873) went on to differentiate between, and accord provisions for, specific Protestant denominations (Anglican, Methodist, Salvation Army, and Pentecostal).

Newfoundland became Canada's tenth province on March 31, 1949. Term 17 of the Terms of Union with Canada gave Newfoundland the exclusive authority to make laws governing primary and secondary education in the province. As Glenn Loveless in Chapter Eight notes, Term 17 also enshrined the rights of the four predominant religious denominations (Anglican, Roman Catholic, Methodist, and Salvation Army) to continue their governance function in education. The Pentecostal Assemblies of Newfoundland were accorded Term 17 status with the Amendment of the Constitution Act 1982.

Although there are numerous references to the denominational education system in the scholarly literature about the Newfoundland and Labrador school system (e.g., McCann, 1988a; Rowe, 1964), during our interviews some doubt was raised as to whether or not the system prior to 1997 was indeed that! At least one long-serving, high-ranking civil servant who worked with the provincial Department of Education claimed that what really existed was a 100 per cent publicly funded education system that was organized along denominational lines. In iterating this point, she noted, "you won't find reference to a denominational system of education in formal [Newfoundland and Labrador] Department of Education documents." This is in contrast to some other provinces (e.g., Ontario) in which religious schools funded by government constitute a private system.

Since Confederation with Canada, there have been three Education Acts (1952, 1960, 1968), followed by the Schools Acts of 1969, 1996, and 1997. The Education Act, 1960 provided for the greatest number of school boards in the province's history, at 335. This number consisted of 95 Anglican, 90 United Church, 80 Roman Catholic, 18 Salvation Army, 9 Methodist, 4 Presbyterian, 1 Congregational, 1 Seventh-Day Adventist, 1 Pentecostal Assembly, and 35 Amalgamated boards (Andrews, 1985b). The peak in the number of school boards loosely coincided with peak number of schools (1266 in 1962–1963) (Government of Newfoundland and Labrador, 1992b) and students (162,818 in 1971–1972) (Government of Newfoundland and Labrador, 2002b).

The 1969 Schools Act further solidified the churches' rights in educational governance and would shape the face of education, in a significant way, for the next 28 years. In addition to the 38 denominational school boards that it created, a denominational governance superstructure was established in the form of a Denominational Education Commission. Under the aegis of the commission, three education committees were established; Roman Catholic, Pentecostal, and Integrated. The Protestant religions, in an Act referred to as the "Act of Integration," had earlier agreed to exercise their rights in education collectively. Under the legislation, until 1997 Denominational Education Committees (DECs) were given authority over new school construction and renovation. School boards' annual priorities and requests for capital works projects were forwarded to the respective DECs which made decisions regarding which projects were to be funded. School boards and directors of education dealt directly with the DECs on these matters with little involvement by the Department of Education, the minister, or local politicians. The elimination of the DECs in 1997 placed decision making related to the distribution of capital funding in the hands of a Department of Education School Construction Committee, whose decisions became more subject to political pressures. To a lesser degree, issues relating to school closures and the location of new schools also became fair game for politicians' comment and involvement. The abolition of the DECs removed a significant intermediary between school boards and government departments, particularly the Department of Education; as a result education decision making seems to have become somewhat politicized. As one former director of education commented:

> The one thing I questioned in all the change was the removal of the Denominational Education Committees (DECs). Up to 1995 this was a significant educational structure in the province. Up to that point politicians were never involved in school construction [or school] closure issues. Previously, when we got into closing schools, we were always in the milieu of the community trying to deal with questions. Politicians were never there. The DECs provided a buffer from the raw politics. In 1996 the DECs were disbanded leaving a void. The provincial politicians began to take on more prominence with respect to educational issues. Cabinet ministers wanted to have involvement. As an administrator I had to learn to work with the new political influence. In the new non-denominational system, in public meetings around school closure and construction, cabinet ministers, and MHAs were [many times] in attendance...sometimes they would pull the rug right out from under me.

Aside from its articulation of the abolition of the DECs, the 1997 Schools Act represented a huge change in the governance of education in the province of Newfoundland and Labrador. The Act reflected the recommendations of the Royal Commission on Primary, Elementary, and Secondary Education, *Our Children, Our Future* (Government of Newfoundland and Labrador, 1992b) and the results of a second provincial referendum on the role of churches in educational governance. The second referendum was triggered by the intransigence of the various denominational groups and their inability to reach a compromise on the level of church involvement in education. While we believe there was no deliberate intent by the designers of the reform initiative to oust the churches from education (e.g., Government of Newfoundland and Labrador, 1992b), when an agreement could not be forged, this was the end result . In the referendum, the voting public opted for a single school system in which all children, regardless of their religious affiliation, attended the same schools. The result was the dismantling of denominational schools, denominational school boards, and DECs. A former employee of the Department of Education, however, explained it this way:

> The objective [of education reform] was to extinguish the role of denominational authorities from the governance of K-12 education...in fairness this was driven by excess duplication in the system. Money was tight, there were many small schools, and busing was a problem.... Also, a lot of people wanted the churches out.

The 1997 Act also decreased the number of school boards in the province to 11. While eliminating a number of educational structures, the 1997 Schools Act created a new one, school councils, the implementation of which had already begun immediately following the 1992 Royal Commission Report. This introduction of school councils represented a significant philosophical shift in the governance of education in Newfoundland and Labrador. Central to this shift was a commitment to changing the decision-making process at the school level to include school staff, parents, community members, and where possible, students. Other support for the establishment of school councils followed the Royal Commission's Report, including *Adjusting the Course: Restructuring the School System for Educational Excellence* (Government of Newfoundland and Labrador, 1993) and *Adjusting the Course: Part Two: Improving the Conditions for Learning* (Government of Newfoundland and Labrador, 1994b). The substance of these discussion documents resulted in the establishment of a steering committee for school council implementation, and pilot school councils were set up in seven schools around Newfoundland and Labrador (Collins, Harte, & Cooper, 1995). In 1996, legislation was introduced mandating that every school in the province was to have a school council by the 1997–1998 school year. This legislation accorded school councils advisory status only.

In a somewhat surprising and less consultative move in 2004, a new provincial government moved to further reduce the number of school boards from 11 to 5, resulting in another amendment to the Schools Act. A former director of education thought that the 2004 consolidation was "clearly a po-litical decision." She indicated that they actually asked the government when they were in opposition, "If elected would a PC government consoli-date school boards?" She indicated she was shocked when the decision was made saying, "We were told in no uncertain terms that the government had no intentions to do this whatsoever." Former high-ranking employees in the Department of Education corroborated this stance and one explained:

> The second consolidation...there were no discussions that I was part of leading up to a decision. The Conservative party was in power and...there was a new minister of education. There was some sense of saving money, but no real rationale was provided... no planning groups had been established. There was only a two- to three-month lead-time for the Department to prepare. At the out-set there was some talk of putting a group of officials within the Department of Education together to oversee the change. But this didn't really happen. There was no formal planning process; to the extent that there was any collaboration... it was kept secret from ev-eryone, except a few officials within the Department of Education. In the budget lockup for directors of education and school board chairs, in March, the district directors of education and chairs first learned the news. They were totally taken off guard.

In a relatively short period of time the educational landscape in Newfound-land has changed dramatically. The most recent published statistics reveals a public school system with five school boards, 280 schools, and just under 69,000 students (Government of Newfoundland and Labrador, 2011).

Accountability and the relationships between government and school boards

Schools Acts typically define the powers and duties of the board, duties of the director, and powers of the minister. In addition, these Acts outline the areas in which the Lieutenant-Governor in Council (Cabinet) can make regulations intended to give effect to the purpose of the Act. A number of school board powers granted through the Schools Acts are somewhat restricted in that they are subject to the approval of the minister. In the current Schools Act this applies to the appointment of directors and assistant directors, entering into employment contracts with directors and assistant directors, selling and leasing of property, and raising of money upon a board's corporate credit.

Broadly speaking, the role of school boards as defined in most legislation is to organize and administer primary, elementary, and secondary education; provide for the instruction of students; and determine policy for the effective operation of schools. In so doing, boards are permitted to appoint and dismiss teachers and other employees, purchase any property it requires, and establish priorities for school construction and maintenance. The current Schools Act states that a board, in carrying out its mandate, is responsible to the minister for the expenditure of public funds, the conduct of programs of instruction and evaluation, and the maintenance of adequate program and performance standards in schools in the district. Among other things, most Schools Acts empower the minister of education to prescribe student programs and resources, and issue policy directives, most notably with respect to student and school evaluation, student transportation, special education, and the allocation and distribution of grants to districts. Under the 1997 Schools Act, a director of education can be required by the minister to attend meetings and institutes, and make annual reports to the Department on the district's education program.

As noted above, although the powers of school boards are laid out in dedicated sections of a Schools Act, these powers are somewhat restricted by clauses in the Act pertaining to the powers of the minister and cabinet. These qualifying powers of the minister and cabinet appear, for the most part, to be imprecisely defined, thereby leaving jurisdictional issues open to interpretation. Consequently, when governments wish to either exercise tight control over boards or when they wish to remove themselves from a contentious issue, they can choose to interpret the legislation in a manner that best suits their needs. Interpretations are communicated directly in the form of a ministerial policy directive, or more indirectly, through actions and stated expectations of the minister and/or the Lieutenant-Governor in Council. Such interpretations are by nature subjective and may not be consistent with either the role and powers of any of the parties as set out in the Schools Act.

Prior to the consolidation of school boards in 2004, there was considerable tension between the boards and the government of the time. Among the most troublesome were the rights of school boards to enter into contracts with their CEOs and to determine their salary and benefits, from which emerged several legal challenges. Other issues related to school board budgeting and school restructuring processes. In the *Supporting Learning: Report of the Ministerial Panel on Education Delivery in the Classroom* (Government of Newfoundland and Labrador, 2000), the government stated, "what is also clear is that the current system of governance and board administration is not fully compatible with the constructs of responsibility and accountability that rest ultimately with the provincial government" (p. 76). The document further notes that government is providing 100 per cent of the funding for the K-12 school system and that elected boards and executive staff hired by the boards are not functionally linked to government in ways that promote and ensure the necessary measures of dual responsibility and accountability (p. 76). As a result, the Panel recommended that "the Schools Act (1997) be amended to accommodate a change to the legislative procedures for the appointment, termination and accountability of school district directors to parallel that of the model in place under the Colleges Act (1996)" (p. 77). Under such a model directors of education would be "charged with dual accountability in that the individual is accountable to the school board for the operation of the district while fostering cooperation between the board and the government" (p. 76). To date, this amendment to the Schools Act has not been made official but there are many (including current and former district executive employees and board members) who think the education system operates under the assumption of a dual accountability to the board and the minister.

There are many models of school governance (e.g., Carver, 2006; McAdams, 2006); however, the model of governance that has evolved in Newfoundland and Labrador most closely resembles policy governance as outlined by Carver. Arguably, under this model, the most important decision a board makes pertains to the selection of its director of education. The director is the person who implements the policies of the board and manages the day-to-day affairs of the district. Under this model, a board has only one employee—the director. Given the magnitude of the board's role and the liability it might incur should it fail to live up to responsibilities outlined in legislation, it can be argued that it is critical that the accountability relationship between the school board and its director be unfettered. The board needs to be assured that the director acts on its behalf only, and that the board's ability to carry out its mandate through the director is not compromised. Conversely, under a model of policy governance the director needs to know that even with the responsibility for fostering cooperation between the board and the government she or he takes direction from only one source, and that she or he is not torn between competing loyalties.

Similar to previous Acts, the current Schools Act (1997) empowers a board to appoint its director, subject to the approval of the minister. Until recently, such approval was mostly a formality with no involvement in the recruitment process by the minister or staff from the minister's office. Prior to the amendment to the Schools Act in 2004, rarely, if ever, was a board's choice of candidate rejected. The power of the board to choose its director, and hold her or him accountable solely to the board, has been tested since the 2004 consolidation of school districts.

As noted in 2004, as part of its budgetary planning process, with little advanced warning and no input from the educational community, the government announced that school boards would be further reduced in number. In short order, a legislative amendment was passed, transitional committees were appointed, and recruiting commenced for new directors and assistant directors to staff the new districts. Three actions taken by the Department of Education throughout the recruitment process, some of which still continue, have impacted boards' autonomy and arms-length relationship from government.

The first action involves the release of a standardized job-advertisement for board executive-level positions. At the direction of the Department, transitional committees released job advertisements containing language that implied accountability of directors and assistant directors to the minister of education, and there are at least two people who were interviewed for those positions who indicated that they were asked questions directly related to dual accountability. The second action was a requirement that Department of Education executive staff participate in the interviewing and selection process for these positions. The third and perhaps the most intrusive of the actions pertained to contracts for new directors and assistant directors. The Department insisted that employment contracts with the new directors contain clauses that would, in effect, have directors reporting to (i.e., be accountable to), both the minister of education and the school board. All of these actions go beyond provisions in the Schools Act and past practices in most jurisdictions across the country. However, in the process, precedents that would affect the working relationship between the director of education, school boards, and the Department of Education were established.

Draft contracts proposed by the Department of Education in 2003 contained clauses making the director accountable to the minister and the board for the expenditure of funds, and required the director to advise the minister when, in her or his opinion, the affairs of the Board were managed in an "irregular, improper or improvident manner." In addition, the draft contract language would have required the strategic plan of the board to be prepared "in consultation with an officer of the Department of Education." As well, the draft contained a clause providing for a member of the Department of Education to sit on a board committee struck for the purpose of conducting an annual performance appraisal of the director. When considered in the context of the final contract clause stating that the director's contract may not be renewed or extended without prior written approval of the minister, concerns were expressed by the directors individually, the Newfoundland and Labrador Association for Directors of Education, and some board members.

Much of the language around *dual accountability* was eventually omitted from final signed director contacts, but in the intervening years of contract negotiations, a vacuum was created wherein boards and directors were uncertain about the directors' reporting/accountability relationships. As one retired school administrator noted:

> the director is very unclear as to who he or she is responsible to.... There is a certain schizophrenia that can take over when you're in that position. Because of the dual accountability there is a tension as to whether you are an advocate of students or whether you're protecting your minister. They are not compatible roles.

Another noted that the dual accountability role has "put directors of education off balance." Most of the people interviewed in this study were, like us, under the impression that the dual accountability requirement was written in legislation and/or in the director's signed contracts. One of the former directors noted that while "it is not recorded in the contracts or the legislation, it gets its power from the Transparency and Accountability Act." However, when we checked the Transparency and Accountability Act no reference could be found to the concept of dual accountability and, in fact, the accountability of the CEO (director of education) in Type 1 bodies, such as school boards, is now clearly defined as being to the chairperson of the public body (Transparency and Accountability Act, 2004).

The chain of events that occurred in the province since the 2004 amendment to the Schools Act has conspired, for good or for bad, to destabilize school board governance and provided an opportunity for the Department of Education to alter their working relationships with school boards and their directors of education. Whether real or imagined, a result of the perception of the dual accountability for directors of education has resulted in the autonomy of school boards being questioned. In the next section we examine the issue of school board autonomy and posit why school boards' autonomy may have eroded since the Education Act of 1997.

The erosion of school board autonomy

In Chapter One, Gerald Galway and David Dibbon present an argument that relies on the political-social-historical review of antecedent policy influencers to represent the events of a decade-and-a-half of education reform. Using the metaphor of a perfect storm of policy drivers, they provide evidence to show that the secularization of education and the reform of the denominational education system in Newfoundland and Labrador was inevitable. One of the drivers that they highlighted in that chapter was a response to the "achievement problem." Although Newfoundland and Labrador students can be seen to have made impressive gains in many areas in recent years, the province's position on many key achievement indicators still remains below the Canadian average and below the position of several other Canadian provinces.

It is well known in Newfoundland and Labrador that the Department of Education has attempted to raise the performance levels of students by raising standards and increasing the accountability of educators to meet those standards as measured by performance on standardized tests (e.g., criterion referenced tests). As well, provincial policies and practices throughout Canada have become increasingly impacted by national and international agendas that appear to be somewhat driven by globalization and the rapidly emerging information and communication technologies (Taylor, Rizvi, Lingard, & Henry, 1997). While these influences are somewhat embedded in ongoing social change, the direct observable shifts in provincial policies, structures, and governance appear to be largely influenced by the OECD and the CMEC as they respond to "the political work of various social movements" (Taylor et al., 1997, p. 3).

Taylor et al. (1997) argue that as "society has become more complex, and interest groups more assertive...education is no longer discussed in terms of broad visions and ideals but in terms of what governments believe to be possible and often expedient, and what interest groups feel they can persuade governments to do" (p. 3). As a result of such a shift, "education is increasingly regarded as an [economic] commodity, [rather than] a public good" (Shaker & Grimmett, 2004, p. 29). Considered as a commodity, it must be quantified so that the educational assets of a province/state or country can be compared to others. Consequently, it is not surprising that although school boards are granted responsibility in law for establishing the policies and regulations that govern the operations of the education system within their geographic boundaries, this control has proved historically to be more apparent than real—resulting in nothing more than the "illusion of local control" (Fleming & Hutton, 1997, p. 4).

Historically, school boards in Newfoundland and Labrador and throughout North America have been shielded from the to-and-fro of provincial and state politics, and as long as they were operating within their mandate, they were free to govern and make independent decisions based upon the best interests of students. In our research, many former directors and assistant directors of education, along with school board members, viewed the 2004 amendment to the Schools Act and the subsequent consolidation of school boards as an attempt by the government to gain greater control over school boards.

A former director of education alluded to a strained relationship between boards and the Department of Education in the years leading up to the 1997 consolidation. He commented that "those of us with history as directors saw the erosion of autonomy and we resisted. This meant we were not working together [with government] to make changes and this frustrated the Department." Corroborating this point of view, two former Department of Education officials noted that prior to 1997 government officials had become somewhat frustrated with the boards because "they were making it difficult to implement province-wide changes." The second official noted that between 1997 and 2003 school boards had grown resentful of what they perceived to be the government's autocratic approach in responding to special-interest groups, and as a result they were resisting government initiatives. He commented:

> Boards felt they were left out there to make decisions as long as the Department/minister agreed with these decisions. When political pressures were brought to bear by the public and special interest groups...government sometimes intervened. We'll let you run the district until decisions impact us. This erodes authority at the district level.

Another former department official expressed concern that the education system had become too centralized. She was under the impression that the current five directors were accountable to the minister and the school board, and as a result she opined that "the directors run their decisions by the minister before final implementation/approval."

School board consolidation also seems to have impacted the Department of Education's view of how school board district offices should function. A former director indicated that after consolidation "district offices were dictated to more...we began to be seen more as an extension of the Department of Education/minister's office as opposed to autonomous organizations, not as a corporation but as a satellite of the Department." A number of interviewees questioned whether under such a centralized model, boards could be effective:

> In 2003 the biggest impact on trustees was the centralization of decision making by the minister...decisions that were historically left to boards to make. People are asking if boards have any authority any more. More and more it is the Department of Education that is the face of education. Even the media goes to the Department first. The common element is the minister.

Some interviewees contend that the residual effects of the events that followed the 2004 amendment are evident in the apparent reluctance of boards and directors to put forward positions and make decisions that may not meet with the approval of the Department. A few interviewees expressed the concern that directors and boards have become compromised in their ability to advocate on behalf of students. A former assistant director rhetorically asked "how do you advocate against an issue that your political masters are for?" One of the former directors indicated that the environment had become more politicized, claiming that for him the biggest impact was the requirement to be more politically astute:

> We now had to be as concerned about the way the province sees things as opposed to what makes sense for our organizations. There were pressures to take certain actions (imposed) that were not necessarily things I agreed with. Sometimes no amount of explanation about local variables and factors could get through— we lost the connectivity with local communities.

Writing on the issue of autonomy and local control of education in the USA in the 1980s, Doyle and Finn (1984), argued that "local control of public education as traditionally conceived is in reality disappearing, even though its facade is nearly everywhere intact" (p. 90). In reality, local school systems appear to be evolving in practice into something that they always were in a constitutional sense: subordinate administrative units of a provincial educational system. Doyle and Finn's observations, together with the work of Elmore (2004), might help us understand, a little more clearly, the shifting relationship between government and schools boards during an era of education reform in Newfoundland and Labrador where government accountability has increased and school board autonomy has been questioned.

Elmore (2004) describes a system of "loose-coupling" (Meyer & Rowan, 1992; Rowan, 1990; Weick, 1976) that he perceives to have been the standard model for school systems in the USA in the 1960s and 1970s. This view, in brief, posits that:

> the "technical core" of education—detailed decisions about what should be taught at any given time, how it should be taught, what students should be expected to learn at any given time, how they should be grouped within classrooms for purposes of instruction, what they should be required to do to demonstrate their knowledge, and, perhaps most importantly, how their learning should be evaluated—resides in individual classrooms, not in the organizations that surround them.
>
> Furthermore, the model posited that knowledge at the technical core is weak and uncertain (Bidwell, 1965; Lortie, 1975). It cannot be clearly translated into reproducible behaviors, it requires a high degree of individual judgement, and it is not susceptible to reliable external evaluation. Therefore, the loose-coupling argument continues, the administrative superstructure of the organization—principals, board members, and administrators—exists to "buffer" the weak technical core of teaching from outside inspection, interference, or disruption. (p. 46)

In what appears to have been well-intended efforts to increase school board accountability and to strengthen the "technical core" of education, it may well be possible that the Department of Education in Newfoundland and Labrador has assumed more than its responsibility for the "technical core" and along the way usurped school board autonomy. The evidence in this chapter would seem to support this possibility. As a result it appears that administration and governance of education in Newfoundland and Labrador has come to mean:

> not the management of instruction but the management of the structures and processes around instruction.... [where] local board members, system-level administrators, and school administrators perform the ritualistic tasks of organizing, budgeting, managing, and dealing with disruptions inside and outside the system, all in the name of creating and maintaining public confidence in the institutions of public education. (Elmore, 2004, pp. 46–47)

If this is the case, the institutional theory of loose-coupling might explain a great deal about the strengths and pathologies of the existing structure of public education in Newfoundland and Labrador.

> It explains why, for example, most innovation in schools (and the most durable innovations) occur in the structures that surround teaching and learning, and only weakly and idiosyncratically in the actual processes of teaching and learning. Most innovation is about maintaining the logic of confidence between the public and the schools, not about changing the conditions of teaching and learning for actual teachers and students. The theory of loose–coupling explains why schools continue to promote structures and to engage in practices that research and experience suggest are manifestly not productive for the learning of certain students. (p. 47)

Reform of the education system in Newfoundland and Labrador appears to have impacted boards and changed the relationship between them, the Department of Education, and government generally. Perceptions of government interference in board decision making has impacted the way boards are viewed by the general public, how boards view themselves, and how board members view their roles. Interviewees described boards as less autonomous, more bureaucratic, and more remote from the publics they are elected to serve. They also described an education system that is more centralized and influenced by politics at the provincial level. Yet, researchers have been told by teachers, and school and district administrators that classrooms remain largely unchanged (Atlantic Evaluation and Research Consultants, 2008).

Conclusion

As historians of education reflect on the late twentieth and early twenty-first century of education in Newfoundland and Labrador, they will almost certainly describe it as a critical period of changing policy perspectives on public education. While a lot has happened in education in Newfoundland and Labrador over the past 15 years, what has probably not been as clear to parents and the public is the development of a more subtle centralization in terms of how the education system is governed. For better or worse, school boards today are in a different place than they were prior to 1997. Education reform in Newfoundland and Labrador resulted in a fundamental shift in the power relationships between the Department of Education, schools boards, and directors of education.

Prior to 1997, the province operated on a decentralized model of governance in which school boards operated very independently of government and their accountability to government was low. Directors of education were fully accountable to their boards and as a result the Department of Education had little control over how boards functioned. Since 1997, an era of high government accountability has emerged and as a result government has imposed a more centralized form of governance that sees the director of education being accountable to the school board for the operation of the district while at the same time being held responsible for the fostering of cooperation between the school board and the government. In principle, this would seem to be a sensible foundation from which school boards and governments should operate. In fact, it appears to us that if the education system in any province is to flourish, the school boards and the Department of Education need to work cooperatively on all issues related to education.

At this point, there are few who would argue that the reforms of public education in Newfoundland and Labrador that commenced in the 1990s have improved education in substantive ways or that teaching and learning has flourished during that time. In fact, Sheppard, in Chapter Ten, indicated that an impact of reform initiatives has been a diversion away from teaching and learning and that much of the diversion may have been due to the attention paid to the (much needed) structural changes. Although these structural changes might very well prove to be a springboard to future improvement and lead to a significant strengthening of the technical core, we agree with Elmore (2004) that it is only when the knowledge and "technical core" of education is strong that we can provide excellence in education for all students.

Although initiatives such as class-size reductions, an increased focus on safe and caring school environments, promoting healthy living, improving guidance and special education policy, making improvements to the teacher and administrator allocation formulas, investing in skilled trades programs and equipment are important to improving our education system and the working conditions that exist within it, these initiatives will only ever realize their full potential if they are accompanied by strategies that lead to a strengthened "technical core." The logical next step, then, is for school boards and the Department of Education to focus on strengthening the knowledge and technical core of education—teaching and learning. This will be the supreme test as to whether or not the current model of governance, with limits on school board autonomy and increased government accountability, represents a form of social innovation or a movement towards centralized control.

We agree with Fullan (1993) that a "two-way relationship of pressure, support and continuous negotiation" (p. 38) that enables the partners to work collaboratively towards systemic solutions is required. As Fullan notes, "centralization errs on the side of over control, decentralization errs towards chaos. We have known for decades that top-down change doesn't work (you can't mandate what matters).... Decentralized solutions...also fail because groups get preoccupied with governance and frequently flounder when left on their own" (p. 37). Although we see no evidence to support a return to the system of governance that operated prior to 1997, neither do we see evidence that placing school boards and their directors of education in a position of subservience to political masters or government bureaucrats will likely result in meaningful educational reform. Rather, we have concluded that a more effective strategy for governments is to work with successful school districts and researchers in the field of leadership to ensure that school boards and district leaders are aware of and understand the emerging empirical evidence in support of collaborative leadership and organizational learning, and to support them as they engage in the challenging work of transforming themselves from traditional hierarchical bureaucracies to dynamic professional learning communities.

Chapter Twelve

Discourses of Care in Educational Reform

Mary G. Green

O ne of the often overlooked consequences of educational restructuring is the turmoil, confusion, and disruption caused in the personal and professional lives of educators and school administrators. In this chapter, I contend that the reformation of education in Newfoundland and Labrador in 1997 and the subsequent school board consolidation of 2004 created a climate of stress and despair as school board staff at all levels struggled to deconstruct systems they had strived to create. The research described here suggests that one of the critical aspects of reorganization—basic care and concern for individuals—was largely absent from the reforms of 1997 and 2004. This work draws on research into the potential of theories and practices of care to act as a viable means to challenge and buffer the negative aspects of globalized, neoliberal reform agendas on people. In earlier chapters, some of my colleagues have described how global market forces have negatively impacted resource levels for education, requiring the production of new policies and practices that are responsive to these new arrangements. The notion of "care" runs counter to these forces. Care takes time, thought, and attention to a non-marketized ideology. It can be used as a way to oppose these imperatives. I offer care as a way to reconstruct work, to be more respectful of relations, to be more democratic and just, and to be more effective.

Methodology and conceptual framework

The ideas and findings presented here are based on an ethnographic study of the individuals in one school district involved in the process of education reform. This qualitative research, from an insider's point of view, focused on a particular educational institution—a school district—in which the pub-lic good is an essential role which may be in conflict with individual and group competition and benefit. It illustrates the clash between modern govern-ment agendas to provide for the public good through education and the newer, neoliberal commitment to the market and economic efficiency (Bar-low & Robertson, 1994).

Data were gathered through interviews and a focus-group session with staff working in the district during a period of radical education reform in the provincial education system of Newfoundland and Labrador from 1997–2004. Data were also derived from my own personal, practical know-ledge as a researcher practitioner in telling the experiences of my work in education administration (Clandinin & Connelly, 1998, 2000). In what follows I examine some of the contradictions and paradoxes that impacted the lives of members of the organization and the influence of caring and (some) uncaring efforts. I explore how care can be facilitated and how con-text can influence and complicate the practice of care and the emergence of new practices and conceptualizations.

The chapter is structured around three themes: (1) conceptions of care and caring relevant to organizational work environments, (2) the new work order—how work in education has changed in response to global work issues and patterns, and (3) organizational learning and the develop-ment of professional learning communities in educational organizations.

Background to the study

Conceptions of care and caring

The concept of care I use draws strongly on the work of Nel Noddings (1984, 1992, 2002) and Joan Tronto (1989, 1993, 2002) and involves both feeling and action, or as Tronto (1993) refers to it, "a practice and a disposition" (p. 104). It is an attitude on the part of those who care which requires con-cern for the well-being of those who are cared-for and an ability to demon-strate connection and responsibility. I start from the position that care should no longer be understood along gender lines, as a feminine ethic, and should no longer be limited to private domains. I want to disrupt the tradi-tional ways of treating care as "women's business" and, by extension, women's work in the public organization. Work relationships in large orga-nizations have been thought to be characterized by qualitatively different relations or demonstrations of care than those at home (Beck, 1994). Home relations are thought of as more personal, closer, and emotive, whereas work relations are thought of as rational, businesslike, impersonal, and detached. Breaking free of these assumptions is a difficult task because the home-work framework is well entrenched and is often assumed in studies throughout the social sciences. My research extends beyond this frame-work. My paradigm requires an extension from thinking of care in the per-sonal, private, and feminine domain to its application in public work places and institutions that ought not to be organized on the basis of tradi-tional gender stereotypes.

The "new work order"

Governments around the world are trying to come to terms with new tech-nologies, new social movements, and a changing global economy. These broad social, economic, cultural, and political changes are aimed at prepar-ing people and nations to be more globally competitive (Apple, 2000; Apple, Kenway, & Singh, 2005; Taylor, Rizvi, Lingard, & Henry, 1997). With-in educational institutions, strategic planning and a move to "professional learning" paradigms seem to have become the capstones of the rational di-rection, but there have also been abuses. Franzway (2001) says that many institutions are "greedy"—demanding increased workloads and unbounded time commitments from loyal and committed employees and expecting volun-tary compliance with these new expectations. Critics of the dominant manage-ment and leadership research literatures contend that incentives and recog-nitions being offered are merely ways to control employees and entice them to give more of themselves (Franzway, 2001; Hochschild, 1983). It is also argued that organizations cannot be ethical because they demand loyalty, insist upon the affirmation of certain beliefs, separate members from non-members on principle, and frequently insist on obedience to rules and adherence to ritual which contribute to the erosion of genuine caring (Noddings, 1984). Employ-ees in such organizations struggle to respond to these imposed constraints, causing uncertainty, stress, withdrawal, or detachment.

Neoliberalism includes a demand for smaller government, faith in market competition, and the belief that old bureaucratic structures are in-efficient and expensive, and that they are unable to respond quickly (Tay-lor et al., 1997). "Government decision making has been captured by and reflects the interests of the world's powerful elites, who are not directly ac-countable for these decisions, and yet they have real effects on people's ev-eryday lives" (Reid, 2005, p. 286) These, according to Halpin (1994), are the "universalizing tendencies in educational reform" (p. 204).

As McCann (Chapter Four) has documented, in the Newfoundland and Labrador context we see evidence of these tendencies embedded within official government documents. For example, in its 2000 report, the Ministerial Panel on Educational Delivery commented that, like other Canadian provinces and other countries, Newfoundland and Labrador must compete in a global marketplace where economies and competitiveness are paramount, populations are transient, and there is competition for scarce resources (Government of Newfoundland and Labrador, 2000).

According to Anderson (2001), an accountability bandwagon is converging on education and is bringing with it a focus on control, efficiency, and testing. As a result, education policy finds itself at the centre of a major political struggle between those who see it only for its instrumental outcomes and those who see its potential for human emancipation. One primary reason given for education reform is the well-accepted connection between education and economic growth, which leads to the notion that citizens must acquire increased educational skill levels to participate effectively in a changing labour market (Government of Newfoundland and Labrador, 1992b, 2000). However, Michael Fullan (2005a) cautions that politically motivated reforms produce overload, unrealistic timelines, uncoordinated demands, simplistic solutions, misdirected efforts, inconsistencies, and underestimation of what it takes to bring about reform. In moving toward a corporate model of education, the structure can become the end in itself, rather than a means to accomplishing something worthwhile:

> Paradoxically, at a time when passion, creativity and caring social relationships were necessary for individual and institutional survival, the tendency of educational reforms has been toward technical expertise, standardization and uniformity, products of both markets that produce risk and the new Managerialism that seeks to manage it. (Blackmore & Sachs, 2007, p. 2)

Budget and personnel cuts are made for efficiency rather than improvement, measures are taken to reduce costs rather than improve education programs and services, and downsizing is emphasized over better serving people's needs. Franzway (2005) has argued that:

> Hope and confidence in the potential of progressive pedagogies and social movements have been severely shaken by the successes of the ideological, political and economic projects of neoliberal globalism. (p. 265)

It appears impervious to human effort, and at some levels, the anonymous forces of the political and global economy are destructive of communities. (p. 277)

Blackmore (1999b) states that "[g]lobalization has produced a frenzy of policy-borrowing of educational solutions across Western nation states (UK, New Zealand, Canada, USA, Sweden, Norway and Australia) to what appear to be common social and economic problems" (p. 9). As Galway (Chapter Five) describes, public sector reforms have been based on corporate sector models and have led to human and material resource cuts in education. This reduced support system, paradoxically, comes at a time when teachers' work has intensified with higher levels of administrative duties, more testing and recording, and greater overall accountability requirements (Barlow & Robertson, 1994; Blackmore, 1999b; Sinclair, 1989; Whitty, Power, & Halpin, 1998). Many teachers have expressed a sense of loss of professional autonomy and judgment. Newmann (1993) says that the dominant discourse of educational reform has been technical, functional, and individualistic: "A preoccupation with competitive performance and with administrative efficiency sanctifies a functionalism and instrumentalism that undermines an ethic of cooperative care [and]...deflect attention from the collective good of the larger community" (p. 8).

Professional learning communities

An encouraging trend in recent school-reform efforts focuses on building communities of learners (Ben-Peretz & Schonmann, 1998; Bingham, 2004; Bingham & Sidorkin, 2004; Dillard, 2003; Fullan, 2005a; Grogan & Van Deman-Blackmon, 2001) that require a balance of authority, control, and power through shared decision-making and management. Although there is no single generally accepted definition of a learning organization, it has been described as a group of people pursuing common purposes (individual purposes as well) with a collective commitment to regularly weighing the value of those purposes, modifying them when that makes sense, and continuously developing more effective and efficient ways of accomplishing those purposes (Leithwood & Aiken, 1995). Organizational learning recognizes that change is implemented through the people within an organization (Silins, Zarins, & Mulford, 2002), and is typified by Peter Senge's (1990) model of the five disciplines of a learning organization: systems thinking, personal mastery, mental models, team learning, and shared vision. Senge explains that the basic meaning of a learning organization is one that is "continually expanding its capacity to create its future" (p. 14). He referred to organizational learning as a group of people collectively enhancing their capacities to produce the outcome they really want to produce (Senge, 2006; Senge, Scharmer, Jaworski, & Flowers, 2004). In organizational learning environments leaders become accountable for the learning needs of each individual as well as the school community as a whole. Decisions are shared among educators, administrators, students, parents, and various other government and community groups. The aim is to develop more people-oriented, relational, and collaborative ways of working in which people care about one another (Sernak, 1998).

I think the application of organizational learning theory to structures and systems is consistent with the notion of caring and commitment to others. I advocate a conceptualization of organizations as processes and relationships rather than as structures and divisions. Education is about human beings who are in relation with one another, who need to meet together, as a group of people, if learning is to take place (Bingham, 2004). As Margonis (2004) states:

> Respectful relationships being built in the process of collective decision making....establishing educationally conducive relationships....free-flowing communicative give-and-take, the willingness to try new methods and fail and return to the drawing board, and the ability to appreciate one another in the process of creating...these are social abilities made possible only by...relationships. (p. 51)

This conceptualization makes room for both male and female educators to learn from the strengths, weaknesses, and various approaches of each other, provided there are open, trusting, and tolerant relationships and environments. In what follows, I explore the spaces within an organizational learning context that could be enriched with more care as a means of determining whether a learning organization can be designed so that caring has a chance to be initiated and completed.

One district's struggle: Caring, power, and education reform

One of the most challenging parts of large-scale structural reform is negotiating its many contradictory messages and actions. As demonstrated by the following observations of participants and district leaders, the reform mandate impacted the people charged with implementing it, leading to low morale and tenuous emotional well-being. Although many "survived" the uncertainty associated with the reforms, the process was intensely negative. Suspicion and mistrust were widespread, and these feelings became extensions of the uneasiness felt by staff and the way interpersonal relationships changed. Information became the new currency. Privileged information was available to some people—who gained new power and status—while others felt devalued and "left out of the loop." Many resisted either engaging in discourse about what was happening or confronting their own fears. Consequently, anxieties, biases, and a communication vacuum surfaced, and these were expressed in various ways. Failure to communicate these feelings, I contend, damaged the potential for collaboration among the staff members who were affected. My experiences as a district administrator left me to ponder ways of working as a leader within education and specifically the impact of the policies that I had a hand in developing and implementing. Often in my work, I found myself contradicting personal values. I have seen many people hurt, discouraged, disheartened, and disillusioned through the course of mandated school reform.

My colleagues and I struggled to work in caring ways from our particular positions as organizational leaders within the school district; however, school board consolidation, by its nature, tends to be centrally controlled, leaving district administrators with limited powers. Uncertainty and communication problems in the district seemed to create tensions around organizational loyalty, pragmatic goals, and care for others. One participant reported how he asked the director to reinstate an organizational mechanism that he perceived to have been an effective communication tool used in the former board structure, an academic council (a full-day monthly meeting of the director with program specialists, and assistant directors). He said:

> I asked the director when he destroyed that old organization, "You believe in team building, right?" He said, "yes." Well if you don't get together you can't build a team. The maintenance that we needed wasn't there and when we came together for an hour or two, you know, there would be 20 or 25 items on the agenda. Well, what time is that for team building?

He was arguing that people need time to talk about and think through issues that are important to them. I discovered multiple and contradictory meanings of care within district policies and practices; often there were references made to sharing decision-making and treating teachers as professionals, yet because of hurried timeframes, decisions were made and announced from the top and imposed throughout the system. As Little (1994) has observed:

> In privileging the institutional and collective view, the language of reform underestimates the intricate ways in which individual and institutional lives are interwoven. It under-examines the points at which certain organizational interests of schools and occupational interests of teachers may collide. (p. 4)

Because of mixed messages conveyed by the leadership of the district, some felt pressured into accepting the views and perspectives of others. References were made to the internal politics of the organization, questions were raised about the manner in which decisions to fill positions were made, and there was skepticism about the fairness of the process. One participant expressed strong views about not feeling a part of important decisions related to the reconfiguration of schooling in the district. He was upset that he had not been consulted on matters affecting his life and work and believed that, too often, decisions were made without consultation. He referenced the process used to close schools and was displeased that some of the professional staff at the district office were not involved in the redesign of school configurations. He said:

> That blew me apart—blew me away! In the former school board... program specialists were integrated in the process. They were asked what they thought, why options would work, and why they would not work. The only times we were asked to do something under the current director's administration was when he felt he needed more information to give to the public.

He further commented that:

> program specialists' opinions were not valued and that in itself can show that there's a lack of caring. Only getting information on a need-to-know basis—that's what the program specialists were relegated to.

Another complication involved the requirement for district personnel to engage with a number of persons and groups whose interests were in conflict with one another. For example, during public hearings, parent groups and community leaders passionately presented their case that a different school than theirs should be the one to close. How district staff (acting as care-givers) navigated these conflicts affected the quality of care and the perceptions of parents and community partners. Consensus building in an environment where there is such a polarization of interests was ineffectual, leading the school board director to introduce a shared decision-making model (a series of charts defining which individuals and groups had the power to veto, act, or advise on a variety of policy issues related to teaching, learning, and finance). This approach is consistent with those processes associated with building learning communities (Gilligan, 1982; Gilligan, Ward, McLean Taylor, & Bardige, 1988; Noddings, 2002) and was intended to give everyone in the organization input, understanding, and a degree of comfort with how decisions were made and where they fit in the process. Webs of relationships developed and care was extended to others, accepted, and returned. The experience of this district provides an interesting study in the ongoing themes of power and authority of educators and the need for activists to respond to key local issues in the context of the global politics of education. Attempts to show care or develop care were central to the existing policy documents. However, responses to administration's attempts to develop and implement caring policies clashed with managerial discourses and provincial restructuring imperatives. One participant commented:

> Some people are seeing the comfort level they've always had disrupted and they can't handle that and are fearing the new system. They're starting to suspect everybody, and thinking "Who is honest?" and "Who knows what?"

The education system's long-entrenched hierarchical system with its top-down decision making and adoption of cost-cutting and restructuring directives had negative effects on employees' morale and confidence. The 2004 decision to amalgamate 10 Anglophone districts into four was initiated for the stated purpose of achieving administrative savings. This was a euphemism for cuts to professional administrative and support positions; indeed, the government carried the exercise to the point of stipulating the number and form of senior positions within each district. Existing staff felt as if they were in a state of limbo; productivity diminished and the impending re-staffing process was a substantial barrier to the district's ability to act in caring ways. The following participant comment emphasizes some of the frustrations and mistrust she or he experienced:

> Is it caring what they've done here with the four districts—the way they've ripped them apart? Now it's "dog-eat-dog"' here! I mean you can tell that tensions and morale are low and I don't

know how organizations can do this.... [We] are competing with each other...we're moving into the process of people trying to find other positions and wondering who will get back with the new board and who won't. That whole cloud of ambiguity is hanging over everybody.

The relationships that existed at the school district developed as a result of the bureaucratic hierarchy, a type of domination exhibited through top-down authority arrangements (Abbott & Caracheo, 1988). Assistant directors reported to the director. The director was considered the sole employee of the elected school board, and as such, was the only person authorized to speak directly to the board. Only upon invitation by the director were assistant directors permitted to address the board in official meetings, and if a Department of Education official called to speak with a district administrator, it often interrupted previously scheduled meetings. There was a sense of urgency and immediacy that the concerns and questions of high-level officials be given priority attention and be responded to promptly.

Prior to the second (2004) structural reform the district management team had been focused the establishment of an organizational learning environment. Following the approach outlined by Senge (1990), we were pursuing interdependence or "systems thinking"—overlapping layers and levels, each with varying degrees of authority or control over others. Unfortunately, the use of power to dominate, subordinate, or manipulate through enforcement of rules and regulations (Kreisberg, 1992) maintained social and organizational divisions among the various groups in the district and situated administration as dominant and staff as subordinate. The processes initiated to develop the shared decision-making matrices defined new hierarchies of power that reinforced aspects of control and provoked power struggles, even as we strove to create an atmosphere of caring for one another and for the whole school district. Despite their attentiveness and willingness to dialogue and listen, there is no guarantee that a leader's decisions are going to be appropriate or acceptable to the whole community. Mistakes do happen and leaders do slip into paternalism, authoritarianism, and dogmatism (Jagger, 1995).

The social, political, and personal consequences of reform efforts may never be fully measured or analyzed. There was so much uncertainty and change that it appears no group or individual in the education system had firm enough footing in their own capacities to be able to think and act very far beyond themselves. Everyone was searching for stability and security but there was no overall organizational forum in which this could be generated.

Some felt a sense of hypocrisy with the notion of continuing any focus on "growth and development" and "lifelong learning" in the face of job losses, reassignments, and fiscal restraint throughout the system. Matters worsened because of the urgency with which positions in the newly restructured district were filled—many jobs were filled quickly to ensure schools were staffed for the new school year. This is how one participant described the changes:

> They [management] went in their offices, took out their stuff, threw it in boxes outside the doors and when the itinerants came back they discovered that they were reassigned to schools. I mean, nobody consulted with them, no one allowed them to come in and take their books off the wall in an orderly fashion, and certain itinerants came back and found other people in their office—moved in. I mean, what does that say about caring?

All this was interpreted by many as evidence of a callous and uncaring management approach, and although there was no indication of "ill intent" on the part of those charged with managing the turnover to a new school board, it appears that traditional, hierarchical management practices became the default procedures during the transition. All participants experienced and expressed some degree of tension between their professional roles and personal commitments to care. A strike by maintenance personnel in the middle of the transitional year added to these tensions. Management personnel spent mornings escorting school buses and teachers across picket lines, afternoons carrying on the educational work of the district, and nights cleaning schools to make them ready for students and teachers the next morning. Most staff members were uncomfortable and conflicted by having to cross the picket lines of people they respected, and some strikers who worked respectfully side-by-side for years with administration, now found themselves on the opposite side of the fence. In the midst of education reform processes and job actions it is often difficult to discern who is a provider of care and who requires care.

A way forward

The foregoing description of one district's struggle with structural and organizational change underscores the difficulty of sustaining mechanisms for caring and collaboration in the face of personal and professional upheaval. Our district made attempts to continue with its pre-reform agenda of distributed leadership, personal and professional growth, shared decision-making, collaborative cultures and dialogue, but implementing a government-imposed reform process in a tightly-compressed timeline is messy business. Talk of caring became just that, and the language and practices of the hierarchical, bureaucratic patriarchy became the dominant discourses. Our decision-making policies reflected managerial mandates; they became the means by which senior officers' work entrenched managerial values, competitive processes, and the economic bottom-lines throughout the organization. Authoritarianism seems to have become the predominant model in the Newfoundland and Labrador education system despite the efforts to move the system toward flatter and more relational work environments. In these times, it will require great energy and commitment, and a willingness to take on considerable risk, if we are to arrive at a place where the actions of school system managers are to be based primarily on caring and collaborative structures. There is a price to pay if the system demands so much that people become worn out, ineffective, and disenfranchised.

For an organization to become more humane and less oppressive, an ethic of caring has to replace the focus on edicts, rules, and chain of duty. The principle of justice must be valued by those who hold power; educational leaders must understand that the particular needs of individuals serve as guidelines for equitable and moral treatment for members of the larger profession. Power of position provides the space in which moral debates of fairness and justice can take place. To encourage this kind of dialogue and debate, leaders need to be driven by moral purpose (Schlechty, 1990), such that caring is as important as efficiency.

Despite growing awareness among senior management of the importance of workers' knowledge, skills, and involvement in decision making, the fact remains that traditional work structures, control systems, and an overriding focus on costs and achievement make it difficult to nurture these human qualities in workplaces. Resolving this contradiction is the most pressing issue on the human-resource policy agenda (Lowe, 2000). On the one hand, organizational learning theory claims to emphasize teamwork, collaboration, and personal mastery, and on the other hand, it sets up structures and systems thinking that seem to reinforce old models and ways of thinking. Ultimately, we are driven not by what we know but rather by what we feel.

How then can traditional power structures be adapted to create an environment in which power could sustain caring? Each participant in this study believed that care had to be linked with justice, respect, trust/honesty, and equity. Each believed that caring promoted trust and vice versa. Each sought to cultivate personal relationships with colleagues and believed that caring required attention to the personal and that it could not be exercised merely through position, policies, or programs.

Within organizations there must be room for the expression of difference, frustration, and anger, as well as feelings of happiness and friendly accord. "Care in relationships does not necessarily mean the suppression of difference in the interest of maintaining interpersonal harmony" (McDaniel, 2004, p. 98). The challenge is to stay in dialogue with each other across differences and come to understand ourselves as being related to one another as human beings whose dignity and uniqueness are dependent on the recognition we receive from others. Individuals who care about each other in this way are able to take an interest in the other's point of view and seek to promote each other's well-being. We know that neither partner in a conversation needs to capitulate to the position of the other in order to maintain a relationship, nor should one partner in the conversation seek to erase, deny, or ignore the claims of the other in order to protect their own position.

To change caring practices in educational organizations, the very nature of governance organizations themselves needs to change. In order to be more caring, organizations must cultivate personal relationships, especially by listening and responding rather than by blaming. A more democratic and person-centred philosophy is needed where collaboration is the norm. As we are all interdependent, we should be mindful of the pressures we bring to bear on others through our words and actions. A caring rapport gets established through informal communications and the sharing of positive encounters, and word spreads when leaders, administrators, and decision makers are approachable and supportive. In this study, communication, collaboration, openness, and networking were identified by most participants as fundamental features of a caring organization.

From an institutional/organizational perspective, caring involves leaders responding not only to the particular needs of individuals but of the entire system. In a knowledge-based economy, education is seen to be the means by which information and technology is converted to economic performance and global competitiveness . Education must produce graduates with the Essential Graduation Learnings (Atlantic Provinces Education Foundation, 1996) to contribute to the fabric of society and shape the future. Education decision-makers must make sense of all the talk and action in terms of what would benefit the entire organization. They have to factor in the expectations of superiors and make decisions that sometimes anger, frustrate, and upset people. Most administrators will recognize the importance of caring within educational settings—which it is crucial for good teaching, learning, and working to occur. They must also respond to corporate demands—for example, the expectation that the school system will be efficient and accountable, and the need to respond promptly and effectively to governmental authorities. Because bureaucratic caring grows out of a political process that precludes control by care-givers, much bureaucratic caring is fragmented and inadequate. Instead of directing attention to people's needs, the political process that creates the bureaucracy defines what it will care about and shapes caring to the agency's changing purposes and needs for self-perpetuation:

> Creation and implementation of an ethic of caring….requires leaders who do not have all the answers, who willingly struggle with ambiguity, who willingly make hard decisions….knowing that at some point they make a decision, unintentionally, that is not in the best interests of an individual or group. They know how to regroup. They dialogue, having a good sense of when to show their weaknesses and when that would be damaging to themselves or to the group. They have a vision clear enough to guide others, while simultaneously working with others to create a collective vision. They are political subjects, understanding the delicate balance of care, justice and power. (Sernak, 1998, p. 161)

For an organization to be caring requires resources, skills, and knowledge. In order to cultivate interdependence, connection, and community, public institutions must be willing to give enough to change a system that has been traditionally preoccupied with competition, autonomy, control, and independence. The foregoing case study illustrates the difficulty in breaking away from these constructs as operational principles, especially when the organization is under threat. But, if we embrace a social justice perspective of equality, we open space for a range of interests to be advanced and legitimatized. Some authors have described how school reform might be different, focusing on partnerships that require a balance of authority and control through decision-making and management that is shared between governmental authorities and educators, administrators, students, parents, and various other community groups (Government of Newfoundland and Labrador, 2000; Grogan & VanDeman-Blackmon,

2001; Taylor et al., 1997). The aim is to develop more people-oriented, relational, and collaborative ways of working where people care about one another (Valentine, 1995; Zimbalist, 2005). This is consistent with feminist notions of organizational structures grounded on an ethic of caring that have been advanced as alternatives to bureaucracy and hierarchy (Brunner & Björk, 2001; Held, 1995; Noddings, 1992, 2002; Tronto, 2002).

What has been learned?

In terms of their objectives, educational organizations and scholarly conceptions of care are not worlds apart. Care and caring are theoretical concepts that have much potential for practice in educational institutions specifically, and in government organizations generally. When caring innovations, intents, and collaborations currently evident within some organizations gain legitimacy, they can diffuse outward and help change the status quo, but this is complex and challenging work. Although the central institutions of modern life claim to promote caring, both marketplaces and bureaucracies seriously distort and fragment caring activities (Fisher & Tronto, 1990), and the performance measures on which bureaucracies rely bear little relationship to the quality of care provided (Abel & Nelson, 1990). As much as parents and the public want improved academic performance, they also expect schools to develop happy, socially well-adjusted, and moral human beings. Students and educators cannot meet these expectations within discouraging and alienating environments. Educational organizations must focus on human relations and address the core of the problem. Perhaps the greatest challenge in educational accountability is keeping the focus on improvement without forgetting the rest of the agenda (Sergiovanni, 2000). A caring orientation may help us to think more deeply and clearly and compensate for some of the inadequacies and limitations of the current rational but less than relational perspectives on work and education reform:

> School reform becomes a question of the possibility of school participants reimagining their professional lives. This imagined middle ground shifts the terms for reform from initiative, control, and urgent problem solving for either outside reformers or individuals working alone or together, to new terms such as... negotiation, improvisation, imagination, and possibility. Such a standpoint allows us to imagine reform as softer; as less impositional on the lives of children, parents, teachers, and others; as

needing to be undertaken with less urgency and with more willingness to listen, to negotiate, and to change as we move forward in this changing parade. (Clandinin & Connelly, 1998, p.
162)

Many organizations continue to struggle with the fallout from neoliberal
movements and the resultant apathy among those who work in and care
about those institutions. I suggest the time has come to cast aside the dehu-
manizing aspects of the restructuring formula, and accept as a primary goal
of future reform campaigns the dignified and respectful treatment of individuals. School systems are not corporations in which efficiency and profit
trumps humanism. Before embarking on more top-down, mandated restructuring, we have to find ways to demonstrate to people that we value
their knowledge and creativity. Being good stewards of the public investment in education demands that we respect the principles of efficiency and
accountability; however, these goals must not be achieved at the expense of
denying basic care for those whose lives are fundamentally changed by
structural education reform.

Conclusions

This chapter suggests that an ethos of caring could be highly beneficial to
learning institutions undergoing external and internal pressure, but in practice this is complicated and difficult to achieve. The challenge in restructuring or downsizing education systems while keeping the needs of disenfranchised employees at the fore is not a straightforward process. As enrolments continue to decline, there will be new opportunities to consolidate.
Now is a good time for reflection on the past—for thinking about how education authorities have operationalized structural reforms and how those
reforms have affected individuals. I think there is great potential for developing caring practices as a means to improve morale and enhance the quality of work relationships, which can positively affect organizational productivity and accomplishment of goals.

My interest is in changing the culture of institutions and the means by
which we change those institutions. In the ideal school system both professional and support staff feel respected and fulfilled and experience personal
satisfaction with themselves and their work. In this system employees are
motivated and willing to learn new strategies and skills that will benefit
learners and the overall organization. The school district profiled in this
chapter was on a path to get closer to this kind of organization but was lim-

ited by external pressures and prevailing patriarchal beliefs and practices. It is difficult to even attempt a transition from the traditional concepts of leadership authority and control toward an ethic/practice of care while being immersed in a structure of power over (Brunner & Björk, 2001) and position power (Northouse, 2004).

Many leaders today seem to be advocating a collaborative team approach towards administration and decision-making. This study suggests that they can expect to experience obstacles that have the potential to derail their efforts to bring about and sustain meaningful change. School systems are complex enterprises in which centralized decision-making, contradictory messages, and agendas imposed from above can undermine the goals of collaboration, trust, and sharing. Notwithstanding these pressures, it is possible to work with others in compassionate, generous, and nurturing ways. People working in today's organizations should not accept the status quo in terms of their expectations for how they should be treated and how they should interact with colleagues. To recast organizations as places in which care for individuals becomes a genuine core value, tensions relating to the distribution of power, decision-making, external accountabilities, the division of male and female roles, and all the other trappings of traditional hierarchical organizations must be deconstructed and rethought. The traditional obstacles which dampen marginalized voices and resist equality through justice and care need to be exposed, and there must be balance and convergence of male and female ways of working. This is an onerous task, particularly because we (researchers, policy-makers, administrators, educators, citizens, and governmental authorities) are not all on the same page in terms of our motives, interests, beliefs, and accountabilities. As the demographic profile of Canada continues to change (to an older and more urbanized population), there will be demands for greater resource levels from social sectors other than education—and this will invariably result in calls for the redistribution of public money and the reorganization of school systems. Among the lessons from this study is the imperative that, in both day-to-day operations and during periods of organizational change, we all take "care" more seriously.

Chapter Thirteen

Stirring Political Pots: Information and Communications Technology, Denominational Reform, Northern Ireland, Newfoundland and Labrador

Roger Austin and William J. Hunter

Mystery writers and television police dramas have made generous use of the notion of the detective's "hunch" or the street cop's "gut feeling." In fiction, such intuitions must be taken seriously, but in academic work, the *sine qua non* is hard evidence, and any form of intuition is generally suspect. There is an exception, however. Historian J. H. Hexter (1971) introduced a notion that he called the "second record." Hexter makes clear that what counts most in historical research is the physical evidence that exists in document form. Unearthing, scrutinizing, and evaluating such documents is the lifeblood of history, but historians generally recognize that something of the imagination of the individual researcher comes to light in the process of interpreting these data and putting them into a broader narrative. Hexter coined the term "second record" to describe a kind of data source that emerges from the life experience of the researcher: "everything that historians bring to their confrontation with the record of the past" (p. 103). The second record, however, cannot replace the documentary evidence that makes up the first record, but it gives the researcher a basis for putting him or herself "in the shoes" of historical characters and for testing the soundness of interpretations against the judgment of their accrued life experience.

We hope in this chapter to argue for a strong use of the notion of the second record. The authors are two highly different academics—a British- and French–educated historian on one hand and a US–educated Canadian educational psychologist on the other. Our academic preparations are liter- ally worlds apart—different research traditions, different interpretive tools, different working and writing environments. Our personal lives have been lived (for the most part) on different continents and in different cultural milieux. However, there is some common ground in our connection to Northern Ireland—born in England, Austin has lived and worked in Northern Ireland for most of his academic career; Hunter was born in Northern Ireland but his family left before he started school, so his educa- tion and academic career have been mostly in the USA and Canada. Both had academic interests in schooling in Northern Ireland and in the use of telecommunications in teaching and learning. On the very day we met in the fall of 2007, our conversation took an interesting turn around the role that churches play in education in Canada and in Northern Ireland. The case of Newfoundland and Labrador's 1997 reform began to loom large as we wondered what lessons Northern Ireland might learn from the New- foundland and Labrador experience of ending denominational schools.

Our initial online searches yielded limited detail on the 1997 reforms, but when we contacted researchers at Memorial University, we discovered that a symposium in the spring of 2008 would be focusing on the reforms, and we submitted a paper focused on our readings of the common issues in Northern Ireland and Newfoundland and Labrador. Parts of this chapter are drawn from our presentation at that symposium (Hunter & Austin, 2008).

Although the other chapters in this book are some of the best infor- mation we have found regarding the 1997 reforms, there is much more that we would like to know about the impact of the reforms on student perfor- mance, attitudes, or social behaviours (as well as the perceptions of teach- ers, administrators, and parents). The change was controversial at the time, and readers will see that strong perspectives still prevail among scholars in Newfoundland and Labrador.

That is where our second records come into play. Any worthwhile project deserves input from a critical friend. Living and working far from

Newfoundland and Labrador (each about 3,000 kilometres away—in different directions), we hope to draw on our two very different second records to find interpretations and insights that make sense to our disparate world-views and disciplinary traditions. Where an interpretation rings true for both of us, we believe we have something of value to offer to our colleagues in Newfoundland and Labrador.

Two key questions have guided us in writing this chapter:

- ❖ Has the process of ending denominational schooling in Newfoundland and Labrador offered insights that might be relevant in other parts of the world and particularly in Northern Ireland?
- ❖ What roles has information and communications technology (ICT) played in examining socially important issues in Northern Ireland and in Newfoundland and Labrador in the recent past?

Ending denominational schooling in Newfoundland and Labrador: Perspectives from Northern Ireland

People from outside Northern Ireland are likely to think of it as having been engaged in some form of religious strife through the latter part of the twentieth century. People living in Northern Ireland (as well as in Ireland and the UK) understand the conflict to also be a political matter concerning the future of Northern Ireland as part of the UK or as part of Ireland. Opinions on this question tend to be strongly aligned with religion because the majority of Catholics in Northern Ireland identify with the Republic of Ireland and most Protestants feel more strongly connected to the UK (Mitchell, 2006). Because 95 per cent of children in Northern Ireland attend either "maintained" schools that are Catholic in ethos, or "controlled" (i.e., "state") schools, which enrol mainly Protestant students, opportunities for contact with those from different political, religious, and cultural backgrounds are, in many cases, minimal. The 5 per cent of pupils who attend "integrated" schools, which were set up specifically to educate children of all faiths or none, have reached a "plateau" in terms of size—even though it is claimed that some 60 per cent of the population in Northern Ireland support "integrated" education (e.g., Alliance Party, 2006). We expected that Newfoundland's decision to abolish denominational schooling might serve to inform our thinking about a broader range of alternatives for examining the religious and political differences that divide the people of Northern Ireland.

We therefore wanted to know more about, and to understand better, *how* Newfoundland and Labrador had ended denominational schooling and with what consequences. It seemed to us that Northern Ireland in 2011 faces some of the same issues that Newfoundland and Labrador faced in the 1990s:

◈ a declining population,
◈ declining traditional industries, and
◈ a denominational school system serving a geographically dispersed population.

In both cases, we saw that the consequences seem to be:

◈ restricted curricular choice, particularly in specialist subjects at advanced levels,
◈ a greater cost to the taxpayer through the duplication of schools, and
◈ uneven patterns of academic performance.

Some might argue that these phenomena are not directly linked to denominational schooling or that addressing these problems need not involve the elimination of denominational schooling (e.g., it is clear that Fagan in Chapter Six argues the latter in the case of Newfoundland and Labrador), but we would say that the connection is, at the very least, plausible. In the case of Northern Ireland, the fact that 95 per cent of students attend religiously separate schools has also been linked to a range of additional problems, including the development of sectarian attitudes (Mitchell, 2006) and a lack of trust (Hudson, Dunford, Hamilton, & Kotter, 1997). Although it is not clear to us whether such links have been made in Newfoundland and Labrador, it is clear that religious differences in the province have historically been linked to socio-political differences, that Newfoundlanders have often struggled bitterly over political questions, and that they have sometimes found novel ways of living with these differences (e.g., "turn-taking" across religions in holding some local political offices).

Our reading of the research about educational reform in Newfoundland and Labrador has focused on how denominational reform was achieved and what its consequences have been. On the first of these questions, we have noted the views of Galway and Dibbon (Chapter One) that the government maintained that the primary reason for the reforms was to improve educational achievement, and that more broadly, this was consistent with the principle of efficiency underpinning the reforms of the 1990s. In other words, ending denominational schooling would both save money and improve educational performance. The provincial government's report, *Adjusting the Course* (Government of Newfoundland and Labrador, 1993, 1994b), indicated that the goal of the reforms was "to transform the system from one of persistent under-achievement to one whose achievement levels rank with the rest of the nation" (preface, ¶2). The Williams Royal Commission report (Government of Newfoundland and Labrador, 1992b), which had called for a radical restructuring of the education system involving the creation of non-denominational school boards, estimated that doing so would save over $13 million annually. On the other hand, Fagan (Chapter Six) claims that government figures on both student performance and estimated savings were unreliable. Fagan believes the government's purpose in ending denominational schooling was actually a desire to take control of school governance, by which he means control of religious education, family life education, and teacher employment. It seems clear to us that the government did indeed take control of governance as the *means* of ending denominational schools, but Galway and Dibbon (Chapter One) have presented persuasive evidence that the schools were not performing well and that enrolment was declining, so the government's stated reasons are at least credible.

That is to say, it appears to us that the government had reason to be concerned about both the performance and efficiency of schools, but we are not in a position to judge whether *Adjusting the Course* presents the government's real motivation or if, as Fagan implies, these conditions were only a pretext that permitted government to act on an agenda that had other objectives/purposes. For example, we do not have information regarding the employment practices of Newfoundland and Labrador schools prior to 1998, but it would be *possible* that the government had reasons for wanting more direct control over teacher employment and that justifying these reasons would have been more politically problematic than justifying change in the service of efficiency and performance.

Hodder (Chapter Nine), meanwhile, presents compelling evidence that the reforms were not introduced with the intention of secularizing the school system; he makes it clear that the amended Term 17 actually meant that Newfoundland and Labrador was the only province in Canada with a religious education program for all grades and legislation that religious education had to be taught. Far from reducing religious education, Hodder contends, the reforms provided a more coherent framework for every student and every school in Newfoundland and Labrador.

When we look at this situation from the Northern Ireland perspective, it is especially interesting that the 1997 Liberal government that Fagan credits with ending denominationalism was not closely aligned to clerical interests and was therefore prepared to push through a change in denominational schooling that was bound to be contentious. Without the political will to drive this through two referenda, it is difficult to believe that the reforms would have been agreed by the citizens of Newfoundland and Labrador or their elected representatives. In contrast, the political context in Northern Ireland in 2009 had a local power-sharing executive composed of two Unionist parties (i.e., supporters of Northern Ireland's membership in the UK) whose membership is predominantly Protestant, and two republican/nationalist parties (i.e., supporters of Northern Ireland's unification with the Republic of Ireland) whose members are predominantly Catholic. In Northern Ireland, education, together with many other policy areas, is an overtly political issue. Denominational schooling in Northern Ireland is also closely tied to several other cultural allegiances in sport, language, and even patterns of housing settlement (Austin & Anderson, 2007, pp. 9–10). Ending denominational schooling in Northern Ireland would require a seismic shift in current attitudes, perhaps to a greater extent than was required in Newfoundland and Labrador in the mid 1990s.

Finally, in terms of the factors behind the reform in Newfoundland, we note the view of Stevens (2008) that there was a correspondence between the decline in the number of schools and a "pan-Canadian initiative to prepare people across the country for the Information Age" (p. 218). However, it does not appear to us that the government's case for ending denominational schools relied much on the idea that amalgamating schools would lead to greater curricular choice, either face-to-face or through e-learning, with benefits to the employment opportunities for young people and the economy of Newfoundland and Labrador.

Given that the reform was bound to lead to conflict with the churches and consume a substantial amount of political energy, it seems to us that the most likely "pay-back" for the government was reduced costs in the educational budget and greater autonomy for government in driving the direction of education policy, including raising educational attainment.

The impact of reform

It is worth asking whether the reforms achieved the goals set forth in *Adjusting the Course* (Government of Newfoundland and Labrador, 1993,

1994b). Here we will examine the evidence available regarding the effects of ending of denominational schooling in Newfoundland and Labrador.

Student achievement

Using the OECD results reported by Bussière, Knighton, and Pennock (2007), Sheppard (Chapter Ten) says that Canadian students were among the best in the world in the OECD's PISA tests. He asserts that "while students in Newfoundland and Labrador had scored slightly below the Canadian average on those tests, when socio-economic status and parent education levels are considered in the analysis, students from Newfoundland and Labrador performed on par or above the Canadian average." Sheppard also notes, however, that 44 per cent of parents in Newfoundland and Labrador have no post-secondary education, the highest in Canada by a long way, and that Newfoundland and Labrador has the lowest socio-economic index. Graduation rates at 75.3 per cent for males and 81 per cent for females are similar to the rest of Canada. On the face of it, therefore, it would seem that student scores have improved, but there is no evidence or analysis to suggest that this is a direct consequence of the ending of denominational schooling. Other factors, such as funding changes unrelated to denominational schooling, changing rates of participation, the impact of out-migration, greater emphasis on accountability, etc., might reasonably be expected to have played a part in this process.

Funding and investment

It is challenging to find from outside the province clear data on education expenditures. In 1998, the government did provide a report on the costs of education (Government of Newfoundland and Labrador, 1998b). While this report predicted an 11.3 per cent reduction in education expenditures for 1998, it made no mention of denominational schooling as a factor contributing to that reduction. By contrast, the 2006 budget highlights (Government of Newfoundland and Labrador, 2006) indicate a $100 million increase in overall education spending (including post-secondary and training). Again, it is clear that the financial situation is different 10 years after the reform, but we are unable to see a basis for attributing the changes to the ending of denominational schooling.

However, we have been struck by the hugely impressive development of ICT for the delivery of distance education in Newfoundland and Labrador both before and after 1997. The details of how e-learning has enabled thousands of students to access specialist courses are explained by Brown and Barry (2008), Furey, Drover, Nash, and Skinner (2008), Rose, Hickey, and Mercer (2008), and Stevens (2008). In some schools 25 per cent of students are accessing courses provided at a distance, and student performance in these courses appears to be comparable to those classes delivered face-to-face. Furey et al. (2008) suggest that students who undertake distance learning courses develop more independence and are better prepared for higher education. It would appear from Brown and Barry (2008) that the Newfoundland and Labrador Ministry of Education was actively involved with the higher education sector in the development of these courses in terms of funding, conceptualizing, and delivery, although Stevens (2008) indicates that it was only in 2007 that "funding was allocated for information technology" (p. 263). We are aware that much of the earlier work was funded through research projects and grants from the federal government and private foundations, but we suspect that a certain amount of support for e-learning was derived from the education budget through decisions made at the local level (e.g., by permitting a teacher to work on school time as a local tutor for a distance delivery course). It may be that changes to schools in Newfoundland and Labrador brought about by the 1997 reforms created the conditions in which distributed distance learning was likely to take root. The rupture with the past and the disruption to traditional ways of teaching and learning may have established an atmosphere of change that supported the innovative practices in ICT that would become e-learning. Certainly, schools in Newfoundland and Labrador were extensively involved in distance delivery much earlier than schools in Northern Ireland and provided these services in a highly cost-effective way across the province as a whole.

Two major changes: Research questions

In the past two decades, Newfoundland and Labrador has been involved in two major changes in public education—the end of denominational schooling and the development of ICT-based distance education. These two major changes seem to have developed relatively independently, but together, they have transformed public education in Newfoundland and Labrador. Much has been done to document this transformation, but much remains to be done. Looking from afar, we would hope to see future research answer such questions as:

◈ To what extent are parents, teachers, and school administrators happy with non-denominational schooling? Are there differences in attitude associated with religious affiliation?

◈ Are key leaders in the government's education bureaucracy satisfied with the impact of the 1997 reform on school finance?

◈ Has the secularization of schooling had an impact on social cohesion? That is, do people in the different religious communities report that they get along better now than they did when schools were denominational? The answer to this question could be of great interest to decision makers in other provinces and internationally, notably in Northern Ireland.

◈ Is the early development of ICT-based distance education in the K-12 schools of Newfoundland and Labrador having economic impact, for example, in employment, in the attraction of new jobs or industries, or in worker mobility?

Denominational schools in Northern Ireland

The Government of Newfoundland and Labrador in the late 1990s eliminated denominational schooling in an attempt to solve a range of problems. Northern Ireland today faces challenges relating to the overall quality of education and getting a return from the investment in ICT at the same time that the number of children in schools is declining.

As context for this discussion, it is important to know that there are four significant factors affecting educational policy in Northern Ireland at this time:

◈ the impact of social and cultural differences,
◈ the role of the churches in education,
◈ the role of the State in education, and
◈ the planned elimination of the "11+" tests.

The ways in which each of these factors operates over the next few years will have considerable impact on the future of schooling in Northern Ireland.

The impact of social and cultural differences

Northern Irish politics is still dominated by political parties that reflect historical divisions between Catholics and Protestants. (The Alliance Party, without denominational ties, attracts only single digit support in local elections. In the 2007 Northern Ireland Assembly elections it polled 5.2 per cent of the vote.)

These divisions are also reflected in the type of schools that young people attend and in housing patterns. Only 5 per cent of students attend religiously "integrated" schools, and in some public sector housing estates, curb stones are painted to denote identity and affirm territorial rights (red, white, and blue to show their "loyalty" to the UK, or white, gold, and green to show allegiance to the Republic of Ireland). Cultural differences are also apparent in sports, with Catholics more likely to be involved in "Gaelic" games such as Gaelic football, hurling, and camogie, whereas Protestants are more likely to play rugby and hockey. Despite a lessening of differences since the 1997 peace accord, Northern Ireland remains deeply divided, with many of its young people often growing up with little knowledge of "the other side." These divisions also affect perceptions of the Republic of Ireland as some Unionists continue to regard "the south" with suspicion, fearing a united Ireland could mean a loss of both their identity and their rights. On the Nationalist/Republican side, some still distrust Britain.

Role of the churches in education

Although church attendance is declining, clerical influence remains strong in daily life and particularly in schools. Representatives of the various churches make up almost half of the board of governors in nearly all schools, giving them a significant role in the appointment of all staff. Employment legislation allows schools, exceptionally, to circumvent equality of opportunity legislation so that, in general, the overwhelming majority of staff in "controlled" or state schools are Protestant and the majority in the "maintained" sector are Catholic (Montgomery & Smith, 2006).

The Northern Ireland Department of Education has proposed that the statutory role of Protestant clergy on school boards of governors be removed. This would have a significant impact on the representation of clergy in controlled schools and there has been considerable opposition to this. Research by Dunn and Gallagher (2002) for the Equality Commission in 2002 revealed that there was little support among teachers for the employment legislation to be repealed.

Further evidence of the strength of the churches' position in education can be seen in the continuing debate about teacher education. In 1980 the Northern Ireland administration tried to push through a merger between two Catholic teacher-training colleges and a "state" teacher-training college (in response to the Chilver Report [1980]) but backed down in the face of fierce resistance. A review of teacher education in 2005–2006 produced an equally stout defense from the Catholic Church about the importance of maintaining a distinctive type of training for Catholic schools.

Role of the state in education

Northern Ireland is experiencing a major change in school administration. Beginning in January 2010, the Northern Ireland Department of Education continued to provide overall policy guidance to schools, but the implementation of policy is the responsibility of a new body, the Education and Skills Authority (ESA), which brings together many of the different administrative agencies which had been running schools. Crucially, the ESA has oversight of *all* schools, whatever the religious composition of their student body. However, the interests of the state remains paramount in some key areas. The Northern Ireland Department of Education:

- ❖ is responsible for approving any new school buildings,
- ❖ continues to pay all teaching salaries, and
- ❖ controls the curriculum, including the recently added "citizenship" course.

The importance given to this "subject" with its focus on human rights, responsibilities, pluralism, and democracy needs to be seen as part of the state's response to the reality of children growing up in a society that remains divided. As the chief inspector for schools in Northern Ireland noted in her report for 2002–2004, "Sectarianism remains a major threat" (Northern Ireland Department of Education, 2004–2006, p. 79) At the very time when the rest of the curriculum is being driven by the need to acquire skills with less emphasis on content, the privileged place that citizenship occupies is one sure way the state can enable teachers and students to examine the reality of difference and the need for respect between citizens within Northern Ireland and in the rest of the world.

The curriculum also requires breadth in its implementation (for 14–18-year-olds) and this will present a significant challenge to many secondary schools with declining enrolments and a loss of subject specialists. The Department of Education's control of salaries (75 per cent of all costs) gives it a key role in the overall management of the school. The Department of Education's sustainable school strategy (Northern Ireland Department of Education, 2009) suggests that many small schools will become increasingly unable to fulfil their legal obligations in terms of providing subject choice, and calls on schools to look for ways to cooperate and share resources.

It should also be noted that under the Education Reform (Northern Ireland) Order 1998, the Northern Ireland Department of Education has a duty to encourage and facilitate the development of integrated education (Article 64). The Catholic Bishops of Northern Ireland (2001) oppose this direction but most politicians recognize the rights of parents to select integrated education for their children.

Planned elimination of the "11+" tests

The present arrangement for transfer from primary to post-primary education is based on two academic tests popularly called the "11+". Children who achieve the highest grades can be "selected" by traditional academic "grammar schools." Those who do not take the examination or who achieve lower grades attend a more general/vocational "high school."

A consequence of this selection process is that some small towns have a "selective" maintained school, a non-selective maintained school, a "selective" controlled school, and a non-selective controlled school. The former minister of education, who belongs to the Sinn Fein party, was seeking to phase out academic selection but this was resisted by both the Unionist parties and by a parental lobby supporting grammar schools. It should be noted that for this to occur there would need to be a consensus in the Assembly's Education Committee and on the executive. So far, there is no sign of this being even close.

Even though the 11+ has been officially abolished, grammar schools have not been convinced that alternative arrangements are in their interests; the majority of these selective schools are now intending to set their own entrance examinations. The intense debate on the issue of academic selection shows how educational policy is now being shaped by party political differences and it underlines how the Northern Ireland Department of Education is subject to these forces. Under the power-sharing agreement set up in 1997, there is a risk that any educational reform will be blocked by one or another of the main political parties.

Insights from Northern Ireland

In summary, although the Northern Ireland Department of Education accepts that with a declining school population there are too many small schools, its policy options for dealing with this problem do not include any suggestion that denominational schooling should be abolished. Instead, the "sustainable schools" policy identifies minimal levels of student numbers and six criteria for a school to be considered "sustainable" and urges schools that cannot offer a sufficiently broad curriculum to collaborate with neighbouring schools (Northern Ireland Department of Education, 2009). It will be the responsibility of a new educational body, the ESA, which has oversight of all schools, to implement these policies.

In 2011, unlike Newfoundland in the 1990s, the political parties in Northern Ireland that hold power are so strongly connected to either traditional "Catholic" and "Protestant" positions there is little chance of the duplication of school places being remedied through the imposition of any limits to denominational schooling. In effect, there is no political will at present to drive such a reform. It remains to be seen whether possible reductions in public expenditure arising from the present economic difficulties will lead to a re-appraisal of this position. With the devolution of powers to Northern Ireland's politicians in 1997 came responsibility for the educational budget; in a future election, the costs of denominational schooling could become an issue.

The role of ICT in Northern Ireland

We have noted above what remarkable steps Newfoundland and Labrador has taken since the mid-1990s to solve one of the problems it faced then and which Northern Ireland faces now, namely the means of ensuring there were equal educational opportunities for advanced study in *all* schools.

When we analyze the place of ICT in Newfoundland and Labrador and Northern Ireland we see a significant difference in the *purpose* for which ICT is used. We have seen from the research of Brown and Barry (2008), Furey et al. (2008), Rose et al. (2008), and Stevens (2008) how ICT has been used to broaden curricular choice through the development of a wide range of specialist courses, particularly for older students. These specialist programs have meant that small schools have been able to retain students by offering them access to distance learning.

In contrast, in Northern Ireland, the Department of Education's "sustainable schools" policy (Northern Ireland Department of Education, 2009) makes only a passing reference to the opportunities to use ICT in the ways it is used in Newfoundland and Labrador. Two purposes have guided educational uses of ICT in the schools of Northern Ireland: first, embedding ICT in the curriculum for all children, including the assessment of ICT skills at ages 11 and 14, has been seen as one way of raising educational standards. Second, ICT is being used to link schools together, both between Northern Ireland and the Republic of Ireland and between Catholic and Protestant students within Northern Ireland. We believe Northern Ireland has been in the forefront of using ICT for this kind of intercultural learning as the following case studies illustrate.

The Dissolving Boundaries program

Set up in 1999 by the Departments of Education in Belfast and Dublin, the Dissolving Boundaries through Technology in Education program has enabled 300 schools to form cross-border partnerships where they have studied aspects of the curriculum through the use of real time video-conferencing and on-line, using Moodle[1] to allow pupils and teachers to interact in secure discussion areas and to build a collaborative project on their chosen aspect of work.

Extensive evaluation of this work has been reported elsewhere (Austin et al., 2009). Here, we highlight four issues that we believe relevant to the works in this book:

(1) *The program has wide appeal to all types of school and student.* Dissolving Boundaries (DB) serves pupils from "Special schools,"[2] primary schools, and secondary schools. Some DB schools make more use of real time video-conferencing; others focus on asynchronous interaction through Moodle. Although all types of school in Northern Ireland have been involved, until recently it was difficult to recruit and retain "Protestant" schools. The most recent figures for 2008–2009 show that 40% of the participating schools are "Protestant" whereas 51% are Catholic. The remaining schools are either integrated, Irish language medium or "Special."

(2) *All curriculum areas are "fair game."* The DB philosophy, that of working together and engaging in productive virtual contact, is central to both learning and to "citizenship." But rather than restricting teachers to work done during official "citizenship" classes, the program has adopted the view that almost any subject can be used as the focus for valuable lessons in listening, respecting difference, and diversity. A very wide range of subject areas, including

mathematics, science, geography, history, art, and music, has seen that having pupils work on common projects with people who have different perspectives adds value to the learning experience.

(3) *The Departments of Education in one University in Northern Ireland and one in the Republic of Ireland collaborate in managing DB.*

The university departments play a critical role as external organizations that coordinate the teacher planning and review conferences, monitor the quality of interaction between schools, and intervene with support when necessary. The two universities also work very closely with education advisers on both sides of the border in the recruitment of schools and in evaluating the impact of the work on teachers and pupils.

(4) *Successive evaluation reports have shown that the program has been successful in embedding ICT in the daily work of many teachers.*

Principal reasons for this success have been the presence of a distant audience, the generally reliable nature of the technology, and the "match" between curriculum content and the focus of the cross-border work. For the pupils, reports have repeatedly shown increases in ICT skills, self-esteem, and a better understanding of both cultural similarity and difference. The most recent research report has identified that teachers and pupils have begun developing a more extended understanding of what is involved in collaborative learning. In our view, this is pivotal not only in terms of cross-border links but between schools within Northern Ireland.

The Digital Citizenship project

In 2007–2008, building on the success of DB, the Northern Ireland Department of Education agreed to fund a pilot program to support five cross-community school links within Northern Ireland—the Digital Citizenship Project. These 10 schools focused on a citizenship-related project for 15-year-old pupils drawn from a mix of both "grammar" schools and "non-selective high schools." The university managing the project brought teachers together to undertake training on Northern Ireland's own virtual learning environment, "LearningNI," and asked them to identify an appropriate part of the citizenship curriculum for a joint project. Teaching staff and pupils selected issues that were very current and in many cases controversial. Some of the issues were: "cultural identity," "living in a divided society," the impact of the 11+ selection examination, "getting my voice heard," and a project on racism.

Some preliminary conclusions from this project are emerging. Presentations given at a review conference in April 2008 indicated that pupils have been able to examine many difficult questions about disputed history, about differences in sport, and about their concerns for the future. One student from a predominantly Protestant school, for example, produced a very dramatic graph of the declining Protestant population in the Republic of Ireland, caused by both migration of Protestants from the Republic of Ireland since partition in 1921 and by the Catholic church's ruling that children of "mixed" marriages (i.e., between Catholic and Protestant) should be brought up as Catholics.

In concluding this analysis of these two programs, we need to make it clear that virtual contact is not the only formal way in which young people in schools in Northern Ireland are encouraged to meet and work together. Since 1987, the Northern Ireland Department of Education has implemented the Schools Community Relations Program designed to help young people develop an "understanding of, and respect for difference"; however, as the Chief Inspector for schools pointed out in her report for 2002–2004, while 53 per cent of primary schools had been involved, only 21 per cent of the children in those schools had taken part (Northern Ireland Department of Education, 2004–2006). In the secondary sector, where 50 per cent of schools had been involved, a mere 3 per cent of young people from those schools had taken part.

It is our contention that this remarkably small percentage of young people should and could be significantly increased through the structured use of ICT.

Undergraduate students' experience of ICT and joint work

Finally, we report on work we did in the fall of 2007 with second-year University of Ulster students who were taking "education" as a minor component of their degree and who were engaged in experiences working with ICT in "mixed" Catholic-Protestant pairings. Most of the students were from Northern Ireland but a small percentage was from the Republic of Ireland. Data came from an on-line forum that was part of an ICT module and from a questionnaire on students' ICT competence and attitudes towards the concept that citizenship education in schools requires cross-community contact to be effective.

When asked if schools would benefit from having an e-partner from a different background within Northern Ireland, 34.4 per cent of the students said this should be "required," 62.1 per cent said they should be "encouraged." Only 3.4 per cent said it was "not a priority." Just over half of the students said they had previous experience of working with a partner as part of their university studies although it was not clear if the partner was of a different religious denomination. On the "ICT and education" module, 80 per cent said they had worked with a partner who had attended a different type of school to themselves; 51.7 per cent said it was either an "extremely valuable experience" or a "very good experience," while 31.1 per cent said it was "satisfactory," and 3.4 per cent said it was "more negative than positive." When asked if "working with a partner" should be one of the criteria for assessing work on the module, 24.1 per cent gave this unconditional support, 17.2 per cent thought it was a "good idea," 41.4 per cent said they were unsure, and 14 per cent opposed this suggestion.

We believe these data mean that Northern Ireland must encourage a higher level of ICT skill in schools to take full advantage of the potential of ICT for intercultural learning. We also think the strong support these students gave to using ICT to forge intercultural links between schools means that there is room for students from Northern Ireland's differing religious traditions to work effectively together in higher education. We also agree with the European Commission (Reading, 2002) that the ability to work in multicultural teams, often in different places, is an essential skill in a global knowledge-based economy.

We think that the evidence from the Dissolving Boundaries program and the Digital Citizens project confirms that ICT can be used effectively to remedy some of the long-term difficulties that have arisen from the history of "separate schooling" both within Northern Ireland and on the island of Ireland. We see the evidence from the undergraduate study as confirmation that 10 years after the signing of the 1997 "Good Friday" peace agreement, there is a mixture of hope and caution among this sample of university students. It is likely that they would be more positive about improved community relations than society as a whole, not least because of their experience of working and studying with students from a different background.

Promoting contacts

The technical infrastructure is in place to enable much greater use to be made of ICT both to redress the anticipated shortage of specialist subjects at 16–18 and to extend the intercultural work between schools within Northern Ireland and on the island of Ireland. Unlike Newfoundland and Labrador, we see no sign that the churches or the main political parties in Northern Ireland are ready to accept the end of religiously "separate" schools. In these circumstances, therefore, the promotion of purposeful educational contact between young people, face-to-face and digitally, is both cost effective and necessary to build trust and prepare them for a knowledge–based economy.

Conclusions and global lessons

Our analysis of the use of ICT in Northern Ireland and Newfoundland leads us to two suggestions about lessons each jurisdiction could learn from the other with respect to the use of ICT. First, the ways ICT is used in Northern Ireland to foster intercultural links might have utility with 8–14-year-old students in Newfoundland and Labrador, both as a desirable educational activity for local and global citizenship and as a way to build the ICT confidence and skills of teachers and students in preparation for participation in distance learning courses. Second, Newfoundland and Labrador's successful use of e-teams in schools (rather than seeking highly skilled individuals) and the development of mediating teachers (m-teachers) who facilitate student learning are practices that deserve to be emulated in Northern Ireland.

We have also been impressed by the level of cooperation between the Ministry of Education in Newfoundland and Labrador and Memorial University in terms of the design and delivery of courses. We see a high level of confidence in Newfoundland and Labrador in the platform being used to provide e-learning, whereas teachers in Northern Ireland do not have the same level of confidence despite considerable government investment in LearningNI (Northern Ireland Education and Training Inspectorate, 2008). We have been especially impressed by the difference in the locus for course development—the provincial department in Newfoundland and Labrador versus a proliferation of local initiatives in Northern Ireland. Following the Bain report (Northern Ireland Department of Education, 2006b) and the Department of Education's policy on sustainable schools (Northern Ireland Department of Education, 2006a), groups of schools in Northern Ireland were established as learning partnerships, with an unstated assumption that sharing of courses would involve students travelling to other neighbouring schools or Further Education colleges. To date, we do not see any evidence that these arrangements will create anything like the wide range of attractive digital courses which have been set up in Newfoundland and Labrador.

Our analysis of Newfoundland and Labrador's reform of denominational schooling leaves us with thoughts rather than suggestions. The interplay between politics, denominational schooling, and digital learning, even in jurisdictions with some shared history and culture, seems too complex and idiosyncratic to be confident that the lessons learned in one place will be of benefit in another. We fully agree with Galway and Dibbon (Chapter One) that a "perfect storm" is necessary to explain how the denominational education reforms in Newfoundland and Labrador were achieved. It is through a comparison with Northern Ireland, and in particular the composition of its power-sharing executive, that we can appreciate how much political will was needed to drive through such ground-breaking reform.

Finally, although accepting that an end to denominational schooling remains a highly unlikely policy solution for Northern Ireland's problems of demographic decline and uneven curricular choice, we believe that one way forward would be the creation of a virtual school that would provide both inter-school links for citizenship and on-line courses for students aged 14-18. To be most effective, such a school would need to be an "integrated" school that would serve students from all religious communities. This proposal would not challenge the role of the churches in the administration of local schools and would be less likely to run into political opposition. It would be cost-effective and would build on the work already carried out. Nonetheless, it would require a kind of political drive akin to what we observed in Newfoundland and Labrador in the 1990s to change some of the underlying assumptions about what schooling in the twenty-first century is for. This includes recognition of the place of values and the role that churches can play in educating young people.

So, perhaps we now see a "third record"—a basis for understanding that is informed by documentary evidence, the life experience of the observer, *and* a communal process that arises from a sustained effort to bring different understandings together around a common interest.

Reflections and Conclusions

Chapter Fourteen

Lessons for the Policy Community

David Dibbon and Gerald Galway

In this volume, we have attempted to present an inclusive and necessarily divergent collection of perspectives on the story of denominational education reform in Newfoundland and Labrador. Like us, those authors who have generously contributed to this volume, believe that the 1997 reform, and the one that followed in 2004, had not been adequately interrogated. In the years leading up to the changes described here, many people on all sides of the debate were heavily invested in the prospect of educational reform. Individual and organizational positions on the issue were often highly polarized and emotions were volatile. But once the changes were announced, the transition seemed to take place without much fanfare and with even less reflection, as if the *process* of school and school district restructuring had nothing to teach us. This book has been our attempt to consolidate the lessons and learnings from the reform process so that we may be in a better position to understand this important history, but more importantly, to suggest options for policy-makers to consider in future restructuring campaigns.

The multiple discourses presented herein capture much of the historical context to the changes that took place in Newfoundland and Labrador, but they also conceptualize the social, religious, and economic drivers that contributed to these events, and examine some of the consequences of these changes from a curricular, governance, and humanistic perspective. The "official version," recorded in government press releases, reports, and policy documents, depicts the educational change process in clinical language, using economic argument and tidy political rhetoric. But the reality of changing a system in which so many individuals were heavily invested is complex and messy. As readers of this book will have noticed, several of the contributing authors have a deeply personal connection to the education reform process. Our original plan, as we began the writing of the book, was to tell *the* story of education reform, but, as the project unfolded and we began to unravel the many facets of the changes, we realized that there are, in fact, *many* stories—each representing valid perspectives on the reform process. Levin (2001a) has observed that reliable empirical research looking at the nature and consequences of reforms in various settings is difficult to find. Although there are still gaps in our knowledge about the effects of reform on the province and its people, we believe this book has come some distance towards capturing the evidence to close *some* of these gaps.

We do not consider these representations to be complete or all encompassing. Nor do we consider the debate surrounding education reform in this province to be closed. Undoubtedly, people will continue to reflect on issues and questions such as the magnitude of the reforms; the constitutional rights of minorities; the nature of the reconstructed education system; the legislative processes required to enact the changes; whether a referendum result is sufficient grounds to impose changes to Charter rights, and whether economic interest necessarily trumps the rights of individual classes of people. The accounts of the reform process presented in this book will also find their way into university classrooms and on-line discussion groups. Thus, it is our fervent hope that the structural, governance, and constitutional issues raised in these chapters will continue to generate debate and discussion for some time to come.

Reform 2.0: Focusing on the technical core

The foregoing notwithstanding, structural and governance change are but two aspects of education reform. Changing the structure of a system can be interpreted as strong and resolute political action by a government, yet it is often at this juncture that systemic reform efforts end or stall. Unless governments and/or school boards are prepared to augment structural reforms with meaningful and systemic improvements to the *conditions for learning*, then restructuring may be nothing more than an economic strategy to take surplus schools out of service and consolidate units of instruction. Those with knowledge of change theory will recognize that structural change alone rarely expresses itself in fundamental and sustainable cultural change.

From structural to systemic change

Structural change, in combination with careful, strategic, collaborative planning, can provide a scaffold for systemic (cultural) change. Although structural change cannot ensure cultural change, we believe the strong commitment to education that exists in Newfoundland and Labrador at this time provides a unique opportunity for systemic change. Systemic change is far more difficult to accomplish than structural change; it is, however, essential for system-wide improvement. Deep, cultural change challenges the basic assumptions or paradigm upon which a system is based, and when the challenge is successful it can result in changes to beliefs and values and lead to improvements to the technical core of education—teaching and learning.

Education reform has been in the public eye, in Newfoundland and Labrador, for at least two decades. With recent improvements to this province's fiscal position, the educational community has been watching to see whether the reinvestment in education, promised by governments past and present, would come to fruition. Our judgment is that these reinvestments are occurring. There can be little doubt that this province's schools are in a better place today than before the system was restructured. There has been substantial investment in learning resources, including free textbooks, and an increase in the instructional grant, new equipment and technology, and significant funding for school buildings. There have also been some improvements in the curriculum, limits on class size in certain grades, enhancements to the model of allocating teachers, development and expansion of e-learning, more emphasis on the fine arts and healthy living, and improvements in programs and services for special-needs students.

Many educational observers, however—both supporters and opponents of reform—would likely argue that while structural and governance change has occurred, and educational funding levels are on the rise, not enough emphasis has been placed on improving the technical core or raison d'être of schooling—teaching and learning. This is not unique to Newfoundland and Labrador. In a 2008 article, Wesch argues that today's students are struggling to find significance in the traditional approaches to classroom instruction:

> Meaning and significance are assured only when our learning fits in with a grand narrative that motivates and guides us. In the past, religious narratives could serve this purpose, or narratives of national progress....but the reality is that, for a substantial portion of the population, these narratives have been dead for a long time and no longer serve. They are simply not grand enough to grapple with an increasingly global, post-industrial, media-saturated world, and not grounded enough to pass the necessary and healthy skepticism towards grand narratives that

we find in an increasingly diverse and informed public. As our focus shifts from the national to the global, our grand narratives must also shift. (p. 6)

Opponents of the reforms of the 1990s were correct when they claimed that changes in the denominational system were not a panacea for all of our educational ills; that further improvements to classroom learning and more funding were necessary to achieve our educational goals. Because we know the link between structural reform and improved student learning is weak (see e.g., Levin, 2001b; Schechty, 2005; Sheppard, Brown, & Dibbon, 2009), we see an opportunity to shift focus and to identify policy initiatives and strategies that will strengthen the technical core. We contend that the improved fiscal position of Newfoundland and Labrador and the current high level of interest in education represent a *new reform opportunity* that could be the catalyst to propel its system towards widespread improvement in teaching and learning. It is not our intention to lay out a comprehensive plan to effect this transition, but we believe strongly in the need to place emphasis in four areas: (1) continued action towards poverty reduction; (2) fostering new approaches to teaching and learning; (3) focusing on what it means to be an instructional leader, and; (4) establishing a program of research, which responds to key policy questions about student learning in the new smaller and more geographically disparate public education system. These four planks, we maintain, would go a long way towards shifting emphasis from structural reform to cultural reform and informing policy and practice—locally, regionally, and in the broader Canadian context.

Poverty reduction

Financial support for schools is one of the most important social investments that governments can make, but we must also understand how essential it is to improve the more general conditions in homes and communities. Schools can be so much more effective when their work with children is reinforced by economically secure, supportive families. The strong link between socio-economic background and educational achievement is now firmly established. Studies continue to show that family background is the single most important predictor of educational outcomes (Willms, 2002). A child's ability to grow and mature into an educated, self-assured, and productive citizen can be seriously impaired by poverty, unemployment, poor housing, poor nutrition, inadequate health care, low levels of literacy in the home, and the absence of appropriate early childhood education programs. Policy initiatives such as the poverty-reduction strategies that have been undertaken in provinces such as Quebec, Ontario, and Newfoundland and Labrador are critical to supporting the educative process at the family and community level, and must be sustained and enhanced. These initiatives and others, such as universal early childhood education and non-stigmatizing school lunch and breakfast programs, all help to level the playing field for disadvantaged families.

The technical core: Teaching and learning

To achieve meaningful improvements also requires a different way of conceptualizing how children learn, in what contexts, and through what means. It means rethinking how we can facilitate that learning so that teachers act to mediate rather than dictate learning, a practice Wesch (2008) describes as "anti-teaching." Students need access to learning tools other than traditional texts and resources, and schools must become less steeped in traditional assumptions about learning and more adept at designing new and engaging learning environments (Bransford, Brown, & Cocking, 2000).

Recent Canadian research confirms that many problems experienced by students in middle and secondary schools, such as disengagement and dissatisfaction with their schooling experience, are significantly linked to the learning environment (Willms, Friesen, & Milton, 2009). As the authors note, "the emergence of a knowledge-based economy, combined with a more diverse and complex society, compels us to rethink schools and learning" (p. 7). Willms and his colleagues go on to argue that teachers, administrators and other important stakeholders must "make schools socially, academically, and intellectually exciting and a worthwhile place to be" (p. 39). These are the hallmarks of today's highly successful school systems. Failure to create such systems will result in students continuing to tune-out traditional ways of learning. Indeed, Richardson (2007) has observed, "our students are beginning to learn in new ways without us. If they have a connection, they know they can begin to build their own networks around whatever they are passionate about" (p. 24).

So we ask: must instruction always take place in a conventional classroom? Can we be more flexible about timetabling? With the cost of laptop computers and iPads/tablets dipping below $500.00 shouldn't all students have one? Shouldn't we begin to transition away from paper resources—at least in the upper grades? Shouldn't most schools have a technology expert on staff? Shouldn't we place as much or more value on knowledge- acquisition processes and collaborations as on content knowledge? To mount a successful challenge to some of the old assumptions about learning will require leadership and cooperation from all participants and stakeholders—government, teachers' associations, district and school leaders, teacher educators, researchers, and classroom teachers. Strengthening the relationships with students, parents, and communities will also be fundamental to achieving this goal.

Leadership for learning

Local leadership, at the school district as well as the school level, is vitally important in the improvement of education. Dibbon has argued elsewhere (Sheppard et al., 2009) that knowledgeable and skilled leadership at the district level is essential to any change effort. Our conceptualization of leadership is articulated well in Sheppard et al. (2009) as systemic and distributed and one which "moves away from the traditional, hierarchical, rational planning, bureaucratic approach towards a more collaborative approach" (p. 15). This model requires that constituents at all levels of the system be actively involved in leading learning initiatives. Changes to classroom environments, such as the use of new media and the adoption of new pedagogy, will only be pervasive if they are promoted, supported, and resourced by formal leaders who enable and empower teachers to take risks. Next to the teacher, the leadership of principals may be the second most important factor in the improvement of student learning. A comprehensive leadership strategy for the development of principals and school system leaders, who are knowledgeable not only about system administration but also about how to strengthen the technical core of education, is a necessity.

The meaningful involvement of the public, particularly parents and students, is also essential to strengthening the technical core. Greater parental and student involvement has been shown to promote student success. One approach, which subverts the traditional hierarchical model of educational delivery, involves locating more educational decision making at the school and school council level. School councils can make a significant contribution to the improvement of student achievement, when they broaden their focus from tasks like fundraising to improving the learning environment. Parents, who may feel powerless and marginalized, can have a major impact in working with and motivating their children as independent learners and by reinforcing their in-school experiences. At a time when school districts are increasing in size, ways need to be found to increase the involvement of parents and the public in educational decision making.

Connecting researchers and policy-makers

Finally, any serious effort to reframe teaching and learning must be mapped to a program of research. Research is required, for example, to determine the effects of the past reform initiatives on student outcomes, including the development of pro-social values—a fundamental aspect of the former denominational schools. Research is needed to consolidate data and identify trends in student achievement, which had been such a pervasive problem under the denominational structure. Research will be required to understand how schools and districts are embracing new technologies and pedagogy, for example, Web 2.0 (Read/Write Web) tools and mediated vs. content-driven instruction. We need to monitor how new ways of organizing teaching and learning play out in terms developing what Richardson (2007) describes as a student's "personal learning practice"(p. 24). We need to devote greater attention towards understanding the middle school/intermediate school student; what changes take place during this transition period that seem to be associated, in some cases, with less rigorous program choices and low academic performance in high school? We need to know how parents and communities affected by educational restructuring and rezoning can establish and maintain strong connections to their regional schools. A robust program of research will provide insight and direction for policymakers. Otherwise, we risk falling into a pattern of enacting strategies without any formal means of monitoring their effectiveness.

As governments and school boards continue to seek out ways and means of improving the quality and efficiency of their smaller and more diverse education systems, there will be no end of proposals and strategies for doing so. However, as Levin (2001b) notes, "reform is complicated business [and] getting it right, either in terms of what is proposed or how things actually develop, is far from easy" (p. 193). As reform and restructuring opportunities emerge, sometimes there are unintended consequences that were not anticipated by the policy entrepreneurs who initiate educational change, or by their opponents.

Educational leaders, therefore, should seek to understand the nature and politics of change and demonstrate a genuine willingness to work with all partners in policy formulation, implementation, and evaluation. Research should be a key aspect of this process. As Galway has suggested elsewhere (Galway, 2007), research needs to occupy a more prominent place in educational decision making and be seen less as a source of political risk and more as a means by which educational policy can be supported. A program of research to guide future decisions about teaching and learning and other policy matters would necessarily involve policy-makers (government and its advisers), school boards, and the academy. Like many of our colleagues, we look forward to contributing to the knowledge base in these areas by following this book with future policy-relevant research.

Twenty years of structural reform: Final reflections

Nationally, it is likely that educational reform will remain on the public agenda for the foreseeable future, particularly in those provinces now experiencing the kinds of enrolment declines felt by Newfoundland and Labrador over the past several decades. At the 2009 conference of Atlantic school board trustees in St. John's, Newfoundland. the issue of how to organize schooling in a contracting education system dominated the agenda. Once a localized problem, enrolment decline is becoming a pan-Canadian phenomenon. It is not a temporary blip or a trend that is going to reverse itself any time soon. Enrolment decline is more a consequence of a more deep-seated social change than the result of a localized demographic shift. We say this because at the root of the startling enrolment shifts we are seeing in this country are fundamental changes in social behaviour and changes in the way people now see their place in the world—changes in religiosity, changes in how we conceptualize the family, changes in our life expectations, changes in our career and educational aspirations, and global changes in how we work and where we work. Young couples will likely continue to marry or engage in serious relationships later in life than their parents and grandparents. Many will opt not to have children. Those that do decide to become parents will have fewer children and be older than their parents and grandparents when they have their first—perhaps their only—child. Many young adults will move and raise their families in other parts of the country or other places in the world. This combination of an alarming drop in fertility rates combined with the migration of younger graduates in their prime childbearing years will continue to present enormous challenges across Canada, both in terms of our immediate concern—organizing and delivering educational programs—and the broader issue of community sustainability.

When we reflect upon the history of the demographic problem in Newfoundland and Labrador, we find in these chapters important lessons for administrators and policy-makers across Canada and abroad. Very often in the past, school boards and government have clashed with parents, municipalities, and community-action groups over the prospect of school closure and consolidation. It strikes us that in these times schools represent more than learning institutions; the school is a symbol of community well-being. While parents are primarily concerned about quality education, there is also the sense that a robust school enrolment is emblematic of a strong and vibrant community; and the converse also holds true—sustained enrolment decline, for many people, seems to be linked to questions of community survival and the loss of a way of life.

The choices governments and school boards make now about the structures for educational delivery are for the long term and are not going to be easily reversible. It is inevitable that some school closure and consolidation will take place, particularly in communities which presently maintain two or more schools or in communities in close proximity to one another. What we are suggesting, however, is that large-scale school closure and consolidation need not be the default policy position towards addressing the challenges of enrolment decline. It is our judgment that policy-makers need to be thinking less in economic-rationalist terms—which almost always leads to school closure and regional uncertainty—and more in terms of community/regional sustainability—being innovative and forward-looking to provide quality and equitable programming within existing schools and communities.

Mary Green (Chapter Twelve) describes how, in 2004, educators and senior staff who had built a school district based on a distributed leadership model, felt detached and demoralized when a surprise fiscal decision of government dissolved the district. The move threw their efforts into disarray, causing an information vacuum and imposing a renewed environment of distrust. She contends that leaders who advocate for a collaborative approach to administration and decision making can expect to experience obstacles that have the potential to nullify their efforts. When governmental authorities impose centralized decision making, contradictory messages, and aggressive change agendas, she writes, the goals of collaboration, trust, and sharing are at great risk and take a long time to become restored, if they are ever fully embraced in the new organization. Thus, the core values that many organizations strive to reach can lost in a sea of mistrust and cynicism where even "true believers" may feel betrayed and abandoned. When the individuals who make an organization work become disenfranchised there are both human costs and broader organizational losses. Green's call to action envisions a less hierarchical system, where "tensions relating to distribution of power, decision making, external accountabilities, and the division of male and female roles" are deconstructed and re-conceptualized.

As enrolment decline and redistribution continues, how will governments adjust their formula for school system change? Can we step away from traditional top-down models of reform and look to a more collaborative approach to disassembling and reconstructing school systems—one in which individuals are respected and their capacity and motivation to excel is retained? Like Green, we believe there is room for policy leaders to do things differently; incorporating the concept of care for individuals is a good point of departure.

We offer these closing thoughts at some risk of sounding utopian in our outlook. After 20 years of reform, who else but the optimist would argue for further changes to education? There can be no doubt that the changes to the denominational system of education, explored in this book were, for many, difficult and protracted. But we are reminded of Oscar Wilde who said, "What seems to us as bitter trials are often blessings in disguise." We are optimistic about the next 20 years as we move towards a stronger education system and a better future for all.

Appendices

Appendix A

Text of Term 17 from the Terms of Union
(Newfoundland and Canada, 1949)

17. In lieu of section ninety-three of the Constitution Act, 1867, the following Term shall apply in respect of the Province of Newfoundland.

In and for the Province of Newfoundland the Legislature shall have exclusive authority to make laws in relation to education, but the Legislature will not have authority to make laws prejudicially affecting any right or privilege with respect to denominational schools, common (amalgamated) schools, or denominational colleges, that any class or classes of persons have by law in Newfoundland at the date of Union, and out of public funds of the Province of Newfoundland, provided for education

(a) all such schools shall receive their share of such funds in accordance with scales determined on a nondiscriminatory basis from time to time by the Legislature for all schools then being conducted under authority of the Legislature; and

(b) all such colleges shall receive their share of any grant from time to time voted for all colleges then being conducted under authority of the Legislature, such grant being distributed on a nondiscriminatory basis.

Appendix B

Aims of public education for Newfoundland and Labrador (Original publication, 1959)

A.   Education is the process by which human beings are enabled to achieve their fullest and best development both as private individuals and as members of human society.

B.   We believe that best and fullest development can be achieved only in a Christian democratic society and that the aims of education, both general and specific, must be conceived in harmony with such a belief.

C.   We believe that those who have achieved their fullest and best development as individuals are those who, to the best of their ability,

(a) are possessed of a religious faith as maintained and taught by the church of their affiliation *(Spiritual: religious training and exercises)*;

(b) are possessed of a sense of moral values, based on a belief in, and an earnest endeavour to practice and exemplify in their daily living, the virtues, both spiritual and moral, affirmed by their religious faith *(Moral: religious training and general moral precept and example)*;

(c) are so developed and matured mentally and emotionally as to be able to live sanely, happily and satisfyingly, in harmony with themselves and their individual circumstances both inherited and acquired *(Mental-Emotional: a wholesome mental and emotional environment)*;

(d) have minds whose critical and other faculties are so developed and trained as to enable them to cope successfully with the varied problems and situations that they may be expected to encounter *(Mental-Intellectual: practical training and situations conducive to this end)*;

(e) have a knowledge, understanding, and appreciation of their human heritage, in all its principal aspects (aesthetic, scientific, economic, political, etc.), as well as a desire to make a positive contribution to it, and a knowledge and appreciation of the natural environment in which the human scene is set *(Intellectual-Cultural: specific training and study in the Arts, Sciences, and the Humanities)*;

(f) have learned to occupy their leisure hours in keeping with their personal interests and capacities, and in a manner which is consistent with their moral and social duties, and the other attributes listed here *(Cultural-Recreational)*;

(g) are possessed of physical health, and a knowledge of, and respect for, their physical bodies; as well as a desire, and a knowledge of how to take care of them and their functions *(Physical: a healthy environment, and specific training to this end)*;

(h) and—by way of summary—are those in whom the attributes and acquirements listed in sub-paragraphs (a) to (g) are harmonized and related in an all-round personality, whose "growth in wisdom and stature" is accompanied by "growth in favour with God and humanity".

D. "In favour with humanity" introduces the second aspect of our definition of education. For, while insisting upon the individual importance and worth of all human beings as such, and the necessity of their preserving their individuality and identity, as well as upon their right to the fullest and best development of which they are capable as individuals, we recognize that in actual fact they are members of human society. Therefore, a primary function of education must also be to enable individuals to achieve their fullest and best development as members of that society. But, in both capacities, or aspects of life, they are, of course, the same person. Thus, what they are as members of society will depend largely upon what they are as private individuals, and what they are as private individuals will depend largely upon what they are as members of society. It is, therefore, self-evident that persons who have reached their best and fullest development as members of society are those who bring to all social relationships, both private and public, the personal attributes and acquirements outlined above.

We also believe that, in addition, these persons are those who

(a) are possessed of other qualities, bearing more specially on their social relationships, that may not be thought of as included in the various subdivisions of paragraph C, such as sympathy, courtesy, tolerance, dependability, recognition of the rights of others, the ability to cooperate, assume responsibility, etc. (*Social-General: a general environment as well as practical training and situations conducive to these ends*);

(b) have a lively sense of their rights and responsibilities as citizens, based on an understanding and appreciation of the various organizations and institutions of the community—municipal, provincial, national and international (*Social-Civic: practical training and situations conducive to these ends*);

(c) have acquired the knowledge and skills of a profession, trade, or occupation that makes a necessary contribution to society; are impressed with the dignity and honourable- ness of labour; and are imbued with a sense of their responsibilities to their professions, fellow-workers, and the public they serve (*Social-Vocational: practical training and situations conducive to these ends*).

This philosophy suggests the following general objectives for education in Newfoundland schools:

1.   To help pupils understand the Christian principles and to guide them in the practice of these principles in their daily living.
2.   To help pupils to develop moral values which will serve as a guide to living.
3.   To acquaint pupils with the principles of democracy and to provide opportunities for the practice of these principles.
4.   To help pupils to mature mentally.
5.   To help pupils to mature emotionally.
6.   To ensure that all pupils master the fundamental skills of learning to the limit of their abilities.
7.   To provide opportunities for the development of pupils' abilities to think critically.

8. To help pupils to understand, appreciate and benefit from what is good and valuable in history, literature, science and the arts.
9. To help pupils make the best of their leisure time.
10. To help pupils understand the human body and practice the principles of good health.
11. To help pupils appreciate their privileges and responsibilities as members of their families and the wider community and so live in harmony with others.
12. To give pupils guidance in the choice of a career and to provide opportunities to begin preparation for occupational life.
13. To encourage pupils to strive for high standards in their work and to develop an appreciation and respect for the work of others.
14. To seek out and develop pupils' special talents and potentialities and to assist them in developing their strengths and in overcoming or adjusting to disabilities and weaknesses.
15. To ensure that both English language and French language pupils are provided the opportunity to study in their own language, where numbers warrant, and also, to study English or French as a second language.

Appendix C

Revised Term 17 (April 1997)

Adopted December 1996 and proclaimed April 1997

In lieu of section ninety-three of the Constitution Act, 1867 the following shall apply in respect of the Province of Newfoundland:

In and for the Province of Newfoundland, the Legislature shall exclusive authority to make laws in relation to education but

(a) Except as provided in paragraphs (b) and (c), schools established, maintained and operated with public funds shall be denominational schools, and any class having rights under this Term as it read on January 1, 1995 shall continue to have the right to provide for religious education, activities and observances for the children of that class in those schools, and the group of classes that formed one integrated school system by agreement in 1969 may exercise the same rights under this Term as a single class of persons;

(b) Subject to provincial legislation that is uniformly applicable to all schools specifying conditions for the establishment or continued operation of schools,

    i. any class of persons referred to in paragraph (a) shall have the right to have a publicly funded denominational school established, maintained and operated especially for that class, and

    ii. the Legislature may approve the establishment, maintenance and operation of a publicly funded school, whether denominational or non-denominational;

(c) where a school is established, maintained and operated pursuant to subparagraph (b) (i), the class of persons referred to in that subparagraph shall continue to have the right to provide for religious education, activities and observances and to direct the teaching aspects of the curriculum affecting religious beliefs, student admission policy and the assignment and dismissal of teachers in that school;

(d) all schools referred to in paragraphs (a) and (b) shall receive their share of public funds in accordance with scales determined on a non-discriminatory basis from time to time by the Legislature; and

(e) if the classes of persons having rights under this Term so desire, they shall have the right to elect not less than two thirds of the members of the school board, and any class so desiring shall have the right to elect the portion of the total that is proportionate to the population of the class in the area under the board's jurisdiction.

Appendix D

Term 17 (1998)

Proclaimed January 1998

17.(1) In lieu of section ninety-three of the Constitution Act, 1867, this term shall apply in respect of the Province of Newfoundland.

(2) In and for the Province of Newfoundland, the Legislature shall have exclusive authority to make laws in relation to education, but shall provide for courses in religion that are not specific to a religious denomination.

(3) Religious observances shall be permitted in a school where requested by parents. (Government of Newfoundland and Labrador, 1997).

Notes

Chapter One

1. Four Systems, if the Seventh-Day Adventist School Board is included.
2. Grade 11 enrolment as compared with Grade 2 enrolment nine years earlier.
3. Based on 2001 census data from Statistics Canada.

Chapter Two

1. Cody (1994), Mawhinney (1992), Pross et al. (1990), and Wilson (1971) offer a further discussion of the use of royal commissions.
2. Cody (1994) has provided an excellent summary of the Commission's activities.
3. See Fagan, Chapter Six, for a fuller discussion of these events from the perspective of the Roman Catholic authorities.

Chapter Five

1. Source: Federal Deposit Insurance Corporation (1997).
2. Defined as the ratio of government debt to gross domestic product (GDP) in Canada.

Chapter Six

1. For discussion of the perceived economic forces at play, refer to Chapters Four (by McCann) and Five (by Galway).

Chapter Seven

1. For a fuller treatment, see Bezeau (2007a), Eidsness, Steeves, & Dolmage (2008), Phillips (1957), and Smith & Foster (2001a, 2001b, 2001c).
2. It is difficult to determine the exact proportion of Catholic school enrolment in Canada as a percentage of the total school enrolment. The Canadian Catholic School Trustees Association (CCSTA) is an organization that consists of Catholic trustee organizations of both the public denominational school systems (Ontario's English and French systems, Alberta including the Yukon, and Saskatchewan) and the private Catholic school trustee associations of British Columbia, Manitoba, and Newfoundland and Labrador but no representation from the private Catholic schools of either Ontario or Nova Scotia. CCSTA maintains numbers of full-time enrolment equivalents of schools but its Director drew attention to the fact that this way of counting students differs somewhat from provincial and national data which counts total enrolment. An important example of the difference might be Junior Kindergarten students who are enrolled for only half days. It would take two such students to count as one in full time equivalent numbers.

Chapter Nine

1. For most of the period while the new religious education program in Newfoundland and Labrador was being developed, Bryce Hodder was the provincial education consultant charged with overseeing the process. He now teaches religious studies methods at Memorial University.
2. Where appropriate, in this chapter, the term living belief system(s) will be used rather than the term religion(s). This is in recognition of, and out of respect for, communities of belief and spirituality that do not wish to be identified as a religion but are included in the curriculum.

Chapter Ten

1. Mother's education level and the number of books in the home are commonly used proxy measures of a family's socio-economic status.

Chapter Eleven

1. The first school board elections in Newfoundland and Labrador were held in 1974 when the revised Schools (Amendment) Act (1970) pro-

vided one-third of the members to be selected by election; the remaining members were appointed by the Denominational Education Committees. From November 1984 to February 1998 two-thirds of the members were elected and one-third was appointed (Schools (Amendment) Act, 1984). Since February 1998, the practice has been for all school board members to be elected (Schools Act, 1997).

Chapter Thirteen

1. Moodle is a Virtual Learning Environment that allows users to engage in asynchronous discussion and to construct knowledge in a shared and private website.
2. Special schools cater for the needs of young people with moderate or severe learning difficulties.

References

Abbott, M. G., & Caracheo, F. (1988). Power, authority, and bureaucracy. In N. J. Boyan (Ed.), *Handbook of research on educational administration* (pp. 239–257). New York, NY: Longman.

Abel, E. K., & Nelson, M. K. (Eds.). (1990). *Circles of care: Work and identity in women's lives*. New York, NY: State University of New York Press.

Adler v. Ontario, [1996] 3 S.C.R. 609 (S.C.C.). Retrieved from http://scc.lexum.org/en/1996/1996scr3-609/1996scr3-609.pdf

Alliance Party of Northern Ireland. (2006, March). *Alliance party policy: Integrated education*. Belfast, NI: Author. Retrieved from http://www.allianceparty.org/pages/policy-integratededucation.html.

Alphonso, C. (2007, September 10). Ontario campaign starts with verbal attacks. *The Globe and Mail*. Retrieved from http://www.theglobeandmail.com/archives/article781289.ece

Amulree, Baron. (1933). *Report of the Newfoundland Royal Commission*. London, UK: Secretary of State for Dominion Affairs, His Majesty's Stationery Office.

Anderson, G. (2001). Disciplining leaders: a critical discourse analysis of the ISLLC National Examination and Performance Standards in educational administration. *International Journal of Leadership in Education, 4*, 199–216.

Andrews v. Law Society of British Columbia, [1989] 1 S.C.R. 143. (S.C.C.). Retrieved from http://scc.lexum.org/en/1989/1989scr1-143/1989scr1-143.pdf

Andrews, R. L. (1985a). *Integration and other developments in Newfoundland education, 1915–1949*. A. E. Wareham (Ed.). St. John's, NL: Harry Cuff.

Andrews, R. L. (1985b). *Post-Confederation developments in Newfoundland education, 1949–1975*. A. E. Wareham (Ed.). St. John's, NL: Harry Cuff.

Appadurai, A. (1996). *Modernity at large: Cultural dimensions of globalization*. Minneapolis, MN: University of Minnesota Press.

Apple, M. W. (2000). Between neoliberalism and neoconservativatism: Education and conservatism in a global context. In N. C. Burbules & C. A. Torres (Eds.), *Globalization and education: Critical perspectives* (pp. 57–77). New York, NY: Routledge.

Apple, M. W. (2004). *Ideology and Curriculum* (3rd. ed.). New York, NY: Routledge Falmer.

Apple, M. W., Kenway, J., & Singh, M. (2005). *Globalizing education: Policies, pedagogies, and politics.* New York, NY: Peter Lang.

Armstrong, S. (2000). Magazines, cultural policy and globalization: The forced retreat of the state. *Canadian Public Policy, 26*, 369–385.

Atlantic Evaluation and Research Consultants. (2008). *Intermediate program review.* Report prepared for the Department of Education. St. John's, NL: Government of Newfoundland and Labrador.

Atlantic Institute for Market Studies. (2008). *AIMS 5th annual high school report card (rc5).* Halifax, NS: Author. Retrieved from http://www.aims.ca/

Atlantic Provinces' Economic Council. (2003). Outlook 2003–A delicate balance: Maximizing growth in turbulent times. *Atlantic Report, 37*(3), 2.

Atlantic Provinces Education Foundation. (1996). *The Atlantic Canada framework for essential graduation learnings in schools.* Halifax, NS: Author.

Aucoin, P. (1995). *The new public management: Canada in comparative perspective.* Montreal, QC: Institute for Research on Public Policy.

Auditor General of Newfoundland and Labrador. (2008). *Report of the Auditor General: Reviews of departments and crown agencies.* St. John's, NL: Author. Retrieved from http://www.aims.ca

Austin, R., & Anderson, J. (2007). *E-schooling: Global messages from a small island.* Abingdon, UK: Routledge.

Austin, R., Smyth. J., Mallon, M., Rickard, A., Flynn, P., & Metcalfe, N. (2009). Cross-border digital school partnerships. *Report of the Dissolving Boundaries Program, 1999–2009.* Retrieved from http://www.dissolvingboundaries.org/research/dbreport2009.pdf

Avis, J. (2000). Policing the subject: Learning, outcomes, managerialism and research in PCET. *British Journal of Educational Studies, 48*, 38–57.

Banting, K., Sharpe, A., & St-Hilaire, F. (Eds.). (2001). *The review of economic performance and social progress: The longest decade: Canada in the 1990s.* Montreal, QC: Institute for Public Policy.

Bard, J., Gardener, C., & Wieland, R. (2006). Rural school consolidation: History, research summary, conclusions and recommendations. National Rural Education Association task force report. *The Rural Educator, 27*(2), 40–48.

Barlow, M., & Robertson, H.-J. (1994). *Class warfare: The assault on Canada's schools.* Toronto, ON: Key Porter.

Barzelay, M. (2001). *The new public management: Improving research and policy dialogue.* Berkeley, CA: University of California Press.

Beck, L. G. (1994). *Reclaiming educational administration as a caring profession.* New York, NY: Teachers College Press.

Ben-Peretz, M., & Schonmann, S. (1998). Informal learning communities and their effects. In K. Leithwood & K. S. Louis (Eds.), *Organizational learning in schools* (pp. 47–66). Lisse, The Netherlands: Swets Zeitlinger.

Bergman, B., & Stokes-Sullivan, D. (1997, September 15). Back to the drawing board. *Maclean's*, 16–17.

Bezeau, L. M. (2002). *Educational administration for Canadian teachers* (4th. ed.). Fredericton, NB: New Brunswick Centre for Educational Administration. Retrieved from www.unb.ca/centres/nbcea/nbeduc90.html

Bezeau, L. M. (2007). *Educational administration for Canadian teachers* (7th. ed.). Fredericton, NB: Author.

Bibby, R. (1993). Secularization and change. In W. E. Hewitt (Ed.), *The sociology of religion: A Canadian focus* (pp. 65–81). Toronto, ON: Butterworths.

Bibby, R. W. (2006). *The boomer factor: What Canada's most famous generation is leaving behind.* Toronto, ON: Bastian Books.

Bidwell, C. (1965). The school as a formal organization. In J. G. March (Ed.), *Handbook of organizations* (pp. 972–1022). Chicago, IL: Rand McNally.

Bingham, C. (2004). Let's treat authority relationally. In C. Bingham & A. M. Sidorkin (Eds.), *No education without relation* (pp. 23–37). New York, NY: Peter Lang.

Bingham, C., & Sidorkin, A. M. (Eds.). (2004). *No education without relation.* New York, NY: Peter Lang.

Blackmore, J. (1999a). Localization/globalization and the midwife state: Strategic dilemmas for state feminism in education? *Journal of Education Policy, 14,* 33–54.

Blackmore, J. (1999b). *Troubling women: Feminism, leadership and educational change.* Philadelphia, PA: Open University Press.

Blackmore, J., & Sachs, J. (2007). *Performing and reforming leaders: Gender, educational restructuring, and organizational change.* Albany, NY: State University of New York Press.

Blouin, P. (2008). *Summary public school indicators for the provinces and territories, 1999/2000 to 2005/2006* (Catalogue no 81-595-M No. 067). Ottawa, ON: Statistics Canada.

Borst, J. (2008). *NWT Appeals Court upholds non-Catholic's right to sit on Catholic Board; Yellowknife Catholic Board will take appeal to Supreme Court.* Retrieved from http://tomorrowstrust.ca/?p=3160

Boswell, P. (1997, August 16). Politics: Referendum opposition is about power not morality. *The Evening Telegram,* p. 11.

Boudreau, S. (1999). *Catholic education: The Quebec experience.* Calgary, AB: Detselig.

Bowker, J. (2002). World religions: The boundaries of belief and unbelief. In L. Broadbent & A. Brown (Eds.), *Issues in religious education* (pp. 210–217). London, UK: Routledge Falmer.

Bransford, J. D., Brown, A. L., & Cocking, R. R. (Eds.). (2000). *How people learn: brain, mind, experience, and school* (Expanded Ed.). Commission on Behavioural and Social Sciences and Education, National Research Council. Washington, DC: National Academy Press.

Brennan, R. (2004). *Revolutions and evolutions in current educational testing.* Occasional paper. Iowa City, IA: Iowa Academy of Education.

Brooks, J. G., & Brooks, M. G. (1999). *In search of understanding: The case for constructivist classrooms.* Alexandria, VA: Association for Supervision and Curriculum Development.

Brown, J., & Barry, M. (2008, May). The evolution of e-learning in small rural and remote schools in Newfoundland and Labrador. In G. Galway & D. Dibbon (Eds.), *Symposium 2008: Post-confederation educational reform: From rhetoric to reality* (pp. 21–32). St. John's, NL: Memorial University.

Brown, R. D. (2000). The impact of the US on Canada's tax strategy. *Isuma, 1*(1), 70–79.

Brunner, C. C., & Björk, L. G. (Eds.). (2001). *The new superintendency.* Amsterdam, The Netherlands: JAI.

Bulcock, J. W. (1990). Public attitudes toward interdenominational sharing of educational facilities and services. *The Morning Watch, 18*(1–2), 22–34.

Bussière, P., Knighton, T., & Pennock, D. (2007). *Measuring up: Canadian results of the OECD PISA study: The performance of Canada's youth in science, reading, and mathematics: 2006 first results for Canadians aged 15.* Ottawa, ON: Statistics Canada.

Callahan, R. E. (1962). *Education and the cult of efficiency: A study of the social forces that have shaped the administration of the public schools.* Chicago, IL: University of Chicago Press.

Callahan, W. R. (2003). *Joseph Roberts Smallwood: Journalist, premier, Newfoundland patriot.* St. John's, NL: Flanker Press.

Canadian Broadcasting Corporation. (2006, December 19). *Squabbling costs school board members their jobs.* Ottawa, ON: Author. Retrieved from http://www.cbc.ca/canada/nova-scotia/story/2006/12/19/hrsb-casey.html.

Canadian Chamber of Commerce. (1989). *Focus 2000: Report of the task force on education and training.* Toronto, ON: Author.

Canadian Church Historical Society. (1960, July). *Occasional publication No. 5.* Toronto, ON: Author.

Canadian Civil Liberties Association (CCLA). (2007, September 21). *CCLA to Kathleen Wynne re: public funding of religious schools.* Retrieved from http://www.ccla.org

Canadian Council on Learning. (2007). *State of learning in Canada: No time for complacency.* Ottawa, ON: Author. Retrieved from http://www.ccl-cca.ca/

Canadian Education Statistics Council. (2003). *Education indicators in Canada: Report of the pan-Canadian indicators program.* Ottawa, ON: Author.

Canadian School Boards Association (CSBA). (1995). *Who's running our schools: Educational governance in the 1990s–Provincial/territorial summaries.* Ottawa, ON: Author.

Carver, J. (2006). *Boards that make a difference: A new design for leadership in nonprofit and public organizations* (3rd. ed.). San Francisco, CA: Jossey-Bass.

Castells, M. (1997). *The power of identity: The information age–economy, society and culture* (Vol. 2). Oxford, UK: Blackwell.

Castells, M. (2000a). *The rise of the network society: The information age–economy, society and Culture* (Vol. 1, 2nd. ed.). Oxford, UK: Blackwell. (Original work published 1996.)

Castells, M. (2000b). *End of millennium: The information age* (Vol. 3, 2nd. ed.). Oxford, UK: Blackwell.

Catholic Bishops of Northern Ireland. (2001). *Building peace, shaping the future*. Armagh, NI: Author. Retrieved from http://www.catholiccommunications.ie/ PastLet/buildingpeace_October.pdf

Catholic Civil Rights League. (2009, September 3). Quebec court rules against Drummondville parents. Retrieved from http://www.ccrl.ca/index.php?id=5062

Catholic Education Council. (1991, April 30). *Brief presented to the Royal Commission of Enquiry into the Delivery of Programs and Services in Primary, Elementary and Secondary Education*. St. John's, NL: Author.

Catholic Education Council. (1997, November 24). *Brief on the legal issue arising in connection with the amendment*. St. John's, NL: Author.

Catholics OK school closures. (1997, July 30). *The Evening Telegram*, pp. 1-2.

Chilver Report. (1980). *The future structure of higher education in Northern Ireland: An interim report of the Higher Education Review Group for Northern Ireland*. Belfast, NI: Her Majesty's Stationery Office.

Clandinin, D. J., & Connelly, F. M. (1998). Stories to live by: Narrative understandings of school reform. *Curriculum Inquiry, 28*, 149-164.

Clandinin, D. J., & Connelly, F. M. (2000). *Narrative inquiry: Experience and story in qualitative research*. San Francisco, CA: Jossey-Bass.

Clarke, A. C. (2004). *Belief with integrity* [Pamphlet]. Oxford, UK: International Association for Religious Freedom.

Cody, A. (1994). *The role of a Royal Commission in educational decision-making* (Unpublished doctoral dissertation). The Ontario Institute for Studies in Education, University of Toronto, Toronto, ON.

Coffin, G. A. (1977). *A profile of shared school services in Newfoundland* (Unpublished master's thesis). Memorial University, St. John's, NL.

Collins, A., Harte, A., & Cooper, J. (1995). Enhancing local involvement in education through quality leadership. *Prospects, 1*(2), 2-4. St. John's, NL: Memorial University. Retrieved from http://www.cdli.ca/Community/Prospects/v1n3/enhaeduc.htm

Commission of Enquiry. (1934). *Report of the Commission of Enquiry into the Present Curriculum of the Colleges and Schools in Newfoundland*. St. John's, NL: Author.

Consolidated school board likes report. (1992). *The Evening Telegram*, p. 1.

Coombs, K. (1990, February 12). Address to *Forum on Denominational Education*. St. John's, NL: Author.

Council of Ministers of Education, Canada (CMEC). (2005). *Measuring up: Canadian results of the OECD PISA study–The performance of Canada's youth in mathematics, reading, science and problem solving (2003 First Findings for Canadians Aged 15)*. Ottawa, ON: Author. Retrieved from http://www.cmec.ca/pisa/2003/indexe.stm

Council of Ministers of Education, Canada (CMEC). (2007). *The Pan-Canadian Assessment Program (PCAP) and the School Achievement Indicators Program (SAIP)*. Toronto, ON: Author. Retrieved from http://www.cmec.ca/pcap/indexe.stm

Council of Ministers of Education, Canada (CMEC). (2008). *Education in Canada*. Retrieved from http://www.cmec.ca/Publications/Lists/Publications/Attachments/64/EducationCanada.en.pdf

Cotton, K. (2001). *New small learning communities: Findings from recent literature*. Portland, OR: Northwest Regional Educational Laboratory. Retrieved from http://citeseerx.ist.psu.edu/viewdoc/download?doi=10.1.1.104.3895&rep=rep1&type=pdf

Cox, H. (1966). *The secular city: Secularization and urbanization in theological perspective* (Rev. ed.). New York, NY: Macmillan.

Crocker, R. (1989). *Towards an achieving society: Report of the task force on mathematics and science education*. St. John's, NL: Government of Newfoundland and Labrador.

Crocker, R. K. (1990). *Catholic education in Newfoundland and Labrador: Report of surveys of members of the Catholic education community* (2 Vols.). St. John's, NL: Catholic Education Council.

Crocker, R., & Riggs, F. (1979). *Improving the quality of education: Challenge and opportunity: Final report of the task force on education*. St. John's, NL: Government of Newfoundland and Labrador.

Cuff, H. A. (1985). *A history of the Newfoundland Teachers' Association, 1890–1930*. St. John's, NL: Creative.

Dale, R. (1999). Specifying globalization effects on national policy: A focus on the mechanisms. *Journal of Education Policy, 14,* 1–17.

Dea, C., Kustec, S., Lapointe, M., & Lawlis, J. (2000). Current labour market conditions and outlook. *Quarterly Labour Market and Income Review, 1*(3), 1–7. Ottawa, ON: Human Resources Development, Canada.

Dehli, K. (1996). Between "market" and "state": Engendering educational change in the 1990s. *Discourse, 7,* 363–376.

DeMont, J., & Stokes-Sullivan, D. (1997, September 18). Voting for change. *Maclean's,* 24–25.

Denis, W. B., & Li, P. S. (1988). The politics of language loss: A Francophone case from western Canada. *Journal of Education Policy, 3,* 351–370. Retrieved from http://www.informaworld.com/smpp/content~content=a757672994~db=all

Denominational Education Councils. (1993, November 23). *Coterminous cooperative school district model and a provincial structure*. St. John's, NL: Author.

Dickinson, G. M., & MacKay, A. W. (1989). *Rights, freedoms and the education systems in Canada: Cases and materials*. Toronto, ON: Emond Montgomery.

Dillard, C. B. (2003). The substance of things hoped for, the evidence of things not seen: Examining an endarkened feminist epistemology in educational research and leadership. In M. D. Young & L. Skrla (Eds.), *Reconsidering feminist research in educational leadership* (pp. 131–159). New York, NY: State University of New York Press.

Dolmage, W. R. (1992). Interest groups, the courts and the development of public policy in Canada. *Journal of Educational Policy, 7,* 313–335.

Donlevy, J. K. (2005). Re-visiting denominational cause and denominational breach in Canada's constitutionally protected Catholic schools. *Education and Law Journal, 15,* 85–112.

Doyle, D. P., & Finn, C. E., Jr. (1984). American schools and the future of local control. *Public Interest, 77,* 77–95.

Dubnik, M. J., & Bardes, B. A. (1983). *Thinking about public policy: A problem-solving approach.* New York, NY: Wiley.

Duffy, F. (2004). Navigating whole-district change: Eight principles for moving an organization upward in times of unpredictability. *School Administrator, 61*(1), 22–26. Retrieved from http://www.aasa.org/publications/sa/2004_01/Duffy.htm

Dunn, B. J. (1991). *Catholic schools in Newfoundland: An investigation into their nature according to the Code of Canon Law* (Unpublished doctoral dissertation). Saint Paul University, Ottawa, ON.

Dunn, S., & Gallagher, T. (2002). *The teacher exception provision and equality in employment in Northern Ireland: Research report.* Belfast, NI: Equality Commission. Retrieved from www.equalityni.org/

Easton, D. (1965). *A systems analysis of political life.* New York, NY: Wiley.

Economic Council of Canada. (1992). *A lot to learn: Education and training in Canada.* Ottawa, ON: Author.

Economic Recovery Commission. (1994). *At the crossroads: The new economy in Newfoundland and Labrador.* St. John's, NL: Author.

Education Act, S.N.L. 1968, s.25.

Education plebiscite is a go. (1995, June 24). *The Evening Telegram,* p. 1.

Education Reform (Amendment) Order (Northern Ireland) 1998, No. 117. Retrieved from http://www.legislation.gov.uk/nisr/1998/117/contents/made

Eidsness, B., Steeves, L., & Dolmage, W. R. (2008). Funding non-minority faith adherents in minority faith schools in Saskatchewan. *Education and Law Journal, 17,* 291–346.

Elmore, R. F. (2002). *Bridging the gap between standards and achievement: The imperative for professional development in education.* Washington, DC: Albert Shanker Institute.

Elmore, R. F. (2004). *School reform from the inside out: Policy, practice, and performance.* Cambridge, MA: Harvard Education Press.

Emery, M. (2006). *The future of schools: How communities and staff can transform their school districts.* Lanham, MD: Rowman & Littlefield.

Fagan, B. (1993). The Royal Commission report, *Our Children, Our Future*: A challenge to Newfoundland's denominational education system. *Grail, 9* (December), 63–81.

Fagan, B. (2004). *Trial: The loss of constitutional rights in education in Newfoundland and Labrador: The Roman Catholic story.* St. John's, NL: Adda Press.

Federal Deposit Insurance Corporation. (1997, December). *History of the Eighties: Lessons for the future: Volume 1: An examination of the banking crisis of the 1980s and early 1990s.* Washington, DC: Author.

Fisher, B., & Tronto, J. C. (1990). Toward a feminist theory of caring. In E. Abel & M. K. Nelson (Eds.), *Circles of care: Work and identity in women's lives* (pp. 35–62). New York, NY: State University of New York Press.

Fleming, T. (1997). Provincial initiatives to restructure Canadian school governance in the 1990s. *Canadian Journal of Educational Administration and Policy, 11.* Retrieved from http://www.umanitoba.ca/publications/cjeap/articles/fleming.html

Fleming, T., & Hutton, B. (1997). School boards, district consolidation, and educational governance in British Columbia, 1872–1995. *Canadian Journal of Educational Administration and Policy, 10.* Retrieved from http://www.umanitoba.ca/publications/cjeap/articles/fleming10.htm

Flynn, J. J. (Ed.). (2003). *Catholic schools across Canada: Into the new millennium* (3rd. ed.). Toronto, ON: Canadian Catholic School Trustees Association.

Foster, R. F. (2008). *Luck and the Irish: A brief history of change from 1970.* New York, NY: Oxford University Press.

Foster, W. F., & Smith, W. J. (2002). Religion and education in Canada: Part II—An alternative framework for the debate. *Education and Law Journal, 11,* 1–67.

Franzway, S. (2001). *Sexual politics and greedy institutions.* Annandale, Australia: Pluto Press Australia.

Franzway, S. (2005). Making progressive educational politics in the current globalization crisis. In M. W. Apple, J. Kenway, & M. Singh (Eds.), *Globalizing education: Policies, pedagogies, and politics* (pp. 265–279). New York, NY: Peter Lang.

Fraser Institute. (2008). *Report cards.* Vancouver, BC: Author. Retrieved from http://www.fraserinstitute.org/reportcards/schoolperformance/

Friedman, M. (1962a). *Capitalism and freedom.* Chicago, IL: University of Chicago Press.

Friedman, M. (1962b). The role of government in education. In M. Friedman, *Capitalism and freedom* (pp. 85–107). Chicago, IL: University of Chicago Press.

Fullan, M. (1993). *Change forces: Probing the depths of education reform.* London, UK: Falmer Press.

Fullan, M. (2005a). *Leadership and sustainability: System thinkers in action.* Thousand Oaks, CA: Corwin Press.

Fullan, M. (2005b). Turnaround leadership. *Educational Forum, 69,* 174–181.

Furey, D., Drover, D., Nash, G., & Skinner, J. (2008, May). From radio broadcasts to virtual reality: A case study of distance education in Hermitage Bay schools. In G. Galway & D. Dibbon (Eds.), *Symposium 2008: Post-confederation educational reform: From rhetoric to reality* (pp. 59–78). St. John's, NL: Memorial University.

Galbraith, J. K. (2004). *The economics of innocent fraud: Truth for our time.* Boston, MA: Houghton Mifflin.

Galway, G. (2004). E-learning as a means of promoting educational equity in rural and remote communities: A Canadian case study. In A. Karpati (Ed.), *Promoting equity through ICT in education: Projects, problems, prospects* (pp. 70–81). Budapest, Hungary: Organisation for Economic Co-operation and Development.

Galway, G. (2006). *An investigation of the uses of evidence and research in education decision making of policy elites* (Unpublished doctoral dissertation). University of South Australia, Adelaide, Australia.

Galway, G. (2007). Education policy making in Canada: Risky business. *The Bulletin, 50*(6), 24–27. St. John's, NL: Newfoundland and Labrador Teachers' Association.

Giddens, A. (1990). *The consequences of modernity.* Stanford, CA: Stanford University Press.

Giddens, A. (1991). *Modernity and self-identity: Self and society in the late modern age.* Stanford, CA: Stanford University Press.

Giddens, A. (1994). *Beyond left and right: The future of radical politics.* Stanford, CA: Stanford University Press.

Giddens, A. (2003). *Runaway world: How globalization is shaping our lives* (2nd. ed.). New York, NY: Routledge.

Giles, C., & Hargreaves, A. (2006). The sustainability of innovative schools as learning organizations and professional learning communities during standardized reform. *Educational Administration Quarterly, 42,* 124–156.

Gilligan, C. (1982). *In a different voice: Psychological theory and women's development.* Cambridge, MA: Harvard University Press.

Gilligan, C., Ward, J., McLean Taylor, J., & Bardige, B. (1988). *Mapping the moral domain.* Cambridge, MA: Harvard University Press.

Glaser, B. G. (1978). *Theoretical sensitivity: Advances in the methodology of grounded theory.* Mill Valley, CA: Sociology Press.

Goodlad, J. I. (2001). Convergence. In R. Soder, J. I. Goodlad, & T. McMannon (Eds.), *Developing democratic character in the young* (pp. 1–25). San Francisco, CA: Jossey-Bass.

Goudge, S. T. (2000). The five most significant decisions in the courts in the past year. Retrieved from http://www.ontariocourts.on.ca/coa/en/ps/speeches/five.htm

Government of Canada. (1987). *Constitutional amendment proclamation, 1987.* Ottawa, ON: Author. Retrieved from http://www.geocities.com/yosemite/rapids/3330/constitution/1987.htm

Government of Canada. (1996). *Journals of the Senate.* 35thParliament, 2nd session, No. 54. November 27, 1996. Retrieved from http://www.parl.gc.ca/35/ 2/parlbus/chambus/senate/jour-e/54jr_1996-11-27-E.htm?Language=E&Parl=35&Ses=2

Government of Canada. (1997a). *Constitutional amendment proclamation, 1998 (Newfoundland Act).* Ottawa, ON: Author. Retrieved from http://www.solon.org/Constitutions/Canada/English/cap_1997nfa.html

Government of Canada. (1997b, October 27). The amendment to Term 17 of Newfoundland's terms of union with Canada: Statement by the Honourable Stéphane Dion. Ottawa, ON: Author. Retrieved from http://www.bcp.gc.ca/aia/index.asp?doc=19971027_e.htm&lang=eng&page=archive&sub=speeches

Government of Canada. (1997c, December). *Report of the special joint committee on the amendment to Term 17 of the terms of union of Newfoundland.* Ottawa, ON: Author. Retrieved from http://www.solon.org/Constitutions/Canada/English/Committees/Term17-1997/SJNSRP01-E.htm

Government of Canada. (1997d, November 25). *Linguistic school boards–Amendment to Section 93 of constitution–Consideration of report of special joint committee.* Ottawa, ON: Author. Retrieved from http://sen.parl.gc.ca/lpepin/index.asp?PgId=814&l=E

Government of Canada. (1997e). Journals of the Senate. 36th Parliament, 1st session, No. 35. December 18, 1997. Retrieved from http://www.parl.gc.ca/36/1/

parlbus/chambus/senate/jour-e/035jr_1997-12-18-E.htm?Language=E& Parl=36 &Ses=1

Government of Canada. (1998). *Constitutional amendment proclamation, 1998 (Newfoundland act).* Ottawa, ON: Author. Retrieved from http://www.solon.org/Constitutions/Canada/English/cap_1998nfa.html

Government of Canada. (2001). *Canada Year Book, 2001.* Ottawa, ON: Author. Retrieved from http://www.canadianeconomy.gc.ca/English/economy/overview. html

Government of Canada. (2008). *The amendment to Term 17 of Newfoundland's terms of union with Canada: Statement by the Honourable Stéphane Dion, October 27, 1997.* Ottawa, ON: Privy Council. Retrieved from http://www.pco-bcp.gc.ca/aia/index.asp?doc=19971027_e.htm&lang=eng&page=archive&sub=speeches

Government of Manitoba. (1959). *Report of the Manitoba Royal Commission on Education.* Winnipeg, MB: Author.

Government of Newfoundland and Labrador. (1959). *Aims of education for Newfoundland.* St. John's, NL: Author.

Government of Newfoundland and Labrador. (1967). *Report of the Royal Commission on Education and Youth, Vol. 1* (The Warren Commission). St. John's, NL: Author.

Government of Newfoundland and Labrador. (1968). *Report of the Royal Commission on Education and Youth, Vol. 2* (The Warren Commission). St. John's, NL: Author.

Government of Newfoundland and Labrador. (1969, April 15). *Hansard.* Third session of the thirty-fourth General Assembly. Vol. I.

Government of Newfoundland and Labrador. (1979). *Task force on education: Improving the quality of education–challenge and opportunity, final report.* St. John's, NL: Task Force on Education.

Government of Newfoundland and Labrador. (1986a). *Building on our strengths: Report of the Royal Commission on Employment and Unemployment* (The House Commission). St. John's, NL: Author.

Government of Newfoundland and Labrador. (1986b). *Education for self-reliance: Education report of the Royal Commission on Employment and Unemployment* (The House Commission). St. John's, NL: Author.

Government of Newfoundland and Labrador. (1989–2000). *Education statistics.* St. John's, NL: Author.

Government of Newfoundland and Labrador. (1991). *Report of the Commissioner into the Response of the Newfoundland Criminal Justice System to Complaints* (The Hughes Commission). St. John's, NL: Author.

Government of Newfoundland and Labrador. (1992a). *Change and challenge: A strategic economic plan for Newfoundland and Labrador.* St. John's, NL: Author.

Government of Newfoundland and Labrador. (1992b). *Our children, our future: Report of the Royal Commission of Inquiry into the Delivery of Programs and Services in Primary, Elementary, Secondary Education* (The Williams Commission). St. John's, NL: Author.

Government of Newfoundland and Labrador. (1992c). *Our children, our future: Report of the Royal Commission of Inquiry into the Delivery of Programs and Service in Primary, Elementary, Secondary Education (Summary Report)* (The Williams Commission). St. John's, NL: Author.

Government of Newfoundland and Labrador. (1993). *Adjusting the course: Restructuring the School System for Educational Excellence.* St. John's, NL: Author.

Government of Newfoundland and Labrador. (1994a). *Meeting the challenge: Status report on the implementation of the strategic economic plan.* St. John's, NL: Author.

Government of Newfoundland and Labrador. (1994b). *Adjusting the course: Part II: Improving the conditions for learning.* St. John's, NL: Author.

Government of Newfoundland and Labrador. (1995a, September 6). *Official results.* Office of the Chief Electoral Officer, September 5, 1995 Plebiscite. St. John's, NL: Author.

Government of Newfoundland and Labrador. (1995b). Resolution to Amend Term 17. *Hansard,* Vol. XLII.

Government of Newfoundland and Labrador. (1996, April 19). *Framework agreement established to set up 10 interim school boards and a provincial construction board* [Press release]. Retrieved from http://www.releases.gov.nl.ca/releases/1996/edu/0419n01.htm

Government of Newfoundland and Labrador. (1997a, September 9). *Official results.* Office of the Chief Electoral Officer, September 2, 1997 Plebiscite. St. John's, NL: Author.

Government of Newfoundland and Labrador. (1997b, November 18). *Education reform in Newfoundland and Labrador: Brief submitted on behalf of the Government of Newfoundland and Labrador by Roger Grimes, Minister of Education, to the Special Joint Committee to Amend Term 17 of the Terms of Union of Newfoundland with Canada.* St. John's, NL: Author. Retrieved from http://www.releases.gov.nl.ca/releases/1997/edu/Term17.htm

Government of Newfoundland and Labrador (1998a, January 8). *Historic day for education in Newfoundland and Labrador* [Press release]. St. John's, NL: Author. Retrieved from http://www.releases.gov.nl.ca/releases/1998/weeks/jan0511.htm

Government of Newfoundland and Labrador. (1998b). *Post-secondary indicators '98: University, public colleges, private colleges.* St. John's, NL: Author.

Government of Newfoundland and Labrador. (1999, August 19). *Ministerial panel announced on delivery of education in the classroom* [Press release]. St. John's, NL: Author. Retrieved from http://www.releases.gov.nl.ca/releases/1999/edu/0819n07.htm

Government of Newfoundland and Labrador. (2000). *Supporting learning: Report of the ministerial panel on educational delivery in the classroom.* St. John's, NL: Author. Retrieved from http://www.ed.gov.nl.ca/edu/ pblications/archives/Education Delivery.pdf

Government of Newfoundland and Labrador. (2002a). *Religious education framework document (draft).* St. John's, NL: Department of Education.

Government of Newfoundland and Labrador. (2002b). *Educational statistics.* St. John's, NL: Author.

Government of Newfoundland and Labrador. (2004). *School board consolidation: Orientation information for transitional committees.* St. John's, NL: Department of Education.

Government of Newfoundland and Labrador. (2005). *Guidelines for multi-year performance-based planning.* St. John's, NL: Transparency & Accountability Office, Newfoundland and Labrador. Retrieved from http://www.exec.gov.nl.ca/ exec/cabinet/ transacc/pdf/ GuidelinesforPlanning.pdf

Government of Newfoundland and Labrador. (2006). *Budget 06: The right choices.* Retrieved from http://www.budget.gov.nl.ca/budget2006/highlights.htm

Government of Newfoundland and Labrador. (2007a). *Speech from the Throne 2007.* Retrieved from http://www.releases.gov.nl.ca/releases/2007/exec/0424n03.htm

Government of of Newfoundland and Labrador. (2007b). *Education statistics 2006–2007.* St. John's, NL: Author. Retrieved from http://www.ed.gov.nl.ca/edu/ pub/stats06_07/stats06_07.htm

Government of Newfoundland and Labrador. (2008a). *Fall update.* St. John's, NL: Department of Finance. Retrieved from http://www.fin.gov.nl.ca/fin/2007-08update.htm

Government of Newfoundland and Labrador. (2008b). *Educational statistics.* St. John's, NL: Author.

Government of Newfoundland and Labrador. (2008c). *Strategic plan: April 1, 2008 to March 31, 2011.* St. John's, NL: Author. Retrieved from http://www.ed.gov. nl.ca/edu/pub/StrategicPlan2008-11.pdf

Government of Newfoundland and Labrador. (2009). *Population and demographics.* St. John's, NL: Author. Retrieved from http://www.stats.gov.nl.ca/Statistics/ Population/

Government of Newfoundland and Labrador. (2011). *Education statistics.* St. John's, NL: Author.

Graesser, M. (1988a). *Attitudes toward denominational education in Newfoundland.* St. John's, NL: Department of Political Science, Memorial University.

Graesser, M. W. (1988b). Public opinion on denominational education: Does the majority rule? In W. A. McKim (Ed.), *The vexed question: Denominational education in a secular age* (pp. 195–220). St. John's, NL: Breakwater.

Graesser, M. W. (1990, May). *Church, state and public policy in Newfoundland: The question of denominational education.* Paper presented at the annual meeting of the Canadian Political Science Association, May 27–29, University of Victoria, Victoria, British Columbia.

Graesser, M. W. (1997, June). *Education reform in Newfoundland, 1990–1995: The impact of constitutional restraints and referendum politics.* Paper presented at the annual meeting of the Canadian Political Science Association, Memorial University, Newfoundland. St. John's, NL: Memorial University.

Grogan, M., & VanDeman-Blackmon, M. (2001). A superintendent's approach to coalition building: Working with diversity to garner support for educational initiatives. In C. C. Brunner & L. G. Björk (Eds.), *The new superintendency* (pp. 95-113). Amsterdam, The Netherlands: JAI.

Grubb, W. N., & Oakes, J. (2007). *"Restoring value" to the high school diploma: The rhetoric and practice of higher standards.* Tempe, AZ: Arizona State University.

Gwyn, R. (1968). *Smallwood: The unlikely revolutionary.* Toronto, ON: McClelland & Stewart.

Hall, G. E., & Hord S. M. (2006). *Implementing change: Patterns, principles, and potholes* (2nd. ed.). Boston, MA: Pearson, Allyn & Bacon.

Halpin, D. (1994). Practice and prospects in education policy research. In D. Halpin & B. Troyna (Eds.), *Researching education policy: Ethical and methodological issues* (pp. 198-206). London, UK: Falmer Press.

Hamel, G. (2001). Strategy innovation and the quest for value. In M. A. Cusumano & C. C. Markides (Eds.), *Strategic thinking for the next economy* (pp. 181-195). San Francisco, CA: Jossey-Bass.

Harder, P. (2001, March). *Canada's competitiveness in the global economy* (Industry Canada's 2001 public policy forum). Ottawa, ON: Industry Canada.

Hargreaves, A., & Fink, D. (2006). *Sustainable leadership.* San Francisco, CA: Jossey-Bass.

Harris, M. (1990). *Unholy orders: Tragedy at Mount Cashel.* Toronto, ON: Penguin.

Harte, A. J. (1989). *The joint service school: A study of interdenominational co-operation in the education system of Newfoundland and Labrador* (Unpublished doctoral dissertation). University of Toronto, Toronto, ON.

Harte, A. J. (1993). The growth of the joint service school in Newfoundland: The traditionalist-modernist conflict. *Curriculum Inquiry, 23,* 85-106.

Harvey, D. (1995, August). *A pastoral letter to all members of the Diocese of Eastern Newfoundland and Labrador.* St. John's, NL.

Harvey, D. (2005). *A brief history of neoliberalism.* London, UK: Oxford University Press.

Hayek, F. A. (1944). *The road to serfdom.* Chicago, IL: University of Chicago Press.

Held, V. (Ed.). (1995). *Justice and care: Essential readings in feminist ethics.* Boulder, CO: Westview Press.

Henry, M., Lingard, B., Rizvi, F., & Taylor, S. (1999). Working with/against globalization in education. *Journal of Education Policy, 14,* 85-97.

Hexter, J. H. (1971). *The history primer.* New York, NY: Basic Books.

Hightower, A., Knapp, M., Marsh, J., & McLaughlin, M. (2002). The district role in instructional renewal: Setting the stage for dialogue. In A. Hightower, M. Knapp, J., Marsh, & M. McLaughlin (Eds.), *School districts and instructional renewal* (pp. 1-6). New York, NY: Teachers College Press.

Hintz, L. (2002). Positive directions for schools and communities. *University of Minnesota Extension Service.* Regents of the University of Minnesota, Minneapolis-St. Paul, MN. Retrieved from http://www.extension.umn.edu/distribution/resourcesandtourism/DB6178.html

Hobsbawm, E. (2008). *On empire: America, war, and global supremacy.* New York, NY: Pantheon.

Hochschild, A. R. (1983). *The managed heart: Commercialization of human feeling.* Berkeley, CA: University of California Press.

Hogan v. Newfoundland (Attorney General), [1998] 163 D.L.R. (4th) 672 (NL C.A.). Retrieved from http://www.canlii.org/en/nl/nlca/doc/1998/1998canlii18115/1998canlii18115.html

Hogan v. Newfoundland (Attorney General), [1999] 173 Nfld. & P.E.I.R. 148, [1999] N.J. No. 5 (QL) (S.C.).

Hogan v. Newfoundland (Attorney General), [2000] 183 D.L.R. (4th) 225 (Nfld. C.A.). Retrieved from http://www.canlii.org/en/nl/nlca/doc/2000/2000nfca12/2000nfca12.html

Hogan v. Newfoundland (School Boards for Ten Districts), [1997a] Docket No. St. J. 1433. (NL S.C.T.D.) Retrieved from http://www.canlii.org/en/nl/nlca/doc/1997/1997canlii14610/1997canlii14610.html

Hogan v. Newfoundland (School Boards for Ten Districts), [1997b] 149 D.L.R. (4th) (NL C.A.) Retrieved from http://www.canlii.org/en/nl/nlsctd/doc/1997/1997canlii10854/1997canlii10854.html

Holmes, M. (1984). The victory, and the failure, of educational modernism. *Issues in Education, 2*(1), 23–25.

Holmes, M. (1986). Traditionalism and educational administration. *Journal of Educational Administration and Foundations, 1*(2), 40–51.

Hoogvelt, A. (1997). *Globalization and the postcolonial world: The new political economy of development.* Baltimore, MD: Johns Hopkins University Press.

House, J. D. (1983). *Newfoundland society and culture* (2nd. ed.). St. John's, NL: Memorial University.

House, J. D. (1999). *Against the tide: Battling for economic renewal in Newfoundland and Labrador.* Toronto, ON: University of Toronto Press.

House of Commons (1996, December 4). Constitutional amendment. *Edited Hansard, 113.* 36th Parliament, 1st session. Retrieved from http://www2.parl.gc.ca/house chamberbusiness/chamberindex.aspx?View=h&Parl=35&Ses=2&Language=E&Mode=1&File=e-35-2_2-e.html

House of Commons (1997, December 9). Amendment to the Constitution of Canada (Newfoundland). *Edited Hansard, 47.* 35th Parliament, 2nd session. Retrieved from http://www2.parl.gc.ca/HousePublications/Publication.aspx?pub=Hansard&doc=47&Language=E&Mode=1&Parl=36&Ses=1&DocId=2332751&File=0#LINK231

Hudson, R., Dunford, M., Hamilton, D., & Kotter, R. (1997). Developing regional strategies for economic success: Lessons from Europe's economically successful regions. *European Urban and Regional Studies, 4,* 365–373.

Hull, J. (2001). The contribution of religious education to religious freedom: A global perspective. In International Association for Religious Freedom (Ed.), *Religious education in schools: Ideas and experiences from around the world* (pp. 1–8). London, UK: IARE.

Hunter, W., & Austin, R. (2008, May). Looking back from Europe: ICT and church-based education in Northern Ireland. In G. Galway & D. Dibbon (Eds.), *Symposium 2008: Post-Confederation educational reform: From rhetoric to reality* (pp. 155–164). St. John's. NL: Memorial University.

Information Technology Association of Canada. (1992). *A knowledge-based Canada: The new national dream.* Mississauga, ON: Author.

ISSP and Pathways Commission. (2007). *Focusing on students.* St. John's, NL: Department of Education, Government of Newfoundland and Labrador. Retrieved from http://www.ed.gov.nl.ca/edu/pub/Focusing_on_Students.pdf

Jackson, C. (1995, August 31). Church leaders in quandary over Term 17. *The Evening Telegram,* pp. 1–2.

Jackson, C. (2005, June 18). Tories scrap planned school closure in contested Exploits district. *The Western Star.* Retrieved from http://archives.cedrom.sni.com

Jackson, R. (1979). Exodus Newfoundland: Some social, economic and educational implications of present out-migration and fertility declines. In E. Cluett & F. Cramm (Eds.), *Declining enrolments: Implications for teacher supply and demand.* St. John's, NL: Memorial University.

Jackson, R., & Steele, K. (2004, September). *Problems and possibilities for relating citizenship education and religious education in Europe.* Paper presented at the global meeting on Teaching for Tolerance, Respect and Recognition with Religion or Belief, Oslo Coalition on Freedom of Religion and Belief, Oslo, Norway. Retrieved from http://folk.uio.zo/leirvik/OsloCoalition/JacksonSteele0904.htm

Jacobowitz, R., Weinstein, M., Maguire, C., Luekens, M., & Fruchter, M. (2007). *The effectiveness of small high schools, 1994–95 to 2003–04.* Institute for Education & Social Policy, Steinhardt School of Culture, Education, and Human Development, New York University, New York, NY. Retrieved from http://steinhardt.nyu.edu/iesp.olde/publications/pubs/IESP_SmallHighSchoolEffectiveness_April2007.pdf

Jagger, A. M. (1995). Caring as a feminist practice of moral reason. In V. Held (Ed.), *Justice and care: Essential readings in feminist ethics* (pp. 179–202). Boulder, CO: Westview Press.

Jenlink, P. M., Reigeluth, C. M., Carr, A. A., & Nelson, L. M. (1998). Guidelines for facilitating systemic change in school districts. *Systems Research and Behavioral Science, 15,* 217–233.

John Paul II (1984, September 12). *Address to Catholic Educators at the Basilica of St. John the Baptist.* St. John's, NL.

Jones, J. T., Toma, E. F., & Zimmer, R. (2008). School attendance and district and school size. *Economics of Education Review, 27*(1), 140–148.

Jukes, I. (2006). *From Gutenberg to Gates to Google (and beyond): Education for the online world.* National Educational Computing Conference, San Diego, CA. Retrieved from http://web.mac.com/iajukes/iWeb/thecommittedsardine/Handouts_files/fgtgtg.pdf

Kagan, S. (1994). *Cooperative learning.* San Juan Capistrano, CA: Kagan Cooperative Learning.

Kettl, D. F. (2000). *The global public management revolution: A report on the transformation of governance.* Washington, DC: The Brookings Institute.

Kim, K. S. (1997). The state and education in Newfoundland in the age of market globalization. *The Morning Watch, 25*(1–2). St. John's, NL: Faculty of Education, Memorial University. Retrieved from http://www.mun.ca/educ/faculty/mwatch/fall97/market.htm

Kingdon, J. W. (1995). *Agendas, alternatives and public policies* (2nd. ed.). New York, NY: Longman. (Originally published in 1984.)

Kohn, A. (2002). Fighting the tests: A practical guide to rescuing our schools. *Our Schools/Our Selves, 11*(3), 85–114.

Kouzes, J. M., & Posner, B. Z. (2003). *Credibility: How leaders gain it and lose; why people demand it.* San Francisco, CA: Jossey-Bass.

Kreisberg, S. (1992). *Transforming power: Domination, empowerment, and education.* Albany, NY: State University of New York Press.

Kuhlthau, C. C., Maniotes, L. K., & Caspari, A. K. (2007) *Guided inquiry: Learning in the 21st century.* Westport, CT: Libraries Unlimited.

Kvale, S. (1996). *Interviews: An introduction to qualitative research interviewing.* Thousand Oaks, CA: Sage.

Laitsch, D. A. (2006) *Assessment, high stakes, and alternative visions: Appropriate use of the right tools to leverage improvement.* Arizona State University, AZ: Educational Policy Research Unit. Retrieved from http://epsi.asu.edu/epru/documents/EPSL-0611-222-EPRU.pdf

Laurin, A. (2007). *A primer on federal personal income taxes* (PRB 07-07E). Ottawa, ON: Parliamentary Information and Research Service, Library of Parliament. Retrieved from http://www.parl.gc.ca/information/library/PRBpubs/prb0707-e.htm#international

Lawton, S. B. (1996). *Financing Canadian education.* Toronto, ON: Canadian Education Association.

Lawton, S. B. (1997). Structures and restructuring in Canadian education. In S. B. Lawton, R. J. Reed, & F. Van Wieringten (Eds.), *Restructuring public schooling: Europe, Canada, America* (pp. 25–36). Berlin, Germany: Waxmann Verlag.

Leavitt, H. (2003). Why hierarchies thrive. *Harvard Business Review, 81*(3), 96–102.

Leithwood, K., & Aiken, R. (1995). *Making schools smarter: A system for monitoring school and district progress.* Thousand Oaks, CA: Corwin Press.

Leithwood, K., Louis, K. S., Anderson, S., & Wahlstrom, K. (2004). *How leadership influences student learning.* Retrieved from the Wallace Foundation web site: http://www.wallacefoundation.org/WF/KnowledgeCenter/KnowledgeTopics/ EducationLeadership/HowLeadershipInfluencesStudentLearning.htm

Lessard, C., & Verdy, J. (2007). Policy narrative for New Brunswick. In Chan, A. S., Fisher, D., & Rubenson, K. (Eds.), *The evolution of professionalism: Educational policy in the provinces and territories of Canada.* Vancouver, BC: Centre for Policy Studies in Higher Education and Training, University of British Columbia. Retrieved from http://chet.educ.ubc.ca/pdf_files/Evolution-Book-CHET.pdf#page=176

Levin, B. (1998). An epidemic of education policy: (What) can we learn from each other? *Comparative Education, 34,* 131–141. Retrieved from http://home.cc.umanitoba.ca/~levin/res_pub_files/an_epidemic_of_education_policy.pdf

Levin, B. (2001a). Governments and school improvement. *International Electronic Journal for Leadership in Learning, 5*(9).

Levin, B. (2001b). *Reforming education: From origins to outcomes.* London, UK: Routledge/Falmer.

Levin, B. (2003). Knowledge and action in educational policy and politics. In P. DeBroucker & A. Sweetman (Eds.), *Towards evidence-based policy for Canadian education* (pp. 15-33). Montreal, QC: McGill-Queen's University Press.

Levin, B., & Riffel, J. A. (1997). *Schools and the changing world: Struggling towards the future.* London, UK: Falmer.

Lipsey, R. G., Ragan C. T. S., & Courant, P. N. (1997). Macroeconomics (9th. Canadian ed.). Scarborough, ON: HarperCollins.

Littky, D. (2004). *The BIG picture: Education is everyone's business.* Alexandria, VA: Association for Supervision and Curriculum Development.

Little, J. W. (1994). *Teachers' professional development in a climate of educational reform.* Retrieved from http://www.ed.gov/pubs/EdReformStudies/SysReforms/little1.html

Lortie, D. (1975). *Schoolteacher: A sociological study.* Chicago, IL: University of Chicago Press.

Loveless, G. (2008). Evolution of the governance of french first language education in Newfoundland and Labrador. In G. Galway & D. Dibbon (Eds.), *Symposium 2008: Post-confederation education reform: From rhetoric to reality* (pp. 197-206). St. John's, NL: Memorial University.

Lowe, G. S. (2000). *The quality of work: A people-centred agenda.* Oxford, UK: Oxford University Press.

Loyola High School, and Zucchi, J. (2008). *Motion to initiate proceedings.* Retrieved from http://www.courthousenews.com/2008/09/18/LoyolaCanada.pdf

MacGilchrist, B., Mortimore, P., Savage, J., & Beresford, C. (1995). *Planning matters: The impact of development planning in primary schools.* London, UK: Paul Chapman.

Macklem, T., Rose, D., & Tetlow, R. (1995). *Government debt and deficits in Canada: A macro simulation analysis* (Working paper 95-4 / document de travail 95-4). Ottawa, ON: The Bank of Canada. Retrieved from http://www1.bank-banque-canada.ca/fr/res/wp/1995/wp95-4.pdf

MacLeod, R., & Poutanen, M.A. (2004). *A meeting of the people: School boards and Protestant communities in Quebec, 1801-1998.* Montreal, QC: McGill-Queen's Press.

Magsino, R. (1988). Teacher and student rights within the denominational schoolhouse gate. In W. A. McKim (Ed.), *The vexed question: Denominational education in a secular age* (pp. 126-157). St. John's, NL: Breakwater.

Mahé, Y. T. M. (2002). French teacher shortages and cultural continuity in Alberta districts, 1892-1940. *Historical studies in education, 14,* 219-246. Retrieved from http://library.queensu.ca/ojs/index.php/edu_hse-rhe/article/viewArticle/1698/1797

Margonis, F. (2004). From student resistance to educative engagement: A case study in building powerful student-teacher relationships. In C. Bingham & A. M.

Sidorkin (Eds.), *No education without relation* (pp. 39-53). New York, NY: Peter Lang.

Martel, A. (1991). *Official language minority education rights in Canada: From instruction to management.* Ottawa, ON: Office of the Commissioner of Official Languages.

Martin, D. T. (1990). A critique of the concept of work and education in the school reform reports. In C. M. Shea, E. Kahane, & P. A. Sola (Eds.), *The new servants of power: A critique of the 1980s school reform movement* (pp. 39-56). New York, NY: Praeger.

Mawhinney, H. B. (1992, June). *The commission of inquiry: An instrument for resolving value conflicts in educational policy change.* Paper presented at the annual meeting of the Canadian Association for Studies in Educational Administration, Charlottetown, Prince Edward Island.

Mayntz, R. (1998). *New challenges to governance theory.* Jean Monnet Chair Paper RSC No 98/50. Fiesole, Italy: European University Institute. Retrieved from http://www.iue.it/EF/mayntz.htm

McAdams, D. R. (2006). *What school boards can do: Reform governance for urban schools.* New York, NY: Teachers College Press.

McCann, P. (1988a). The politics of denominational education in the nineteenth century in Newfoundland. In W. A. McKim (Ed.), *The vexed question: Denominational education in a secular age* (pp. 30-59). St. John's, NL: Breakwater.

McCann, P. (1988b). Denominational education in the twentieth century in Newfoundland. In W. A. McKim (Ed.), *The vexed question: Denominational education in a secular age* (pp. 60-78). St. John's, NL: Breakwater.

McCann, P. (1994). *Schooling in a fishing society: Education and economic conditions in Newfoundland and Labrador, 1836-1986.* Institute for Social and Economic Research. St. John's, NL: Memorial University.

McCann, P. (2002). The background to the Royal Commission on Education. *The Morning Watch, 29*(3-4). St. John's, NL: Faculty of Education, Memorial University. Retrieved from http://www.mun.ca/educ/faculty/mwatch/win22/mccann.htm

McDaniel, B. L. (2004). Between strangers and soul mates: Care and moral dialogue. In C. Bingham & A. M. Sidorkin (Eds.), *No education without relation* (pp. 91-101). New York, NY: Peter Lang.

McKim, W. A. (Ed.). (1988). *The vexed question: Denominational education in a secular age.* St. John's, NL: Breakwater.

McLaughlin, M., & Talbert, J. (2003). *Reforming districts: How districts support school reform: A research report.* Seattle, WA: Center for the Study of Teaching and Policy, University of Washington.

McWilliam, E. (2000). The perfect corporate fit: New knowledge for new times. *International Journal of Leadership in Education, 3,* 75-83.

Meier, D. (2004). Smallness, autonomy and choice: Scaling up. *Educational Horizons, 82,* 290-300.

Meyer, J., & Rowan, B. (Eds.). (1992). *The structure of educational organizations, organizational environments: Rituals and rationality.* Newbury Park, CA: Sage.

Miles, M. B., & Huberman, A. M. (1994). *Qualitative data analysis: An expanded sourcebook* (2nd. ed.). Beverly Hills, CA: Sage.

Miller, J. M. (2007). Challenges facing Catholic schools: A view from Rome. In G. R. Grace & J. O'Keefe (Eds.), *International handbook of Catholic education: Challenges for school systems in the 21st century* (Part one, pp. 449–480). Dordrecht, The Netherlands: Springer.

Mintzberg, H. (1994). *The rise and fall of strategic planning: Reconceiving roles for planning, plans, planners.* New York, NY: Free Press.

Mintzberg, H., & Lampel, J. (2001). Reflecting on the strategic process. In M. Cusumano & C. C. Markides (Eds.), *Strategic thinking for the next economy* (pp. 33–54). San Francisco, CA: Jossey-Bass.

Mitchell, C. (2006). *Religion, identity and politics in Northern Ireland: Boundaries of belonging and belief.* Aldershot, UK: Ashgate.

Montgomery, A., & Smith, A. (2006). Teacher education in Northern Ireland: Policy variations since devolution. *Scottish Educational Review, 37,* 46–58.

Mulford, W., Silins, H., & Leithwood, K. (2004). *Educational leadership for organizational learning and improved student outcomes.* Boston, MA: Kluwer.

Murphy, J. (2007, June). *Teacher leadership: Barriers and supports.* Paper presented at Teacher Working Conditions that Matter: The Symposium. Toronto, ON: Elementary Teachers Federation of Ontario.

National Commission on Excellence in Education (1983). *A nation at risk: The imperative for educational reform.* Washington, DC: US Government.

Neary, P. (Ed.). (1996). *White tie and decorations: Sir John and Lady Hope Simpson in Newfoundland, 1934–1936.* Toronto, ON: University of Toronto Press.

Newfoundland Teachers' Association (NTA). (1986a). *Exploring new pathways: A brief presented to the Government of Newfoundland and Labrador.* St. John's, NL: Author.

Newfoundland Teachers' Association (NTA). (1986b, December 1). *Newsletter: The NTA brief–Exploring New Pathways.* St. John's, NL: Author.

Newfoundland and Labrador Teachers' Association (NLTA). (1989a). *Brief to the Government of Newfoundland and Labrador Task Force on Educational Finance.* St. John's, NL: Author.

Newfoundland and Labrador Teachers' Association (NLTA). (1989b). *Reaction to the report of the Task Force on Educational Finance.* St. John's, NL: Author.

Newfoundland and Labrador Teachers' Association (NLTA). (1990). *An introductory presentation to the Royal Commission on Education.* St. John's, NL: Author.

Newfoundland and Labrador Teachers' Association (NLTA). (1991). *Building a vision for the future: A submission to the Royal Commission on Education.* St. John's, NL: Author.

Newfoundland and Labrador Teachers' Association (NLTA). (1992a, March). *Presidential Update, 5*(3). St. John's, NL: Author.

Newfoundland and Labrador Teachers' Association (NLTA). (1992b). *Reaction of the Newfoundland Teachers' Association to the report of the Royal Commission on Education.* St. John's, NL: Author.

Newfoundland and Labrador Teachers' Association (NLTA). (1997a). *NLTA position paper re: September 2nd referendum.* St. John's, NL: Author

Newfoundland and Labrador Teachers' Association (NLTA). (1997b). *Brief to the Joint Committee.* St. John's, NL: Author.

Newfoundland and Labrador Teachers' Association (NLTA). (2003). *Putting the teacher back in teaching.* Retrieved from https://www.nlta.nl.ca/files/documents/reports/brief_tchr_bk_tching_feb03.pdf

Newmann, F. M. (1993). Beyond common sense in educational restructuring: The issues of content and linkage. *Educational Researcher, 22*(2), 4–13, 22.

Nichols, S. L., & Berliner, D. C. (2005). *The inevitable corruption of indicators and educators through high-stakes testing.* Tempe, AZ: Educational Policies Studies Laboratory.

Noddings, N. (1984). *Caring: A feminine approach to ethics and moral education.* Berkeley, CA: University of California Press.

Noddings, N. (1992). *The challenge to care in schools: An alternative approach to education.* New York, NY: Teachers College Press.

Noddings, N. (2002). *Starting at home: Caring and social policy.* Berkeley, CA: University of California Press.

Nolasco Mulcahy, M. (1988). The philosophical-theological foundations of the denominational system of education. In W. A. McKim (Ed.), *The vexed question: Denominational education in a secular age* (pp. 11–29). St. John's, NL: Breakwater.

Nord, W. A., & Haynes, C. C. (1998). *Taking religion seriously across the curriculum.* Alexandria, VA: Association for Supervision and Curriculum Development.

Northern Ireland Department of Education. (2004). *emPowering schools in Northern Ireland.* Belfast, NI: Author. Retrieved from http://www.empoweringschools.com/docs/emPowering.doc

Northern Ireland Department of Education. (2004–2006). *The Chief Inspector's report 2002–2004, Northern Ireland.* Bangor, NI: Author. Retrieved from http://www.etini.gov.uk/index/survey_theme_reports/general_reports/the_chief_inspector_ s_report_2002-2004.htm

Northern Ireland Department of Education. (2006a). *Schools for the future: unding, strategy and sharing.* Belfast, NI: Independent Strategic Review of Education. Retrieved from http://www.deni.gov.uk/index/8-admin_of_education_pg/101-strategic-review-of-education.htm

Northern Ireland Department of Education. (2006b). *Strategic review of education* (The Bain report). Belfast, NI: Author. Retrieved from http://www.deni.gov.uk/index/8-admin_of_education_pg/101-strategic-review-of-education.htm

Northern Ireland Department of Education. (2009, January). *Schools for the future: A policy for sustainable schools.* Belfast, NI: Author. Retrieved from http://www.deni.gov.uk/index/85-schools/13-schools_estate_pg/14-schools_-_estate-new page.htm

Northern Ireland Education and Training Inspectorate. (2008). *An evaluation of the use and impact of learning environments in schools and in the wider education service.*

Belfast, NI: Author. Retrieved from http://www.etini.gov.uk/le_in_schools_
in_wes.pdf

Northouse, P. G. (2004). *Leadership theory and practice* (3rd ed.). Thousand Oaks, CA: Sage.

Nova Central School District. (2006, April 11). Proposed Year 2 changes—5 year plan. *Minutes of Special School Board Meeting.* Gander, NL: Author.

Nova Scotia Department of Education. (2009). *Business plan 2008-2009.* Halifax, NS: Author. Retrieved from http://www.ednet.ns.ca/pdfdocs/businessplan/bp2008-09.pdf

Ontario English Catholic Teachers' Assn. v. Ontario (Attorney General), [2001] 1 S.C.R. 470 (S.C.C.). Retrieved from http://scc.lexum.org/en/2001/2001scc15/2001scc15.pdf

Ontario Ministry of Education. (2008). *Reach every student: Energizing Ontario education.* Toronto, ON: Author. Retrieved from www.edu.goc.on.ca/eng/document/ energize

Organization for Economic Co-operation and Development (OECD). (2001). *Education at a glance: OECD indicators.* Paris, France: OECD Publications.

Organization for Economic Co-operation and Development (OECD). (2004). *Private health insurance in OECD countries.* Retrieved from http://books.google.ca/books?id=oUM39nDp2s4C&printsec=frontcover&source=gbs_v2_summary_r&cad=0#v=onepage&q=&f=false

Organization for Economic Co-operation and Development (OECD). (2008). *Education at a glance 2008: OECD Indicators.* Retrieved from http://www.oecd.org/document/9/0,3343,en_2649_39263238_41266761_1_1_1_1,00.html

Ozga, J. (2000). *Policy research in educational settings: Contested terrain.* Philadelphia, PA: Open University Press.

Palmer, P. J. (1998). *The courage to teach: Exploring the inner landscape of a teacher's life.* San Francisco, CA: Jossey-Bass.

Pascale, R. T. (2001). Surfing the edge of chaos. In M. A. Cusumano & C. C. Markides (Eds.), *Strategic thinking for the next economy* (pp. 105-129). San Francisco, CA: Jossey-Bass.

Penney, R. G. (1988). The constitutional status of denominational education in Newfoundland. In W. A. McKim (Ed.), *The vexed question: Denominational education in a secular age* (pp. 80-101). St. John's, NL: Breakwater.

People for Education. (2008). *Declining enrolment in Ontario's schools: An excerpt from the 2008 Annual Report on Ontario's Public Schools.* Retrieved from http://www.peopleforeducation.com

Phillips, C. E. (1957). *The development of education in Canada.* Toronto, ON: Gage.

Ponder, A. (1987, Winter). Denominational education at what cost? *The Morning Watch, 14*(3/4), 21-23.

Pottle, H. L. (1979). *Newfoundland: Dawn without light: Politics, power and people in the Smallwood era.* St. John's, NL: Breakwater.

Press, H. (1986). *Trends in education: Part I: Demographic projections.* St. John's, NL: Department of Education, Government of Newfoundland and Labrador.

Press, H. (1992). *Costs and consequences: An examination of the potential for consolidation within the education system and the associated costs. Background report prepared for the*

Royal Commission on Education. St. John's, NL: Department of Education, Government of Newfoundland and Labrador. ERIC ED 370159.

Press, H., Galway, G., & Collins, A. (2003). Maintaining quality programming in rural Newfoundland and Labrador: A case study in policy and structural change. *Education Canada*, *43*(3), 20–23, 38–39.

Pross, A. P., Christie, I., & Yogis, J. A. (Eds). (1990). *Commissions of inquiry*. Toronto, ON: Carswell.

Pusey, M. A. (1991). *Economic rationalism in Canberra: A nation-building state changes its mind*. New York, NY: Cambridge University Press.

Queen's Printer for Ontario. (2008–2009a). *Minister appoints supervisor to manage TCDSB's finances*. Retrieved from http://www.news.ontario.ca/edu/en/2008/06/minister-appoints-supervisor-to-manage-tcdsbs-finances.html

Queen's Printer for Ontario. (2008–2009b). *Strengthening accountability on trustee expenses*. Retrieved from http://www.news.ontario.ca/edu/en/2008/11/strengthening-accountability-on-trustee-expenses.html

Raudenbush, S. W. (2004). *Schooling, statistics, and poverty: Can we measure school improvement?* Ninth Annual William H. Angoff Memorial Lecture. Princeton, NJ: Educational Testing Service. Retrieved from http://www.ets.org/research/researcher/PIC-ANG9.html

Reading, V. (2002, Autumn). Knowledge is power: *Extracts from the Public Service Review*, European Commissioner for Education and Culture. Brussels, Belgium: European Union.

Redding, J., & Catalanello, R. (1992, May). The fourth iteration: The learning organization as a model of strategic change. *Thresholds in Education*, *18*, 47–53.

Reference re Secession of Quebec, [1998] 2 S.C.R. 217. Retrieved from http://scc.lexum.org/en/1998/1998scr2-217/1998scr2-217.html

Reid, A. (2005). Rethinking the democratic purposes of public schooling in a globalizing world. In M. W. Apple, J. Kenway, & M. Singh (Eds.), *Globalizing education policies, pedagogies, and politics* (pp. 281–296). New York, NY: Peter Lang.

Richardson, W. (2007). Locked in an irrelevant system: Network building and the new literacy. *Education Canada*, *47*(4), 23–25.

Robitaille, D. F., Taylor, A. R., Orpwood, G., & Donn, J. S. (1998). *The TIMSS-Canada Report* (Vol. 1). Vancouver, BC: Department of Curriculum Studies, University of British Columbia.

Roebothan, C. (1989). *Financing greater equality and excellence in the Newfoundland school system: Report of the Task Force on Educational Finance*. St. John's, NL: Government of Newfoundland and Labrador.

Roman Catholic Archdiocese of St. John's. (1990). *The Report of the Archdiocesan Commission of Inquiry into the Sexual Abuse of Children by Members of the Clergy* (2 Vols) (The Winter Commission). St. John's, NL: Archdiocesan Office.

Rose, A., Hickey, A., & Mercer, A. (2008, May). E-Teaching and learning in arts education—Newfoundland and Labrador. In G. Galway & D. Dibbon (Eds), *Symposium 2008: Post-confederation educational reform: From rhetoric to reality* (pp.

237-252). St. John's, NL: Memorial University. Retrieved from http://www. mun.ca/educ/symposium2008/Rose,_Hickey_Mercer.pdf

Ross, D., Roberts, P., & Scott, K. (2000). Family income and child well-being. *Isuma*, *1*(2), 51-54.

Rowan, B. (1990). Commitment and control: Alternative strategies for the organizational design of schools. *Review of Educational Research*, *16*, 353-389.

Rowe, F. W. (1952). *The history of education in Newfoundland*. Toronto, ON: Ryerson Press.

Rowe, F. W. (1964). *The development of education in Newfoundland*. Toronto, ON: Ryerson Press.

Rushowy, K., & Brown, L. (2008, June 5). Province takes over Catholic school board. *The Toronto Star*. Retrieved from http://www.thestar.com/printArticle/437502

Russell, W. (1991). Where once we feared to tread: An examination of the denominational education system. In A. Singh & I. J. Baksh (Eds.), *Dimensions of Newfoundland Society and Education* (Vol. 1, pp. 99-105). St. John's, NL: Faculty of Education, Memorial University. (Originally published in 1989).

Sackney, L. (2007). Systemic reform for sustainability. Saskatoon, SK: Government of Saskatchewan. Retrieved from http://www.publications.gov.sk.ca/

Sacred Congregation for Catholic Education. (1965). *Gravissimum Educationis (Declaration on Christian education)*. Documents of the Vatican II Council. Retrieved from http://www.vatican.va/archive/hist_councils/ii_vatican_council/index.htm

Sacred Congregation for Catholic Education. (1997). *The Catholic school on the threshold of the third millennium*. Address of the Holy Father Pope John Paul II to Congregation for Catholic Education. Retrieved from http://www.vatican.va/ holy_father/john_paul_ii/speeches/1998/october/documents?hf_jp-ii_spe_ 19981026_ed-cattolica_en.html

Salamon, L. M. (1991). Overview: Why human capital? Why now? In D. W. Hornbeck & L. M. Salamon (Eds.), *Human capital and America's future: An economic strategy for the 90s* (pp. 1-39). Baltimore, MD: Johns Hopkins University Press.

Schlechty, P. C. (1990). *Schools for the 21st century: Leadership imperatives for educational reform*. San Francisco, CA: Jossey-Bass.

Schlechty, P. C. (1997). *Inventing better schools: An action plan for educational reform*. San Francisco, CA: Jossey-Bass.

Schlechty, P. C. (2001). *Shaking up the school house: How to support and sustain educational innovation*. San Francisco, CA: Jossey-Bass.

Schlechty, P. C. (2005). *Creating great schools: Six critical systems at the heart of educational innovation*. San Francisco, CA: Jossey Bass.

Schools Act, S.N.L. 1997, C.5-12.2.

Schools (Amendment) Act, R.S.N. 1970, c.55.

Schools (Amendment) Act, R.S.N. 1984, c.36.

Schultz, T. W. (1961). Investment in human capital. *American Economic Review*, *51*(1), 1-17.

Science Council of Canada. (1991). *Reaching for tomorrow: Science and technology policy in Canada.* Ottawa, ON: Author.

Senge, P. M. (1990). *The fifth discipline: The art and practice of the learning organization.* New York, NY: Currency/Doubleday.

Senge, P. M. (2006). Systems citizenship: The leadership mandate for this millennium. *Leader to Leader,* No. 41, 21-26.

Senge, P. M., Scharmer, C. O., Jaworski, J., & Flowers, B. S. (2004). *Presence: Exploring profound change in people, organizations, and society.* New York, NY: Doubleday.

Sergiovanni, T. J. (2000). *The lifeworld of leadership: Creating culture, community, and personal meaning in our schools.* San Francisco, CA: Jossey-Bass.

Sernak, K. (1998). *School leadership–Balancing power with caring.* New York, NY: Teachers College Press.

Shaker, P., & Grimmett, P. (2004). Public schools as public good: A question of values. *Education Canada,* 44(3), 29-31.

Shakrani, S. (2008). A big idea: Smaller high schools. *New Educator.* Michigan State University College of Education. ERIC ED 502129. Retrieved from http:// www.epc.msu.edu/publications/REPORT/A%20Big%20Idea_Smaller%20 High%20Schools.pdf

Shapiro, B. J. (1985). *The report of the Commission on Private Schools in Ontario.* Toronto, ON: The Commission on Private Schools in Ontario.

Sheppard, B., Brown, J., & Dibbon, D. (2009). *School district leadership matters.* Dordrecht, The Netherlands: Springer.

Silins, H., Zarins, S., & Mulford, B. (2002). What characteristics and processes define a school as a learning organization? Is this a useful concept to apply to schools? *International Education Journal,* 3, 24-32.

Sinclair, A. (1989). Public sector culture: Managerialism or multiculturalism? *Australian Journal of Public Administration,* 48, 382-397.

Smallwood, J. R. (1967). *The book of Newfoundland.* St. John's, NL: Newfoundland Book Publishers.

Smallwood, J. R. (1973). *I chose Canada: The memoirs of the Honourable Joseph R. "Joey" Smallwood.* Toronto, ON: Macmillan.

Smith, W. J., & Foster, W. F. (2001a). Religion and education in Canada–Part I: The traditional framework. *Education and Law Journal,* 10, 393-447.

Smith, W. J., & Foster, W. F. (2001b). Religion and education in Canada–Part II: An alternative framework for the debate. *Education and Law Journal,* 11, 1-67.

Smith, W. J., & Foster, W. F. (2001c). Religion and education in Canada–Part III: An analysis of provincial legislation. *Education and Law Journal,* 11, 203-261.

Sparks, D. (2005). The final 2%: What it takes to create profound change in leaders. *Journal of Staff Development,* 26(2), 8-15.

Starratt, R. J. (2004). *Ethical leadership.* San Francisco, CA: Jossey-Bass.

St. John's Board of Trade. (1990-1993). *Business news.* St. John's, NL: Author.

Statistics Canada. (1999). *Historical statistics of Canada.* Ottawa, ON: Author. Retrieved from http://www.statcan.ca/english/freepub/11-516-XIE/sectionw/ sectionw.htm

Statistics Canada. (2001). *Census data.* Ottawa, ON: Author. Retrieved from http://www.nfstats.gov.nf.ca/Statistics/Census2001/PDF/2001_Pop_AgeSex_CMA.PDF

Statistics Canada. (2003). *Canadian statistics on primary industries.* Ottawa, ON: Author. Retrieved from http://www.statcan.ca/english/Pgdb/primar.htm#pri

Statistics Canada. (2004). *Educational Quarterly Review, 9*(4). Retrieved from http://www.statcan.ca/english/studies/81-003/feature/eqar2004009004s0a01.pdf

Statistics Canada. (2005, February 2). Secondary school graduates. *The Daily.* Ottawa, ON: Author. Retrieved from www.statcan/Daily/English/o50202/do5o402b.htm

Statistics Canada. (2006). *Consumer price indexes for Canada, monthly, 1914–2006* (V41690973 series). Ottawa, ON: Author. Retrieved from http://www.statcan.ca/english/clf/query.html?col=alle&qt=Consumer+price+indexes+for+Canada%2C+&qi=3&charset=iso-8859-1

Statistics Canada. (2007a). *Education Indicators in Canada, 2007.* Catalogue No. 81-582-XPE. Ottawa, ON: Author. Retrieved from http://www.statcan.ca/english/freepub/81-582-XIE/81-582-XIE2007001.pdf

Statistics Canada. (2007b). *Portrait of the Canadian population in 2006, by age and sex: Provincial/territorial populations by age and sex.* Ottawa, ON: Author. Retrieved from http://www12.statcan.ca/english/census06/analysis/agesex/ProvTerr1.cfm

Statistics Canada. (2007c). *Summary public school indicators for the provinces and territories.* Ottawa, ON: Author. Retrieved from http://www.statcan.gc.ca/daily-quotidien/070830/dq070830d-eng.htm

Statistics Canada. (2008). *Total fertility rate in Canada, provinces and territories, 1981 and 2005.* Ottawa, ON: Author. Retrieved from http://www.statcan.gc.ca/pub/91-003-x/2007001/t/4129898-eng.htm

Statistics Canada. (2009a). *Median total income, by family type, by province and territory.* Ottawa, ON: Author. Retrieved from http://www40.statcan.ca/l01/cst01/famil108a-eng.htm

Statistics Canada. (2009b). *Gross domestic product, expenditure-based, by province and territory.* Ottawa, ON: Author. Retrieved from http://www40.statcan.gc.ca/l01/cst01/econ15-eng.htm

Statistics Canada. (2009c). *Population by year, by province and territory.* Ottawa, ON: Author. Retrieved from http://www40.statcan.gc.ca/l01/cst01/demo02a-eng.htm

Statistics Canada and Human Resources Development Canada. (2001). *Learning a living: A report on adult education and training in Canada* (Catalogue #81-586-XPE). Ottawa, ON: Author.

Steering Group on Prosperity. (1992). *Inventing out future: An action plan for Canada's prosperity.* Montreal, QC: Author.

Stevens, K. (2008, May). Lessons for the global community in building sustainable rural schools: The case of post-confederation Newfoundland and Labrador. In G. Galway & D. Dibbon (Eds.), *Symposium 2008: Post-confederation educational reform: From rhetoric to reality* (pp. 267–276). St. John's, NL: Memorial University.

Stoll, L., & Fink, D. (1996). *Changing our schools Linking school effectiveness and school improvement*. Philadelphia, PA: Open University Press.

Taylor, S., Rizvi, F., Lingard, B., & Henry, M. (1997). *Educational policy and the politics of change*. New York, NY: RoutledgeFalmer.

Teacher Allocation Commission. (2007). *Education and our future: A road map to innovation and excellence*. St. John's, NL: Government of Newfoundland and Labrador. Retrieved from http://www.ed.gov.nl.ca/edu/pub/TACReport.pdf

Transparency and Accountability Act, S.N.L. 2004, C.T-8.1.

Trinczek, R., & West, A. (1999). Using statistics and indicators to evaluate universities in Europe: Aims, fields, problems and recommendations. *European Journal of Education, 34*, 343–356.

Tronto, J. C. (1989). Women and caring: What can feminists learn about morality from caring? In V. Held (Ed.), *Justice and care: Essential readings in feminist ethics* (pp. 101–115). New York, NY: Westview Press.

Tronto, J. C. (1993). *Moral boundaries: A political argument for an ethic of care*. New York, NY: Routledge.

Tronto, J. C. (2002, February). The value of care. *Boston Review*, 16–17. Retrieved from http://bostonreview.net/BR27.1/tronto.html

Ungerleider, C. (2003). *Failing our kids: How we are ruining our public schools*. Ottawa, ON: McClelland & Stewart.

Ungerleider, C. (2006). Government, neo-liberal media, and education in Canada. *Canadian Journal of Education, 29*, 70–90.

US Department of Education. (1988). *Religious education in public schools: A statement of principle*. Washington, DC: Author.

Valentine, P. (1995). Women's working worlds: A case study of a female organization. In D. M. Dunlap & P. A. Schmuck (Eds.), *Women leading in education* (pp. 340–357). New York, NY: State University of New York Press.

Valpy, M. (2007, October 11). Michael Valpy's winners and losers. *The Globe and Mail*. Retrieved from http://www.theglobeandmail.com/servlet/story/RTGAM 20071011.welectionattic11/BNStory/ontarioelection2007

Wagner, K. (1997). Trends in public education governance—Canada. *Education Analyst, 1*(1). Kelowna, BC: Society for the Advancement of Excellence in Education.

Wang, M. C., & Walberg, H. J. (1991). Teaching and educational effectiveness: Research synthesis and consensus from the field. In H. C. Waxman & H. J. Walberg (Eds.), *Effective teaching: Current research* (pp. 63–80). Berkeley, CA: McCutchan.

Warren. P. J. (1973a). *Quality and equality in secondary education in Newfoundland*. St. John's, NL: Faculty of Education, Memorial University.

Warren, P. J. (1973b). *Public attitudes toward education in Newfoundland and Labrador*. St. John's, NL: Committee on Publications, Faculty of Education, Memorial University.

Warren, P. J. (1988). Church and state in Canadian education. In W. A. McKim (Ed.), *The vexed question: denominational education in a secular age* (pp. 102–125). St. John's, NL: Breakwater.

Warren, P. J. (2008, May). Address to *Symposium 2008: Post-Confederation Education Reform– From Rhetoric to Reality*. St. John's, NL: Faculty of Education, Memorial University.

Warren, P., Curtis, D., Sheppard, B., Hillier, R., & Roberts, B. (2003). *Facing the challenge: A report of the study group on hours of work*. St. John's, NL: Department of Education, Government of Newfoundland and Labrador. Retrieved from http://www.ed.gov.nl.ca/edu/pub/study/report.pdf

Weick, K. E. (1976). Educational organizations as loosely-coupled systems. *Administrative Science Quarterly, 21*, 1–19.

Wells, C. K. (1996, October 17). A church man with responsibility for government. R. T. Orr Lecture, Huron College, London, Ontario.

Wesch, M. (2008). Anti-teaching: Confronting the crisis of significance. *Education Canada, 48*(2), 4–7.

Whitty, G., Power, S., & Halpin, D. (1998). *Devolution and choice in education: The school, the state and the market*. Buckingham, UK: Open University Press.

Willms, J. D. (Ed.) (2002). *Vulnerable children: Findings from Canada's National Longitudinal Survey of Children and Youth*. Edmonton, AB: University of Alberta Press.

Willms, J. D., Friesen, S., & Milton, P. (2009). *What did you do in school today?: Transforming classrooms through social, academic and intellectual engagement*. Toronto, ON: Canadian Education Association.

Wilson, V. S. (1971). The role of royal commissions and task forces. In G. B. Doern & P. Aucion (Eds.), *The structures of policy making in Canada* (pp. 113–129). Toronto, ON: Macmillan.

World Health Organization. (2001). *World health report, 2000*. Geneva, Switzerland: Author. Retrieved from http://www.who.int/whr2001/2001/archives/2000/en/

Yeatman, A. (1998). Activism and the policy process. In A. Yeatman (Ed.), *Activism and the policy process* (pp. 16–35). St. Leonards, NSW: Allen & Unwin.

Young, D., & Bezeau, L. (2003). Moving from denominational to linguistic education in Quebec. *Canadian Journal of Educational Administration and Policy, 24*. Retrieved from http://www.umanitoba.ca/publications/cjeap/articles/youngbezeau.html

Young, J., & Levin, B. (1999). The origins of educational reform: A comparative perspective. *Canadian Journal of Educational Administration and Policy, 12*. Retrieved from http://www.umanitoba.ca/publications/cjeap/articles/younglevin.html

Young, J., & Levin, B. (2000). Education in transition: Canada. In D. Coulby, R. Cowan, & C. Jones (Eds.), *Education in times of transition: World Year Book of Education 2000* (pp. 50–62). New York, NY: Routledge.

Young, J., Levin, B., & Wallin, D. (2007). *Understanding Canadian schools: An introduction to educational administration* (4th. ed.). Toronto, ON: Thomson/Nelson.

Zimbalist, R. A. (2005). *The human factor in change*. Lanham, MD: Scarecrow Education.

Zinga, D. (2008). Ontario's challenge: Denominational rights in education. *Canadian Journal of Educational Administration and Policy, 80*. Retrieved from http://www.umanitoba.ca/publications/cjeap/articles/zinga2.html

Zur, A. (2003). Ontario's private schools funding policy and international human rights: Waldman v. Canada. *Education and Law Journal, 13*, 277–298.

Index

A

accountability movement, 99–101, 238
Act of Integration, 221
Adjusting the Course, 124–125, 127, 257–258
Aims of Education, 91–92
Alliance for Choice in Education, 64
Amulree Report, 40
Anglican, 17, 39–42, 52–53, 56, 64–65, 120, 124, 157, 220

B

Barry, Judge Leo, 62–63, 69, 164
Bill 30 (Ontario), 167
Bond, Sir Robert, 28
British North America Act; *see* Constitution of Canada (Act of 1867)

C

Canadian Charter of Rights & Freedoms
  Section 1, 161
  Section 2, 141, 157–158
  Section 7, 141
  Section 15, 141, 144, 148, 157–158, 167, 169–170
  Section 23, 148, 159
  Section 25, 149
  Section 29, 43, 57, 120, 142, 145, 157–158, 160–161, 169
Canadian School Boards Association, 104, 194
care
  concept of, 235–237

in educational reform, 8, 249–251
  practices, 247–249
Catholic Education Council/Committee, 6, 55, 64, 121–122
catholicity, 122
Change and Challenge, 89–90, 92
Chrétien, J., *see* Prime Ministers
Christian humanism, 85, 91
Christian view of education, 27
Church of England, *see* Anglican
Confederation with Canada (Newfoundland)
  impact on education, 13–14, 20, 41–42
Constitution of Canada
  Act of 1867, 138–139, 141, 145, 155–158, 160, 165–166, 169–172
  Act of 1871, 140
  Act of 1982, 138, 148, 154–155, 157–161, 167–173
  amending formula, 65–66, 130–131
  amendment, 34, 42, 66, 130–131, 138, 141, 143, 150, 160–163, 165–167, 171–173
  Confederation compromise, 139, 148
  denominational rights, 140, 155–158, 161, 166–170
  minority language education rights, 158–160
  minority rights, 65, 129–132, 164–165, 169
  Section 43, 162, 165
  Section 46, 162
  Section 93, 139–141, 160–161, 166, 169–171

V

Verge, L., *see* Ministers of Education

W

Warren Commission, 4, 15, 17, 20–22,
  24, 29, 42, 44, 54, 57, 77, 83
Warren, P., *see* Warren Commission
Wells, C., *see* Premiers of Newfoundland
  and Labrador
Williams Commission, 4, 15, 27, 29–34,
  43–48, 51–52, 55, 59, 68, 78–82, 108–
  112, 114, 121–123, 132, 222, 257
Winter Commission, 50, 55